The Battle of
the River Plate

Also by Dudley Pope

The Battle of
the River Plate

DUDLEY POPE

NAVAL
INSTITUTE
PRESS

First published in Great Britain 1956 by William Kimber and Co Ltd
Revised edition published by Pan Books Ltd 1974

Re-issued 1987 by The Alison Press/Martin Secker & Warburg Limited,
54 Poland Street, London W1V 3DF

Published and distributed in the United States of America
by the Naval Institute Press
Annapolis, Maryland 21402

Library of Congress Catalog Card No. 88-60816

ISBN 0–87021–018–1

Printed in Great Britain

Contents

Illustrations

Drawings and Charts

―――――

Foreword

By ADMIRAL SIR EDWARD PARRY, KCB

THE BATTLE of the River Plate received a great deal of publicity at the time, largely because it was fought during the first winter of the war when little else was happening. Moreover, the picture of a comparatively large enemy vessel being pursued by two smaller British ships appealed to the imagination. To this day I do not know why the *Admiral Graf Spee* did not dispose of us in the *Ajax* and the *Achilles* as soon as she had finished with the *Exeter*.

This book gives a far more complete story of the battle, and of the events leading up to it, than any that have previously been written. The author has made full use of the German naval records captured by us at the end of the war. He is therefore able to trace the rebirth of the German Navy after its defeat in the First World War, and the intentions of that great strategist who planned its growth, Grand Admiral Raeder.

Dudley Pope reminds us that a battle is the culmination of years of planning, of production, and of practice. On our side we certainly owed our success to our pre-war training. It is perhaps fortunate that, on the German side, Hitler did not always follow the far-seeing advice of his naval staff.

This book poses some very interesting questions. Why did the captain of the *Admiral Graf Spee* think that his ship was so seriously damaged that he must make for a neutral port instead of finishing off his two small opponents?

Why was he so easily persuaded that large British warships were waiting for him outside Montevideo, when in fact there was only one new arrival, far inferior in gunpower to his own ship?

Why, even when he received definite intelligence that the *Ark Royal* and *Renown* had arrived at Rio de Janeiro, a thousand miles away, and were therefore not in the River Plate estuary, did he persist in his plan to scuttle his ship? And why were his ship's company considerably demoralized by the comparatively light hammering they had received, whereas the officers and men of the far worse damaged *Exeter* behaved so magnificently?

My last question may appear to give an answer to the others. Yet we must not think that the Germany Navy was inefficient or that its officers and men were lacking in courage. On the contrary, one can but admire the maintenance of their morale throughout the war, and particularly that of their submarine crews, in spite of the appalling losses which they suffered.

If therefore the answer to my questions is that Captain Langsdorff felt that he had been defeated, and if consequently he was determined not to fight it out, his decision is a real tribute to the dominating influence of Commodore Harwood's leadership in the battle.

How I wish that he could have written the foreword to this book!

Preface

By Admiral Sir Charles Woodhouse, KCB

I SERVED in South America Division under Commodore Harwood for more than a year before the war. He was then in command of HMS *Exeter*, I was in HMS *Ajax*.

No one could have been kinder and more helpful to a captain in his first command than Harwood. He was the sort of man to whom one wanted to take one's doubts and difficulties in the certainty that one would get a sympathetic hearing and wise advice.

Harwood was constantly considering the special problems with which the South America Division would be faced in war, and thinking out the best means of dealing with every foreseeable contingency.

Apart from seeing to the fighting efficiency of his ships, he took endless trouble to explain to all those whose understanding cooperation would be required in an emergency the measures which he anticipated would be necessary.

He had a gift of winning the confidence and esteem of those he met, whether leading government officials or British residents in South America.

Dudley Pope's book gives a picture of the problem of protecting our trade against surface raiders in the early days of the war, and describes the success which rewarded Harwood's years of work on his station. It fell to him to strike the blow with perhaps the least powerful of the several forces which, under the direction of the Admiralty and commanders-in-chief, were all seeking the *Graf Spee* with the same determination to find her if they could, and to fight her wherever she was found.

Author's Introduction

THIS IS the story of a British naval victory, written from the British and German official records with the help of the men who fought in it. That it was won at a time when it had great propaganda value is incidental to my narrative, which aims to show what goes into such a victorious battle – the last of the great naval actions fought before aircraft and radar* completely changed sea warfare and put an end to tactics that Nelson might have used.

Had Nelson or one of his 'band of brothers' been in Commodore Harwood's place at the Battle of the River Plate, where we were fighting an enemy which had a heavier armament, they would undoubtedly have adopted similar unorthodox tactics. A few months afterwards, radar, aircraft and U-boats revolutionized naval warfare, thus severing the link between the tactics which stemmed from Nelson and those employed after 1940.

But apart from the actual battle – in itself only the calculated end of a strategic concept – I have tried to tell of the men behind it: Britons, Germans, neutrals, diplomats, admirals, able-seamen and spies. And one should not forget how the men and women working in the government offices, in factories, dockyards and the harvest fields all contributed to the final victory.

I have done this because it is not enough to give details of how three battleships, three aircraft carriers and fourteen cruisers hunted the *Graf Spee*, and how three cruisers found her; that is not a tenth of the full story. Mistakes were made by both sides, and since I have tried to

---

*The *Graf Spee* had a simple type of rangefinding radar which was of little or no use for search purposes.

present an objective account they are described as impartially as possible.

One fact must be borne in mind by the reader who wants to comprehend the *significance* of the story: the success of the commerce raider cannot be measured in terms of her scoreboard of sinkings. The *Graf Spee* sank nine ships, totalling 50,089 tons, in just over three months at sea; but she would have been no less useful to the Germans and dangerous to the Allies had she sunk half or ten times that number.

A commerce raider has another, even more important task: to disorganize her enemy's seaborne commerce. She can do this by simply letting the enemy know she is at sea. Twenty powerful ships in nine hunting groups were eventually hunting the *Graf Spee* – and all but a few of them had to be withdrawn from other theatres of operations where they were badly needed.

Thus the fact that the *Graf Spee* was at sea ultimately affected the ships sailing the oceans of the world and soldiers and airmen fighting on many battlefields; and although she was destroyed in the last days of 1939, the Allies were still reaping the benefit of Commodore Harwood's victory in 1943 and 1944.

But victories at sea are, in the final analysis, the scoring of hits on enemy ships by shells or torpedoes; shells and torpedoes made by thousands of civilians involved in such widespread jobs as coal-mining, iron-smelting, lathe-operating, ammunition-filling – and even typing – and fired by men both skilled and resolute. That, then, is why this story does not open dramatically with the thunder of broadsides from the *Ajax*, *Achilles* and *Exeter*, and end at sunset off Montevideo with the pocket battleship *Admiral Graf Spee* blowing up like an erupting volcano.

Many people have given me valuable assistance in writing this narrative, and I am especially grateful to Admiral Sir Edward Parry, KCB, and Admiral Sir Charles Woodhouse, KCB, both of whom gave me a great deal of help and advice. They also read the completed manuscript and suggested certain alterations. I am most grateful to Lady Harwood for her help and encouragement.

The Board of Admiralty were kind enough to grant me access to all the British and German documents I needed to write this account, and I am particularly indebted to members of the Historical Section, Records Section, Information Room, Foreign Documents Section, and Department of the Chief of Naval Information.

Officers who served in the three cruisers have provided me with a great deal of detail, and I am especially grateful to Rear Admiral R.E. Washbourn, DSO, OBE, RN, formerly Gunnery Officer of the *Achilles*; Captain E.D.G. Lewin, CB, CBE, DSO, DSC, RN, formerly of the *Ajax*; Cdr R.B. Jennings, DSO, DSC, RN (Retd), formerly Gunnery Officer of the *Exeter*; Lt-Cdr A.P. Monk, DSC, RN (Retd), formerly of the *Ajax*; Surgeon-Cdr J. Cussen, MB, BCh, RN (Retd), formerly of the *Exeter*; and Mr C.A. Pittar, MB, BS, FRACS, surgeon of the *Achilles*.

It remains to thank two people unconnected with the Navy – Count Henry Bentinck, a friend with whom I spent many hours discussing the construction of my narrative, and my wife, who was perhaps my sternest critic, and who typed the manuscript.

Times given in the narrative are frequently zone times; and much of the naval terminology and procedure in use in 1939 has now been changed.

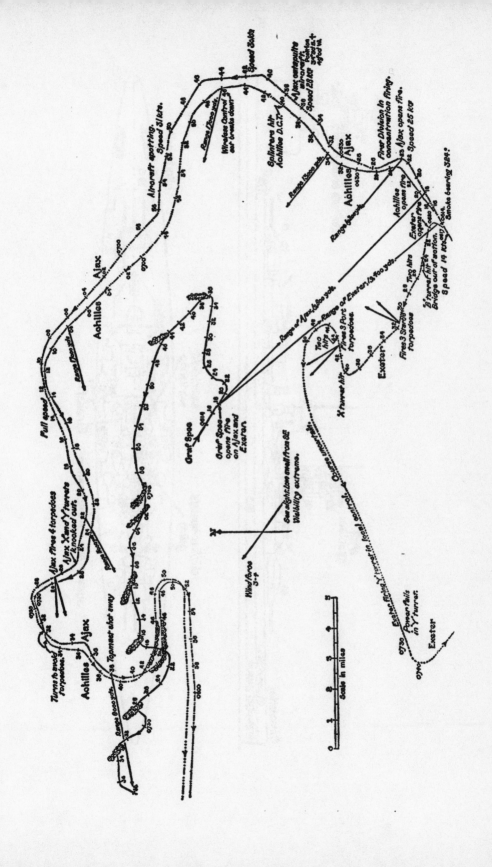

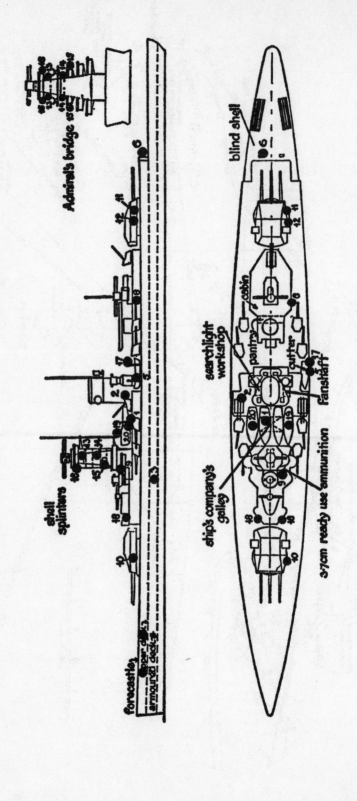

Admiral's bridge section

shell
splinters

forecastle,
armoured deck

blind shell

searchlight
workshop

cabin

pantry

cutter

fanshaft

ship's company's
galley

3·7cm ready use ammunition

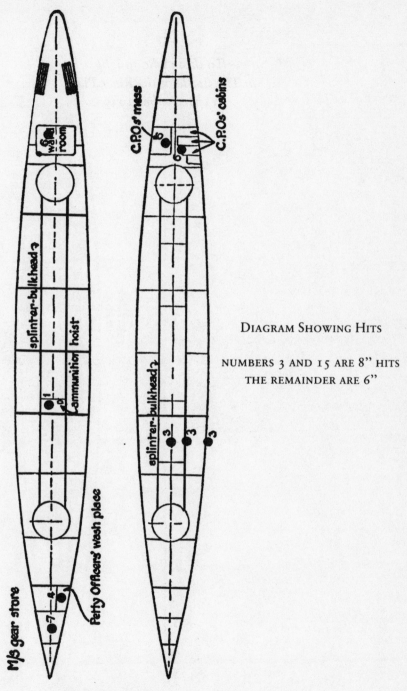

C.P.O.s' mess

C.P.O.s' cabins

splinter-bulkhead

splinter-bulkhead

Communition hoist

6 in. wash room

M/s gear store

Petty Officers' wash place

DIAGRAM SHOWING HITS

NUMBERS 3 AND 15 ARE 8" HITS
THE REMAINDER ARE 6"

Admiral Graf Spee

*To those who fought
in The Battle of the River Plate
13 December 1939*

I

Loading the Dice

On 6 January 1936 rain was falling over most of Europe, and the suave voices of radio commentators speaking in many languages had warned of gales sweeping the coasts. In France the rain was torrential; in Paris fire pumps stood by as the Seine rose three feet and work stopped when many commercial quays flooded. Swollen rivers teeming through other parts of Northern France damaged road and rail bridges, and at Poitiers flood waters submerged the station amid much shrugging of Gallic shoulders.

Apart from the weather, London was a cheerful city; people wanting to see a good film at a West End cinema that evening had the usual moments of indecision while choosing between Charles Laughton in *Mutiny on the Bounty* at the Empire, Leicester Square; George Arliss in *The Governor* at the Rialto, or Conrad Veidt and Helen Vinson in *King of the Damned* at the Tivoli.

Those who preferred a play were trying to get seats for Bobby Howes in *Please Teacher* at the Hippodrome or the Old Vic's inevitable *School for Scandal* in the Waterloo Road. For the millions staying at home beside the fire there was always the wireless, and Claude Hulbert was due on the Regional Programme at 7.45 in *The Scarlet Caramel*, a gentle skit on Baroness Orczy's elusive hero.

There was not much of interest in the evening newspapers: Lloyd George was planning to sell 3,000 head of poultry at his farm in Churt; gossip-writers were describing the interior of the new liner *Queen Mary*, due to sail shortly on her maiden voyage; Sir Alan Cobham had a new scheme for refuelling aircraft in mid-air; and Mr Anthony Eden had been elected president of the London Naval Conference which had just started meetings. Radiograms were advertised at ten guineas each.

Although it was not reported in the evening papers, it had been quite a stirring day for the German Navy at Kiel, where Hitler's third and latest pocket battleship, the £3,750,000 *Admiral Graf Spee*, had been ceremonially commissioned amid rain, Nazi pomp and noisy circumstance.

She was a ship of which Germany could be justifiably proud: as the world's latest capital ship she incorporated many new ideas. The plates and frames of her 609-foot hull were electrically welded and, in a vessel of her size, that was something new and showed daring on the part of her designers. In addition she had diesel engines instead of steam turbines, and these gave her a relatively high economical speed and increased her radius of action.

Her 11-inch guns were the new Krupp model which fired a 670-lb shell and had a range of fifteen miles; her rangefinders and other such gear were the finest that German technicians could devise. A radar set for obtaining accurate ranges was being secretly developed. Altogether, the builders at the Wilhelmshaven yard where she was laid down in October 1932 and launched on 30 June 1934 were proud of the *Panzerschiffe* which they had created.

But perhaps the proudest man in Germany on that wet day in January 1936 was Captain Patzig, the *Admiral Graf Spee*'s commanding officer. He paraded his crew of just under a thousand men on the quarterdeck and read a mesage from Admiral Erich Raeder, the Navy's Commander-in-Chief.

The uninhibited message pointed out that the ship bore the name of the Admiral who commanded the German Cruiser Squadron 'on the glorious day [of] Coronel and in the heroic battle at the Falkland Islands'. It added that 'the motto of the battleship's complement, like that of Admiral Graf von Spee and his men, would be now and for all time "Faithful unto Death" '.

So the *Admiral Graf Spee** joined her two sister ships, the *Deutschland* and the *Admiral Scheer*, and Admiral Raeder was satisfied. He had explained to Hitler that building up a balanced fleet from nothing was a slow process, but unfortunately the Fuehrer did not understand naval strategy. Still, like the build-up of the entire German armed forces, it was at least a steady one.

Germany had been – at least ostensibly – limited by the Treaty of Versailles, and the naval clauses held her to a navy comprising a

* The *von* was dropped from the ship's name.

maximum of 15,000 men, with six heavy ships, six light cruisers, twelve destroyers and twelve torpedo boats, with a limit on displacement in each class. The construction of U-boats was entirely forbidden. But Germany had been secretly breaking the Treaty for some years.

In 1928, for example, within ten years of the end of the First World War and five years before Hitler came to power, the construction of a pocket battleship had begun. She would be much larger than allowed under the Treaty, but by then the former Allies were complacent in enforcing its terms, and by using the description 'pocket battleship' and giving false displacement figures, with the explanation that new methods of welded construction and diesel propulsion saved weight, the Germans had made sure no awkward questions were asked.

When Hitler was appointed Chancellor he had given Raeder a free hand to go ahead with his construction plans and set about ridding himself of the terms of the Versailles Treaty, which was repudiated in 1935. This was little more than a formality – although the Treaty limit for capital ships had been 10,000 tons, the pocket battleships exceeded that and Raeder already had under construction the battle cruisers *Scharnhorst* and *Gneisenau*, each of 32,000 tons, while submarines were built secretly in Holland and Finland.

In 1936 the Anglo-German Naval Treaty was signed. Although he had seen that Britain and France had shown an almost lackadaisical unconcern about enforcing the naval clauses of the Versailles Treaty, Hitler was careful to make sure the British negotiators left the conference table content. It was agreed that Germany could build to thirty-five per cent of British naval strength, and could have submarines. In terms of ships it meant five capital ships, two aircraft carriers, twenty-one cruisers and sixty-four destroyers. Hitler was quite content because it was the maximum number that German shipyards could build for the next few years, and by then he knew he would be in a position to repudiate that Treaty too.

But Germany was not a party to either the Washington Naval Agreement or the London Conference, under which Britain, France and the United States could not – and did not – build battleships of more than 35,000 tons. Meanwhile Hitler allowed Raeder to build the *Bismarck* and *Tirpitz*, each of 45,000 tons. . .

Thus by early 1937, while Britain, France and the USA had voluntarily tied their own hands by treaties, the great expansion of the German Navy went ahead. In making his long-term plans, Raeder had two courses open to him:

(a) Build up to the Treaty limit of thirty-five per cent of the Royal Navy, planning to reach that total in 1940, on the assumption war would break out then.

(b) Assume war would start later – possibly in 1944–5 – and plan a more balanced fleet. This would mean having a weaker fleet in the meantime.

Although Raeder chose the second course, by 1938 he felt that Britain's reaction to the European crisis caused by Hitler's activities was stiffening (a view not shared by Hitler) and drew up the so-called Z Plan, which provided for a more immediately powerful offensive force and to a certain extent abandoned the idea of a fully balanced fleet.

Since the actual strategy that a navy can follow is governed by the types of ships it has, Raeder visualized that under the Z Plan Germany's naval operations against Britain would be directed more against the merchant shipping in her sea lanes than Britain's fighting fleet. In the circumstances this was sensible strategy, particularly since the U-boat arm was being built up.

By the time it was completed in 1945, the Z Plan was intended to provide Germany with a formidable navy comprising thirteen battle-ships, thirty-three cruisers, four aircraft carriers, 250 U-boats and a large number of destroyers. And every ship would be of a modern design, compared with the majority of the larger ships of the Royal Navy which dated from the First World War. The Anglo-German Naval Treaty would, of course, have long since been repudiated by Hitler.

Yet the Z plan was soon aborted by Hitler's changes of policy. Although a voracious reader, much of the material which Hitler read passed through his brain without leaving much impression. But he was an instinctive and effective politician, his major mistake being that he considered himself a statesman. He dreamed of himself as a master strategist, following great soldiers like Napoleon. And in some ways he did resemble Napoleon – initial successes on land in Europe led to the same suicidal attack on Russia, and at no time did he understand naval strategy. Nor was any member of the German Navy, least of all Raeder, among Hitler's 'inner circle'.

4

But for these factors, he might well have kept his hands off Poland until the Z Plan was more advanced, if not completed. In addition he believed that Britain could be persuaded to stay out of a continental war. It is certain he never visualized a long war – yet, in the event, there were only two places where he could effectively attack Britain, the only enemy left in the field against him.

One was at sea, but his timetable wrecked the Z Plan and prevented Raeder from building a navy capable of decisive action. The other was in the Mediterranean, the only area where he could bring Britain to battle on land. Of the two, Britain could only be defeated at sea.

Early in 1939 Admiral Raeder was still working to his Z Plan when Hitler began planning the actual invasion of Poland and in April issued a directive to the Armed Forces to prepare the details. The directive said, 'Policy aims at limiting the war to Poland, and this is considered possible in view of the internal crisis in France and consequent British restraint. . .'

Raeder disagreed over Britain's probable role, quite apart from his dismay at being faced with a war for which he had a completely unbalanced navy. A month later another directive, indicating that Hitler too was now having doubts, gave instructions for 'the economic war and the protection of our own economy', and said that the Navy and *Luftwaffe* were to prepare for the immediate opening of economic warfare against Britain and, as a second priority, against France. The Navy, Hitler added, was to plan for a war against British and French merchant shipping.

In fact, because of Raeder's doubts, the Naval War Staff was already drawing up its Atlantic Trade Warfare Plan, and in order to understand the significance of the subsequent operations by the *Graf Spee*, described in this volume, it is necessary to discuss briefly the strategy of commerce raiding as planned by Raeder.

There are two main objects of commerce warfare: the obvious one of the destruction of enemy ships, and the less obvious one of so disorganizing the sailing of merchant ships that restrictions on the enemy's seagoing trade become unbearable and finally impossible.

The surface raider can assist in three ways:-

1. Sinking or capturing ships.
2. Dislocating normal traffic through the fear of her presence (or by

minelaying), thus slowing up the regular arrival of food, supplies and raw materials. This eventually cuts down imports so much that the blockaded country collapses economically.

3. By making the enemy so scatter his surface warships hunting for the raiders that other arms – the submarines and aircraft, for example – have a better chance of successfully attacking convoys whose escorts (both close escorts and the more remote patrols by larger ships) have been weakened.

So when one tries to estimate the value of a surface raider one has to take these three points into consideration: the actual total sinkings or captures is only a part – and a small part – of the story, as will be seen in the case of the *Graf Spee*.*

In the First World War, as very few merchant ships had radio transmitters or receivers, the surface raider had it more or less her own way, especially as she used coal and could easily refuel from captured colliers. The task of discovering her whereabouts and destroying her was incredibly difficult. In August 1914 the Germans had in fact stationed their warships abroad in favourable positions. But although the losses inflicted by these raiders were not great, the potentialities of this type of warfare were enormous: and it was this which made a great impression on Admiral Raeder's mind when planning the course of a possible second war against Britain. The ships used in the First World War by the Germans had not been really suitable for the task of commerce raiding, and Admiral Raeder, reviewing the results, concluded that independence and deception were more useful qualities in a raider than speed and gunfire and the cruiser designed for Fleet work was unsuitable. Some other design of warship was therefore needed.

While still outwardly limited by the Versailles Treaty, the German Naval Staff had decided to concentrate on the construction of a type of warship which, while ostensibly keeping inside the tonnage restrictions of the Treaty, would have long endurance and a reasonably high speed.

The three twenty-eight-knot pocket battleships, with six 11-inch, eight 5.9-inch, six 4.1-inch (high-angle) guns, torpedo tubes and two aircraft, were the result. Their power was underestimated by the British, who assumed they were inside the then Treaty limit of 10,000 tons. If this had

---

*Commerce raiders in both wars claimed only a small proportion of total Allied ship losses – 4.1 per cent in the First World War and 6.2 in the Second. (See Appendix C.)

been the case, either operational range, speed or armour would have had to be sacrificed. As it was they were of more than 12,000 tons and had a great range, sufficient armour and a speed appropriate to their role.

With an OKW* directive of 3 April setting down the date for the attack on Poland for any time after 1 September, events moved fast in Germany. While the Operations Division of the Naval War Staff drew up detailed plans for commerce raiding by the *Admiral Graf Spee* and the *Deutschland*, Raeder was not unnaturally far from satisfied with the Navy he had created.

The 45,000-ton *Bismarck* and *Tirpitz*, of advanced design and the most powerful warships under construction by any European power, were not yet completed; the 32,000-ton battlecruisers *Scharnhorst* and *Gneisenau* were neither operationally satisfactory nor fully worked up. The new 8-inch heavy cruisers *Admiral Hipper* and *Prinz Eugen* were not yet available, and by August one of the three pocket battleships, the *Admiral Scheer*, would be in need of a long overhaul.

However, he had the consolation that the pocket battleships were brilliantly conceived ships. He considered that the combined British and French Navies had only five or six ships individually capable of both catching and sinking any one of them.

The odds against the pocket battleships in ocean raiding against British and French merchant shipping were not as heavy as Germany's numerical weakness and lack of foreign bases might suggest. The sheer vastness of the oceans is not often fully appreciated: the Atlantic comprises more than 34,000,000 square miles and the Indian Ocean 28,000,000 compared with the area of Europe (3,947,000), South America (6,970,000), Africa (11,688,000) and Asia (17,276,000). Any British warship searching for a pocket battleship in perfect visibility could at best hope to sight her at a range of about twelve miles, so the problem in the Atlantic was finding a ship while looking round a circle with a diameter of twenty-four miles in an area twice the size of Asia and its offshore islands.

In addition, the raider inevitably enjoys the initiative. To fulfil her objective of disrupting trade – far more important than actually sinking ships – she need do little more than make her presence known in one area and move swiftly to another.

After sinking a ship in one position, the *Graf Spee* could be 500 miles

* *Ober Kommando Wehrmacht* – the High Command of the Armed Forces.

away within twenty-four hours without using up fuel at an excessive rate. Cruising at twenty knots, she could easily travel in a week the distance between London and New York.

The German plan, as yet untried, for operating the pocket battleships at sea for long periods anticipated using auxiliary vessels specially designed for fuelling, supplying and prison-ship duties. These supply ships, usually disguised as neutral tankers, were to cruise in the general area of the raiders' operations, making rendezvous as ordered and when possible waiting in unfrequented areas of the ocean.

So the spring of 1939 gave way to a lazy summer. 'Munich', with all that it implied, had passed and British public opinion was rapidly realizing that Neville Chamberlain's 'Peace in our time' was to be measured in months rather than years. In Berlin the Naval War Staff had completed its Atlantic Trade Warfare Plan and, because of the increasing international tension, put it into operation.

On 27 July secret orders were sent to Captain Heinrich Dau, master of the tanker *Altmark*, telling him to store his ship with three month's supplies by 2 August so that the ship could sail to the United States, embark fuel oil and be under way again before war broke out. The *Altmark* was to be a supply ship for a commerce raiding pocket battleship.

Dispatching Dau's orders was the first actual move made by Germany against Britain, and it was swiftly followed by several more. The pocket battleship *Graf Spee*, at sea on torpedo-firing exercises, was recalled to Wilhelmshaven on 17 August to be docked, over-hauled and secretly stored at top speed.

Meanwhile the *Altmark* had crossed the Atlantic and was in Port Arthur, New Mexico, taking on 9,400 tons of diesel fuel as the *Graf Spee* entered Wilhelmshaven. Two days later, on 19 August, Dau sailed after receiving orders in cipher from the Naval War Staff telling him to make for an area near the Canary Islands, where he was to wait for the *Graf Spee*.

The detailed operational orders for the *Graf Spee* and *Deutschland* had been ready since 4 August. They told the two captains that as far as the political situation was concerned, in the event of war with Poland, it was now considered that Britain and France would intervene, and Italy would probably be on Germany's side. Russia's attitude would be uncertain but neutral at first.

The ships' task in wartime, the orders added, would be 'the disruption and destruction of enemy shipping by all possible means'. Enemy naval forces, even if inferior in strength, were to be engaged only if it furthered the principal task of commerce raiding. Frequent changes of position in the specified operational area 'would create uncertainty and will restrict enemy shipping'.

While these orders were being digested, the *Graf Spee*'s men, helped by ratings from the barracks, got on with the work in Wilhelmshaven. The second in command, Kapitän zur See Kay, made sure of the stowage of food and supplies for the fifty-four officers, 217 petty officers, 833 ratings, twenty-four civilians and six Chinese, forming the *Graf Spee*'s crew – and enough paint and gear to keep the ship smart and, if necessary, alter her appearance with dummy funnels from time to time. It was Kay's job to have the ship running smoothly – he was responsible to Kapitän zur See Langsdorff, the '*Graf Spee*'s present captain. One last-minute job he had when it was made known that the ship was going to the tropics was to find out if every man had his own sleeping quarters. He discovered forty-seven men had not. After arguing with the staff on shore it was agreed to cut down the number of crew, and Kay used this opportunity to get rid of some unreliable men. He also had to find accommodation for Reserve officers forming boarding parties. Several of these were carefully chosen former Merchant Marine officers who had served in South American and African waters.

The Chief Gunnery Officer, in charge of the main armament, was Fregattenkapitän Ascher: he had the job of making sure he had enough shells, charges and spares stowed away for the 11-inch and 5.9-inch guns. The Second Gunnery Officer, Korvettenkapitän Meusermann, was responsible for the 4.1-inch high-angle guns; his shells, too, had to be stowed in magazines and ready-use lockers.

Kapitänleutnant Brutzer was the Torpedo Officer: his task, in addition to handling the torpedo tubes on the *Graf Spee*'s quarterdeck, included the checking and stowing of the bombs which would be used to sink captured merchant ships.

The man who would be responsible for navigating the *Graf Spee* was Korvettenkapitän Wattenberg: in the pocket battleship's chart room he had stowed folios of charts enough to navigate the warship round the world – along with the latest Lloyd's Register of Merchant Ships, *Jane's Fighting Ships*, and German and British pilot books for all coasts.

Perhaps the busiest man in these hurried days was Korvettenkapitän (Ing) Klepp: he was the Chief Engineer. In addition to taking hundreds of tons of oil fuel on board through snaking hose, he had to order and stow spare parts – from electric light bulbs to pieces of metal weighing several hundredweights – for the great diesel engines.

Late on 20 August the Captain, Hans Langsdorff, reported to the Naval War Staff* that the *Admiral Graf Spee* was ready for sea. For this slim elegant young commander the test was just beginning: all his adult life had been spent in preparation for the day when he would be captain of his own ship at sea – and at war.

That night, 20 August, was the last the *Graf Spee* was destined to spend in a home port; and although the sailing date and destination was a closely guarded secret since the world was still at peace, few men on board the grey-painted battleship could fail to realize that they were on the eve of departure.

In Britain the three Services were rapidly preparing. While the Admiralty put the finishing touches to their own plans, Coastal Command were having a full-scale exercise to test out their search scheme designed to prevent surface raiders breaking out of the North Sea.

At the completion of the exercises the squadrons of planes were to fly to their war stations and, although war had not started, they were to begin with war-time reconnaissance flights over the North Sea immediately. The days chosen for the exercise were 15 August to 21 August, the last flights ending at dusk. . .

Monday, 21 August, started off as a hot summer's day and rapidly the temperature in London and the south-east of England rose to about 27°C. From Brussels came reports that King Leopold was inviting representatives of several small nations to Brussels for a conference to discuss the sending of a peace appeal to the great nations.

In London, the Prime Minister, Mr Neville Chamberlain, was talking with his Foreign Secretary, Lord Halifax, about the latest reports of the situation in Danzig. Reports of big purchases of copper, lead and rubber on the London market came in the afternoon, and all were for early

*Control of the *Graf Spee* and the *Deutschland* and eleven U-boats was retained by the High Command instead of being left to the C-in-C, West, at Wilhelmshaven.

delivery. 'In some cases,' reported the *Evening News*, 'Dutch firms have made the first enquiries, but on coming down to details have readily disclosed that the deliveries are ultimately to reach a German destination. . .'

At the Oval the West Indies had passed England's total with five wickets in hand, and by lunchtime the atmosphere was oppressive with a damp and heavy, foreboding heat. In the afternoon the thunder clouds which had been gathering swirled into a heavy storm; lightning flickered and struck houses (at Ilford several people were killed). Many London roads were flooded and railways affected.

As usual there was a good choice of films, plays and cabaret for those who wanted entertainment in the West End. So if you wanted fun that evening you could have had it. But on that evening, when the Coastal Command's exercise over the North Sea had finished, eight sets of diesel engines in the *Graf Spee* started their rhythmical thumping and her two great bronze propellers spun almost lazily as Captain Langsdorff took her at 8 PM out of Wilhelmshaven down the Jade river, through the Schillig Roads, and into the North Sea.

Quietly, without fuss, the propellers increased their spinning until dials recorded 250 revolutions, taking the pocket battleship at full speed north-north-eastward past the rock that is Heligoland, past the island of Sylt and Horns Rev off Denmark . . . By noon next day Langsdorff wanted to be in a position west of Bergen.

The ship was sailing on a route already taken by several U-boats since 19 August as they headed for their war stations in the Atlantic, and by 29 August seventeen of them were to have sailed. Thus that night an operation began which, as the Germans themselves observed, made the heaviest claims not only on the strength, endurance and constant operational readiness of the ships' officers and men, but in demands on technical resources and material efficiency.

Carefully Langsdorff moved his ship northward through the night, keeping thirty miles off the Norwegian coast and altering course as soon as a ship's lights were sighted. Only one ship and several fishing vessels had been seen by noon on the 24th, when the *Graf Spee* was south-east of Iceland.

Now he was at sea, Langsdorff was able to digest his instructions more easily. The operational areas allocated to him were (a) the South American–Cape Verde Islands–Biscay trade route; and (b) the South and

Central Atlantic sea area, the Cape Town–Cape Verde Islands route, or the South Indian Ocean. However, these orders were not binding on Langsdorff: he was free to choose his operational area according to the opposition he encountered and the density of the traffic. Until the war began, his instructions said, the *Graf Spee* was to wait in an area to the north-westward of the Cape Verde Islands. In the meantime the pocket battleship was to maintain wireless silence. The next move would come from the Naval High Command.

The supply ship *Westerwald* sailed on 22 August for a position south of Greenland, where she would work with the pocket battleship *Deutschland*; and on the same day Hitler added to the confusion in the minds of the Naval High Command by a speech at Obersalzberg (near Berchtesgaden, in Bavaria, where Hitler had his mountain retreat, the Berghof) to the Commanders-in-Chief of the Armed Forces.

He was in a jubilant mood, and first he told them that a pact was about to be signed with Russia – which meant Poland was isolated. But, he said, he did not know whether Britain and France would go to Poland's help when she was attacked. He felt the pact with Russia would deter them.

The next day, 23 August, saw one of the first British operational moves which affect this story: the cruiser *Exeter* was at Devonport with her crew on foreign-service leave when she was recalled to South American waters. Captain F.S. Bell assumed command of the ship two days later, and she continued to fly Commodore Henry Harwood's broad pendant as Commodore, South America Division. That evening she sailed.

The *Deutschland* sailed on Thursday, 24 August, from Wilhelmshaven under the command of Captain Paul Wenneker. Her operational area was the North Atlantic, and she was due to rendezvous with the *Westerwald* south of Greenland. The Air Ministry in London, warned by the Admiralty that something of this nature was happening, gave orders to Coastal Command to start dawn reconnaissance with the object of shadowing, 'in an unobtrusive manner', any German forces sighted.

On the same day Hitler announced to a surprised world that a non-aggression pact had been signed in Moscow between Germany and Russia. In Poland the Government knew that Hitler's net was closing in on them. Help was many hundreds of miles away, and now the Kremlin was backing Hitler.

It was the same Thursday that the Admiralty signalled orders to the Home Fleet and all ships at home ports to proceed to their war stations, and this was followed on Tuesday, 29 August, by the order to mobilize the Fleet 'in accordance with instructions for war with a European power...'

Slowly and perhaps almost unwillingly the British moved towards readiness for war. Two days later, on 31 August, a signal reached the Admiralty saying there was some indication that a large German ship had left Wilhelmshaven PM on 30 August or AM on the 31st. This was followed by a signal from the First Sea Lord, Admiral Sir Dudley Pound, ordering all forces to proceed to sea and patrol in the area between the Shetlands and Norway; but they found nothing ... the *Graf Spee* had passed through ten days and the *Deutschland* seven days earlier ...

On the same day Hitler issued his 'Directive No. 1 for the Conduct of the War'. He said that now all political possibilities of disposing of the situation on the Eastern Front were exhausted, 'I have determined on a solution by force.' *Fall Weiss*, the attack on Poland, was to start next day. The time, 4.45 AM, was inserted in red pencil. The German land frontiers in the west, he added, were not to be crossed, and 'the same applies to warlike actions at sea, or any which may be so interpreted.'

At dawn the next day German forces swarmed across the Polish frontier at the time written down by Hitler's red pencil. *Fall Weiss*, and with it the Second World War, had started. It was to be a war the like of which had never been seen; a war waged by the Germans in complete disregard of international law and humanitarian considerations; and which saw them, among other things, establish *Einsatzkommandos* (Extermination Squads) expressly to murder Jews.

II

'Total Germany'

ON THE morning of Sunday, 3 September, the voice of the Prime Minister was heard through radio loudspeakers in almost every home in Britain saying that a state of war now existed with Germany. Almost immediately the air-raid sirens sounded and the great silver barrage balloons rose into the sky over a strangely hushed and sunlit London.

From the Admiralty the following signal was broadcast in plain language to all home commands and ships: *11 AM COMMENCE HOSTILITIES AT ONCE AGAINST GERMANY*. A similar signal was sent to all British merchantmen by the powerful Rugby transmitter. (One of the ships that picked it up was the *Graf Spee*, giving Captain Langsdorff the first news that the war had begun.) To its own ships at sea the Admiralty radioed the prearranged signal *TOTAL GERMANY*.

Almost at once, German U-boats struck their first blow, torpedoing the liner *Athenia* in the Atlantic. Four ships heard her SSS signal* and managed to rescue 1,300 civilians, including many children, before the ship sank, drowning about 100 people. However, the *Athenia* was not the war's first casualty although she was the first merchant ship sunk without warning.

The credit for being the first warship to capture and sink an enemy merchant ship in the Second World War fell to the British cruiser *Ajax*, which was later to play a major part in the destruction of the *Graf Spee*. Commanded by Captain Charles Woodhouse, she was in Rio de Janeiro the week before the war began, and as events in Europe reached a climax Captain Woodhouse found himself responsible for 4,000 miles of coastline while being nearly 2,000 miles from the nearest British base.

*The traditional SOS was superseded by SSS for attack by submarine, RRR for attack by a surface raider, and AAA for aircraft.

14

There are few men who would not have felt lonely under these circmstances, and he admitted he was not one of them.

There were a large number of German merchantmen at sea and in port along his 'beat', some reported by Intelligence to have guns on board and to be manned by Nazis. Feeling that war was imminent, Woodhouse decided he ought to be at sea, so that the Germans would not know where *Ajax* was, and the prospect of being intercepted by a British cruiser might deter some ships from sailing. He was heading for the River Plate area when he received the Admiralty signal *TOTAL GERMANY*, and three hours later a merchant ship was sighted.

She proved to be the *Olinda*, bound for Germany from Montevideo with a cargo of wool, hides, cotton, scrap iron and wood. Her crew was taken off and since it was not practical to make a prize of her, she was sunk by gunfire. Next day, yet another German merchantman, the *Carl Fritzen*, was sighted and her crew taken off. One of the *Ajax*'s first shells happened to hit a tank just above the *Carl Fritzen*'s waterline, so that instead of sea water rushing in the hole the British were rather embarrassed to see fresh water pouring out!

Three days later in Berlin Admiral Raeder had his first war conference with Hitler, and the main problem he raised was the future role of the two pocket battleships already at sea. In view of the French restraint 'and the still hesitant conduct of British warfare', he said, the pocket battleships should be withdrawn from their operational area. British trade was being stopped and British forces were being sent out in planned attacks against raiders, so 'the risk was out of all proportion with the chances of success'. After listening to the Admiral, Hitler agreed that the *Graf Spee* and *Deutschland* 'are to hold back and withdraw for the present'.

So far we have dealt only with German naval policy, but the broad lines of Admiralty policy had been approved by the Board eight months before the outbreak of war. The United Kingdom's geographical position has for centuries been one of the most important factors in British power: it has formed a barrier and a fortress between Northern Europe and the Atlantic, and all ships bound for the oceans of the world have to pass either through the Channel or round the north of Scotland. The arrival of high-speed surface vessels, submarines and aircraft had increased the importance of that factor since the gap between Scotland and Norway, the so-called northern passage, is a scant three hundred miles. In the Second World War German ships could get in or out only by passing through the northern passage. If the Royal Navy could prevent this, then Germany would be blockaded and her Navy trapped.

However, there was another side to this: even if the Royal Navy controlled all the ocean highways to Britain completely but lost control round our coasts – to German aircraft, submarines, surface craft or even minefields – then Britain would still be cut off. Her supply ships would be sunk almost literally at the harbour entrance after sailing perhaps half-way round the world.

Some idea of the magnitude of the Navy's commerce-protection task is given by the fact that in 1939 more than 3,000 foreign-going merchant ships were registered in Britain, and more than 1,000 coasters. An average of 2,500 ships flying the Red Ensign were at sea on any one day in positions ranging from the east coast of England to the far ends of the Pacific. So the first priority in the Admiralty's plan was the defence of home waters. Second was the Mediterranean, across which came tankers with oil from the Middle East, and ships with cargoes from India and the Far East. Third came the Far East itself where Japan, with a vast and powerful fleet, stood smiling and inscrutable.

After the bitter experience of the First World War, the Admiralty had always maintained that the minimum number of cruisers needed to meet our commitments was seventy. When the Second World War began, we had only fifty-eight, some of which were unsuitable because of age or lack of endurance. The shortage was due to many things, all political, and the most important of which were the limitations caused by naval treaties. The Washington Conference produced the large 8-inch cruisers, which the Navy never wanted. Later the 8-inch tonnage allowed to each nation was limited and resulted in our last two, the *Exeter* and *York*, having only six instead of eight 8-inch guns.

Although its estimate of the potential of the German pocket battle-ships (based upon their supposed displacement) was wrong, the Admiralty was accurate in its forecast of the way Raeder would make use of commerce raiding, and its War Memorandum specified 'traditional and well-proved methods' of protecting the trade routes. These, it said, consisted in the dispersal of shipping (i.e. the special and often devious routeing of ships to keep them away from known or suspected danger spots); the stationing of naval patrols in focal areas (one might almost

16

call them the ocean crossroads where one trade route crossed another or several met off a large port) and where cruisers could concentrate in pairs; and the formation of adequately escorted convoys. Detachments from the main fleet could be used if required.

The plans outlined in the Memorandum came into force the day war broke out, but British ships were obviously extremely vulnerable for several weeks after that, since many of them on their way to and from Britain were already scattered along regular trade routes.

Changes had just been made concerning the naval command in the South Atlantic, where the events to be described in this volume took place. The designation of Vice-Admiral George D'Oyly Lyon was changed from Commander-in-Chief, Africa Station, to Commander-in-Chief, South Atlantic, and he transferred his headquarters from the Cape to Freetown, in Sierra Leone – a move which brought him 3,000 miles north and put him in a better position to control British warships ranging over the whole of the South Atlantic.

At the same time the South America Division of the America and West Indies Squadron (based at Bermuda) was transferred to his command. The Division at the time comprised the cruisers *Exeter* and *Ajax* and was under the immediate command of Commodore Henry Harwood, who had been in South American waters for the past three years.

Commanded by Captain F.S. Bell, the *Exeter* was an 8,390-ton cruiser carrying 1,900 tons of fuel, giving her a range of only 10,000 miles at eleven to fourteen knots – not nearly enough for the task the Admiralty had given her, as will be seen later. She was a far from satisfactory warship, apart from her short range, the treaty limitations forcing her to carry only six 8-inch guns, instead of eight, leading those taking a charitable view to assume she was built to sell to a potential enemy.

Commodore Harwood was anxious to meet his new Commander-in-Chief, so that when the *Exeter* sailed from Devonport she made for Freetown, where she could also refuel. She arrived there the day Hitler marched into Poland.

The situation Commodore Harwood described to Admiral Lyon was a difficult one. The South American Division was operating off an entirely neutral coastline. The nearest British base was in the bleak Falkland Islands, 1,000 miles south of Buenos Aires and Montevideo, and nearly 2,000 miles from Rio de Janerio. This meant that if a cruiser like the *Exeter*, with her range of 10,000 miles, had to go from Rio to fuel at the

Falklands and return, she would have to use nearly half her fuel to get there and back – and that was assuming she did not exceed fourteen knots.

The entry of belligerent warships into neutral ports was governed by international law and varied from country to country (though the laws were all very similar and based on the 13th Hague Convention of 1907). Whereas a belligerent soldier or aircraft landing in a neutral country was automatically interned, a warship could stay for twenty-four hours, and this period could be extended for certain reasons, which included repairs to make the vessel seaworthy.

Although the Hague Convention did not specify the number of times a warship might visit a neutral port, it did say that she could take on enough fuel to reach the nearest port in her own country. Some neutral countries interpreted this as allowing a warship to fill up all the spaces built to carry fuel, but once having done this she could not fuel again in the same country for three months. This meant, in fact, that Harwood could only refuel his ships in any port belonging to each of the three neutral republics once every three months. The main ports were Buenos Aires (Argentine), Montevideo (Uruguay) and Rio de Janeiro (Brazil). However, the interpretation of the rules finally rested with the neutral governments concerned, and it was vitally necessary for Britain to be on friendly terms with them.

After discussions with the Admiral, Commodore Harwood sailed for Rio de Janeiro where he had to sort out various problems. Arriving on the 7th, he talked with Sir Hugh Gurney, the British Ambassador, knowing that fuelling was now going to be even more of a problem since the 8-inch cruiser *Cumberland* was on her way from Plymouth to reinforce him and two destroyers, the *Hotspur* and *Havock*, were coming from Freetown.

It is on these occasions that the value of the peacetime 'showing the flag' cruises is revealed. The Commodore's three years on the South America Station had been well spent. He was a good mixer and had taken the trouble to learn Spanish. He was noted more for his brave attempts than his fluency; but nevertheless the South American governments had a high regard for him. They considered him a typical Englishman whom they could trust, and the fact that he could talk to them in somewhat unconventional Spanish helped considerably – his grammatical errors were guaranteed to liven up any diplomatic party.

Whereas Drake was famous for his game of bowls, it might well be said that Commodore Harwood's golf and pleasing, 'typically British' personality were two factors which did much to ensure that at the outbreak of war the South American republics (despite the high percentage of Germans living there and forming a virulent and noisy Fifth Column) were all pro-British and willing to stretch a point or two in Harwood's favour.

Over the next few days Harwood received permission from Brazil to fuel at frequent intervals 'provided that such visits were made discreetly and at different ports'. The Commander-in-Chief of the Argentine Navy raised no objections to Harwood's force refuelling from a British tanker in the Plate estuary, going so far as to suggest a particularly sheltered anchorage. The Uruguayan Government was equally helpful, but in each case Harwood had to bear in mind that concessions applied to both belligerents: he could not ask for anything that would also benefit the Germans.

In addition to the twin handicaps of a small force of ships and the difficulty of fuelling them, Harwood suffered to some extent from being afloat. While at sea, his ship had to keep wireless silence. She was of course free to receive signals from the Admiralty or Admiral Lyon in Freetown, but transmitting any message meant she gave her position away to the enemy.

These were the three basic handicaps facing Harwood and the South America Division. And on 8 September, when the *Exeter* sailed from Rio after a stay of less than twenty-four hours, Harwood received a signal from the Admiralty which underlined them. Three German merchant ships, the Admiralty warned, were assembling off the Patagonian coast (at the extreme tip of South America). The position was more than 2,000 miles to the south of the *Exeter*.

The three ships could do a number of things, from mounting guns and acting as surface raiders to launching an attack on the undefended Falkland Islands. So while the cruiser *Ajax* went south to guard the Falklands, the Commodore started short-distance convoys from the Plate and Rio de Janeiro, the merchantmen being escorted clear of the coast and dispersed at night on different routes.

However, unsuspected by either the Admiralty or Harwood, a German pocket battleship was already ranging the South Atlantic.

III

'Make the Challenge'

THE *GRAF SPEE*'s voyage down towards the Tropics had been uneventful. On 24 August, the day the *Deutschland* sailed from Wilhelmshaven, she was midway between Iceland and the Faeroes; by the 27th the noon position noted in her log put her on the same latitude as London and midway between Britain and Newfoundland. On the 28th Berlin passed a radiogram from the SKL giving the position for a rendezvous with the tanker *Altmark* on 1 September.

The world was still at peace and the merchant ships steaming along well-defined shipping lanes of the Atlantic carried the normal navigation and accommodation lights. Since it was essential that the *Graf Spee* reach the waiting area near the Cape Verde Islands, off the West African coast, without being sighted, Langsdorff decided to cross the shipping lanes at night with his ship darkened. And whether it was daylight or darkness, he knew that his lookouts in their positions high over the bridge, scores of feet above sea level, and other men watching through the immensely powerful rangefinder which revolved twenty-four hours a day, would see lights or smoke long before any other ship would sight the *Graf Spee*.

And – even though it was always breaking down – the *Dt-Geraet* was useful for dodging ships. *Dt-Geraet* was the rudimentary radar set mounted in a revolving pillar on the foretop. Although intended for rangefinding, it could be used, with its eighteen-and-a-half mile range, for searching. The trouble was that the vibration all over the ship from the diesel engines caused breaks in the cables feeding the set. However, when it was working it was quite accurate and one great advantage was that the British did not know the Germans had a form of radar installed.

Thus, using his speed, the *Dt-Geraet* and the rangefinders, Langsdorff could evade surface ships. The only thing he had to worry about was aircraft, and he was sufficiently far out into the Atlantic not to have any great fears. The mainstay of the British Coastal Command, the Anson, then had a range of only 510 miles at 144 knots; not even enough for it to reach the Norwegian coast from England and return.

So the hours slipped by as her diesel engines thrust the pocket battleship through the Atlantic swell. Korvettenkapitän (Ing) Klepp, the Chief Engineer, made his daily report to the Captain: all was well, the engines were behaving perfectly, and every man in the engine room, down to the greasers responsible for lubricating the two great propeller shafts, was settling down to the sea routine. And it was a good time for exercising all the guns' crews. Even Kapitänleutnant Brutzer had a chance for exercising his men at the torpedo tubes.

The man with the least work on his hands was Dr Kartzendorff, the ship's surgeon. Apart from the usual cases of sea-sickness and constipation he had no sick or injured men to attend to. However, he had a chance to sort out instruments and check up on the spare supplies – which he might well be wanting within a very short time.

The two busiest men, apart from Langsdorff, were undoubtedly Kay, the second in command, and Wattenberg, the Navigating Officer. Kay was responsible to Langsdorff for the state of the ship and the crew. It was his task to see that all the departments ran smoothly, that the crew were efficient, and the ship was in good trim. And if anything happened to Langsdorff he would take over the command.

In worsening weather the *Graf Spee* ploughed her way to the southwest. The *Dt-Geraet* searched with its invisible eye; the powerful motor slowly revolved the big rangefinder; and ratings, their faces pressed to the rubber-rimmed eye-pieces, watched for the first telltale sign of smoke on the horizon which would mean a quick warning to the bridge and an alteration of course to keep the ship clear.

Watches were changing with what was becoming monotonous regularity. The Navigating Officer, Wattenberg, and his assistant regularly took sun sights, plotted their position on the large North Atlantic track charts, and made neat entries in the log which Wattenberg signed. The amount of cloud, strength of wind, height and length of sea, amount of fuel consumed, courses steered, visibility, revolutions at which the propellers were turning – all were noted at hourly intervals and initialled by the officer of the watch. With a comparatively inexperienced crew the note for 26 August, 'great deterioration in weather', also told a story of widespread sea-sickness.

On 31 August, as Commodore Harwood approached Freetown in the *Exeter*, the *Graf Spee* was more than 1,500 miles away to the north-west, steering south for her first meeting with the tanker *Altmark*; and that evening an officer went as fast as dignity allowed from the wireless office to the Captain's cabin, knocked on the door and entered. He had just deciphered a long signal and he handed a signal pad to Langsdorff. 'Radiogram from Berlin, sir,' he said.

It was from the Naval War Staff and signed by Grand Admiral Raeder. The radiogram contained the gist of Hitler's 'Directive No. 1 for the Conduct of the War' – *Fall Weiss*, the invasion of Poland, was timed to begin at 4.45 AM next day; and Langsdorff was expressly ordered that, owing to the uncertain attitude of the Western Powers, the *Graf Spee* was to open fire only if attacked . . .

During the night Wattenberg was busy with his sextant taking star sights to get a final fix before meeting the *Altmark*. After the usual session in the chart room solving neat problems in spherical trigonometry, Wattenberg announced that the *Graf Spee* should sight the *Altmark* – providing Captain Dau was in position – at about 0800.

Shortly after dawn next day, Friday, 1 September, Langsdorff was on the bridge, joining a group of officers who had also gone up there – although they were not on watch – to wait for one thing: the meeting with the *Altmark*.

Suddenly, at 0805, there was a shout from a lookout: 'Two masts in sight fine on the starboard bow.' The operator at the rangefinder could, at first, see a double image of two masts, then he quickly spun a dial until they merged into a single image. Another rating read off the range of the strange vessel and this was passed to the bridge.

Was it the *Altmark* or was it, by some awful coincidence, a British cruiser? Langsdorff waited for more reports from the rangefinder. 'It's a tanker . . . about 10,000 tons . . .'

'Make the challenge,' Langsdorff ordered: and the shutter of the big searchlight directly above the bridge rattled as a signalman tapped out the Morse letters.

On the bridge of the *Altmark* all available binoculars were trained on the warship, still almost hull-down on the horizon. Was it, wondered

Captain Dau, the *Graf Spee* – or a British cruiser? If it was the Royal Navy he stood a good chance of bluffing his way out – there were plenty of merchant ships about (he had dodged several in the previous few days), and the *Altmark* bore little resemblance to a German supply ship. The Norwegian flag was flying aft and the name painted on either bow was *Sogne*,* and it was repeated on the stern, with the port of registry underneath – 'Oslo'.

The chances were, reasoned Dau, that a British cruiser would come close alongside, identify her as Norwegian and therefore neutral, and after asking her destination, steam on and leave him in peace.

Dau and his Chief Officer, Paulsen, spelled out the Morse letters: it was the *Graf Spee*. He ordered the answer to be made, and in a few seconds a rating with a signal lamp was flashing the reply. Rapidly the word spread round the *Altmark*'s crew and they lined the rails to watch the pocket battleship approach.

Since the two ships were approaching at a mean speed of thirty-five knots, it was a matter of minutes before the details of the *Graf Spee* could be picked out with the naked eye, and Dau rang down to the engine room to stop engines. Slowly the *Altmark* lost way and started to wallow gently while the *Graf Spee* manoeuvred to within a cable length and stopped.

Soon Dau was in Langsdorff's cabin where he was introduced to Kay and the other senior officers, including Wattenberg, the Navigator, who had brought along a roll of charts.

After hearing his report, Langsdorff told him that he considered the *Graf Spee* had, so far, not been sighted. Dau, although overawed by Langsdorff, could not help making a joke about the fact that the *Altmark*'s lookouts had sighted the *Graf Spee*'s smoke before her masts had come into sight over the horizon.

This astonished Langsdorff, especially since the *Graf Spee* had diesel engines. Making a lot of smoke in wartime, for a battleship or a humble merchantman trying to keep station in convoy, is a great offence, apart from being a standing invitation to an inquiring enemy.

So the entry appeared in *Graf Spee*'s log on 1 September: 'Sighted *Altmark* 0805 in 24° 25' north, 36° 15' west. *Altmark* reported they were able to sight our smoke before seeing masts.' And Korvettenkapitän

*The Norwegian *Sogne*, of Oslo, was not listed in Lloyd's Register.

(Ing) Klepp, the *Graf Spee*'s Chief Engineer, was warned that it must not happen again.

Then Langsdorff, Dau, Kay and Wattenberg discussed future operations. Wattenberg had the *Graf Spee*'s first operational area – between 5° and 10° north, and 25° and 35° west (some 400–500 miles due west of Freetown) marked on his chart; but until the diplomatic situation cleared itself up, Langsdorff told Dau, the *Altmark* would steam in company with the *Graf Spee*.

While the officers talked, a large hose was being passed across to the *Graf Spee*, and as soon as it was connected the pumps started the precious oil fuel flowing into the pocket battleship's bunkers. They did not stop until 785 cubic metres of it had poured across.

The *Graf Spee* had brought Dr Harting to join the *Altmark*, but as she already had a doctor on board, Dau and Langsdorff decided he should stay in the *Graf Spee*. After transferring some signalmen and certain stores to the *Altmark*, the two ships got under way and moved southward in company. And all the time the wireless operators in both ships were listening to broadcasts from European stations giving the latest news of the Fuehrer's march on Poland.

All seemed to be going well the next day, Saturday, 2 September; and everyone on board was jubilant. Only the more thoughtful of them stopped to wonder if Britain and France would honour their pledges to Poland.

Still the two ships moved southward at a slow speed. All the time they were moving into warmer water and Dr Kartzendorff had to treat some of the *Graf Spee*'s crew, who had unwisely bared their Nordic skin for too long under the tropical sun.

During the morning the *Altmark* altered course from time to time so that her position varied in relation to the *Graf Spee*. This gave the *Graf Spee*'s gunnery officers a chance to exercise their men. Both the *Dt-Geraet* and optical rangefinders were used and the results were compared.

Later Langsdorff was brought an intercepted radio signal from the British Admiralty to all British merchant shipping homeward bound, warning them to follow certain routes. At dusk both ships altered course to the northward; by midnight the officer of the watch noted the weather as being fine, with a Force 3–4 easterly wind.

At 0800 on Sunday, 3 September, the *Graf Spee* was just over three days from her first operational area, according to Wattenberg, and course was altered south again. As usual, a receiver in the radio room was tuned in to the Rugby transmitter to see what the British were talking about, and a startled operator took down a plain-language (i.e. not in cipher) broadcast in English of an Admiralty special telegram which said: *11 AM COMMENCE HOSTILITIES AT ONCE AGAINST GERMANY.*

This was rushed to Langsdorff, who called his officers together and read it to them. Over the ship's loudspeakers, the crew were told that Britain had declared war against Germany. Then, thirty-nine minutes after the Rugby broadcast, operators in Berlin started to transmit a radiogram in code addressed to the *Graf Spee* from the *Seekriegsleitung.* It read: *COMMENCE HOSTILITIES WITH ENGLAND IMMEDI-ATELY.*

Later that evening a further message from SKL told Langsdorff that from 1700 hours France considered herself at war with Germany; but it added that French shipping was not to be attacked, so that Hitler's efforts to dissuade the Western Powers from assisting Poland would not be prejudiced.

As Langsdorff observed in his War Diary, these orders tied his hands even more in relation to French shipping than they were tied over neutral vessels. French ships could report the position of the *Graf Spee* by wireless, and he could take no action to stop them; whereas with neutral ships the ban on the use of wireless for unneutral purposes could be enforced.

At this time Langsdorff had a reasonably clear idea of what opposition he was up against, thanks to *B-Dienst*. This consisted of a group of cipher experts on board *Graf Spee* whose only task was to take enemy cipher signals as they were received and try to break down the code.

In many cases they were able to do this successfully; and the signals often revealed present or future movements of British warships. This information, coupled with similar reports from Berlin, where other signals were intercepted, was often invaluable to Langsdorff. The *Graf Spee* was equipped with special wireless receivers which automatically combed all the frequencies, and stopped at any one on which a message was being transmitted. If it was in code which the *B-Dienst* group could not break, it was – if wireless silence was not vital – rebroadcast to the SKL in Berlin. There a special computer was set to work on it. The SKL boasted at this time that the computer could break down a code in twenty minutes.

On 7 September another long radiogram addressed to Langsdorff was received from SKL in Berlin, and it gave the gist of Raeder's conference with Hitler, ending up with the order to the *Graf Spee* to move away from the operational area.

By now thoroughly exasperated, Langsdorff decided, in view of these orders, to move rapidly to the open wastes of the South Atlantic, where both the *Graf Spee* and the *Altmark* could wait without fear of being spotted.

The area he chose was a triangle 2,500 miles to the south-east, and just to the westward of Ascension and St Helena. Langsdorff considered that it would be free of merchant ships, unpatrolled by warships, and the weather would be calm enough for both the *Altmark* and *Graf Spee* to carry out such necessary tasks as overhauling engines, storing and fuelling.

On the following Sunday, 10 September, the *Graf Spee* and *Altmark* arrived at the northern limit of the waiting area chosen by Langsdorff as being free of British ships, and at noon slowed down so that they just had steerage way. Langsdorff, however, was wrong. The next day was a Monday, 11 September, and he ordered that refuelling was to start early; but just as a precaution the pocket battleship's reconnaissance aircraft, an Arado 196 float-plane, would take off and make a wide sweep round their position to ensure they were not disturbed.

Just after dawn the plane's tanks were filled, and the pilot, Flugzeug Unteroffizier Heinrich Bongardts, and the observer, Oberleutnant zur See Spiering, donned their flying clothes. At 0610 Bongardts opened up the throttle of the Arado's single engine and took off.

Spiering told Bongardts to steer a south-westerly course, and as the Arado climbed, the two men carefully watched for any sign of smoke or ships. After a few minutes, when they had flown thirty miles and reached latitude 9° south, Spiering gave the pilot another course – this time due north.

Still they sighted nothing until they had covered twenty-nine miles; then almost on the horizon to the north-east, they saw a ship. While Spiering watched it closely through binoculars, Bongardts swung the Arado away to starboard through 180 degrees, until they were flying back along their own track. The time was 0638.

Had they been sighted? Spiering was not sure – but as they were almost at extreme visibility range he thought they probably had not. Unless, of course, the ship carried *Dt-Geraet*.

However, Spiering was certain of two things – the ship was steering a course of 170 degrees when sighted, but she had then turned to 200 degrees and increased speed. And he was fairly certain she was a British cruiser.

It was far too risky to send a wireless signal to warn the *Graf Spee* that an enemy cruiser was only twenty miles away and might any second alter course directly towards the *Graf Spee* to the south-eastward. Bongardts opened the throttle and steered south for about ten miles until Spiering gave him an easterly course which would bring them to the *Graf Spee* and the *Altmark*, lying stopped and unaware of the danger they were in.

By the time the two ships were in sight Spiering had the signal lamp ready and Bongardts put the aircraft into a shallow dive towards the pocket battleship. Rapidly Spiering called her up, received the answering signal, then passed the warning. Immediately Langsdorff ordered all boats to return to their respective ships and passed a signal to the *Altmark* that he intended moving away east-south-east.

In the meantime the *Dt-Geraet* operators were given an approximate bearing to search, and the *B-Dienst*, the code experts, were told to stand by as the *Graf Spee*'s wireless operators listened on the enemy wavelengths to see if any increase in signalling would give an answer to the vital question as to whether or not Spiering's aircraft had been sighted.

But the enemy cruiser – if indeed it was a cruiser – was too far away for the radar, and there was no sign of smoke on the horizon. Soon the operators reported that there was no increase in wireless traffic on the enemy wavelengths. In fact there were no indications, Langsdorff decided, that the pocket battleship's presence in the Atlantic had been discovered. But it had been an extremely narrow escape. It was not that he considered the cruiser was any particular menace to him, but apart from any damage she might do, which would perhaps prove impossible to repair without a base, there was the danger that one brief signal to the British Admiralty would bring swarms of powerful warships hunting for him – from Freetown, Gibraltar, Bermuda, the South American coast and from South Africa.

However, the danger passed. For the moment the problem was to refuel from the *Altmark* and get the stores on board. Shortly before 0715 Langsdorff told Kay that the two ships could stop and resume their interrupted task. As the Arado aircraft was running short of fuel it came in, landed nearby and was hoisted on board.

Within a few minutes launches were plying between them; cases were lowered overside from the *Altmark*, taken over to the *Graf Spee* and taken on board. The long hose and its floats were being prepared when suddenly a lookout in the *Altmark* shouted excitedly to Captain Dau and pointed to the south-east.

Through binoculars the tops of two masts could be seen on the horizon. From the angle they made, Dau roughly estimated the ship was steering a course of 220 degrees and was making about fifteen knots. Within seconds a signal lamp was flickering a warning to the *Graf Spee*. But the unknown ship was steaming fast and soon two thin yellow funnels could be seen.

As 'Action Stations' alarms rattled through the *Graf Spee*, Langsdorff decided that the ship was probably an armed cruiser; and once again the launches were hurriedly retrieved and the pocket battleship, followed by the *Altmark*, turned and steered north-eastward at full speed, away from the unknown ship. Again the operators listened carefully for any wireless signals which might indicate that the *Graf Spee* had been sighted; but they picked up nothing. It seemed that Langsdorff's luck was holding.*

The first ship sighted by the Arado, and which Spiering thought was a cruiser, was in fact the *Cumberland*. As mentioned earlier, she had left Plymouth after being detached from the 2nd Cruiser Squadron of the Home Fleet with orders to reinforce Commodore Harwood in the Rio de Janeiro area.

She had arrived in Freetown, Sierra Leone, on the 7th, refuelled and then sailed again next day for Rio, more than 2,000 miles to the south-west. Three days earlier Langsdorff had chosen his waiting area – and the *Cumberland*'s course for Rio ran through the northern end of it. So, after steaming more than 4,000 miles from Plymouth to join in the hunt for possible commerce raiders in the South Atlantic, the *Cumberland*, by one of those strange and dangerous coincidences that happen in war, was at 0637 steering 170 degrees – a course which would have taken her within ten miles of the *Graf Spee*. But at 0638 she altered course thirty degrees to starboard, on one leg of a zig-zag, to 200 degrees.

*The identity of this second ship has never been discovered.

Had she steered a course which took her ten miles farther to the south-east she would probably not have been sighted by Spiering in the Arado and would have come upon the *Graf Spee* and *Altmark*. How the course of the ensuing action would have gone is not hard to guess. The *Cumberland*'s eight 8-inch guns would have been out-ranged by the *Graf Spee*'s six 11-inch, and Langsdorff would have had to choose between risking engaging the *Cumberland* and possibly being severely damaged by hits, or withdrawing and trying to nullify the enemy's advantage of speed by using his superior fire power.

But far more important is the fact that the *Cumberland* would firstly transmit the all-important enemy report. This would have been picked up at Freetown and passed to the Commander-in-Chief, South Atlantic, and to the Admiralty in London. Then the *Cumberland* would have tried to fulfil the cruiser's traditional role of shadower. However, we cannot speculate too much: the *Cumberland* did in fact alter course 30 degrees at 0638 and was spotted by Spiering at extreme visibility range, and by that chance the *Graf Spee* escaped detection.

For the next fortnight the *Graf Spee* and *Altmark* cruised in the waiting area. Langsdorff kept his ship's company exercising and the Arado float-plane was sent up frequently to act as 'target' for Meusermann's anti-aircraft guns. From time to time the two ships stopped to carry out machinery overhauls, and by the 13th the *Graf Spee*'s navigator noted that the pocket battleship had so far covered 7,079 miles. Langsdorff was wisely keeping her fuel tanks topped up, so that although the *Graf Spee* could operate for six weeks without refuelling, oil was taken in on 12, 20 and 22 September.

So the days slipped by, one very much like another, until the 25th. Although it was to prove a turning point in the *Graf Spee*'s career, it started off badly. She and the *Altmark* had stopped early in the morning in a calm sea to transfer more crates and barrels of stores. Among the barrels was one containing three months' supply of special oil for the pocket battleship's refrigeration equipment (which was required for the magazines as well as food). As it was being hoisted on board from one of the *Altmark*'s launches, a sling slipped and the barrel fell into the sea, sinking immediately.

However, that was soon forgotten when the *Graf Spee*'s wireless operators picked up a long coded radiogram from Berlin which

Langsdorff was overjoyed to read: the SKL announced an imminent change of objective for the *Graf Spee* from a passive waiting *(Abwarten)* to an active participation in the trade war.

The radiogram also gave a list of British warship dispositions. From agents' reports and radio intercepts, SKL placed the cruisers *Cumberland, Exeter, Ajax* and *Despatch*, the destroyers *Hotspur* and *Havock*, and the submarine *Severn* on the east coast of South America, and three cruisers and a submarine on the West Africa coast.

With this information, plus all radio traffic intercepted by his own operators and decoded by *B-Dienst*, Langsdorff was able to build up a fairly clear picture in his mind of the naval situation in the South Atlantic and make plans to begin commerce raiding the moment the SKL sent the order.

Although Langsdorff did not know it, the signal warning of a change of objective was the result of a long argument with Hitler two days earlier. Eventually the Fuehrer had agreed to lift restrictions on French ships and, on being told that 'it will be necessary to commit the pocket battleships by about the beginning of October so that their supplies will not be exhausted or their morale undermined', finally gave permission. On 26 September, more than three weeks after the beginning of the war, the SKL ordered Langdorff to 'commence active participation in the trade war'.

On the day the war began, Admiral Raeder had written: 'Today the war against France and Britain broke out, the war which, according to the Fuehrer, we had no need to expect before about 1944 . . .' After the events and political reassurances of the previous years, he added: 'The surface forces, moreover, are so inferior in number and strength to the British Fleet that, even at full strength they can do little more than show that they know how to die gallantly. . .The pocket battleships – with the outbreak of war only the *Deutschland* and *Graf Spee* are ready for operations in the Atlantic – if skilfully used should be able to carry out cruiser warfare on the high seas for some time . . .'

After the end of the war the man who had succeeded Admiral Raeder in command of the German Navy, Admiral Karl Doenitz, wrote: 'Once Germany was committed to war against the United Kingdom, her whole naval effort was directed against British shipping and sea communications. If this campaign failed to achieve decisive results, then

Germany's defeat, whatever form it might happen to take, became inevitable.'

Both men were correct, and the SKL's signals to the *Graf Spee* and the *Deutschland* were the beginning . . .

The day after receiving the SKL's signal, Langsdorff noted down in his War Diary his thoughts on the future, and his salient points were:

(a) The choice of operational areas is limited to south of 5° south because of defects in the *Graf Spee*'s refrigeration plant affecting magazine temperatures. [Certain explosives are very sensitive to heat changes and for safety's sake must be kept below a certain temperature. The refrigeration plant had been giving trouble for some time and had constantly affected Langsdorff's decisions. It was eventually repaired.]

(b) The South American trade route is more vital to the British and French than the Cape route since the Mediterranean is open to the Allies and in any case provides a shorter route to Europe from the Far East.

Langsdorff decided to take the *Graf Spee* to an area off Pernambuco (in Brazil, forming the easternmost part of South America) and then sweep south to find the British shipping route off the Brazilian coast. After finding a convoy and attacking it energetically, he intended withdrawing at high speed eastward across the Atlantic to attack again on the South African shipping routes off the Cape of Good Hope.

Shortly after noon on 27 September, when Langsdorff had told Captain Dau of his plans and arranged to rendezvous on 14 October, the *Graf Spee* left the *Altmark* in the waiting area and moved off to the north-west at cruising speed.

For all the fifty-four officers and more than one thousand other men it was a moment of elation: all the days and weeks of wearisome preparations on board the pocket battleship were now going to pay dividends. For Langsdorff it was the culmination of years of study and training which started as midshipman in the Kaiser's Navy. Now, at long last, he was commanding one of Germany's greatest warships and he was steering her into action.

But first he must tell the crew what lay ahead of them. He told Kay to muster as many men as could be spared at 1700 because he wanted to address them. They fell in and Langsdorff, smart in his uniform, the Iron Cross pinned on his left breast, came out to deliver his speech. Briefly he outlined the situation. The waiting period was over; the Fuehrer had ordered that from now on the *Graf Spee* was to act as a commerce raider. Even as he spoke, he said, they were heading for their first operational area off the Brazilian coast, where they would find some prey on the old peace-time shipping routes. Their task, he concluded, was not going to be an easy one: the *Seekriegsleitung* had signalled the whereabouts of several enemy cruisers, but the *Graf Spee* would have to run from them if she was to fulfil her role as a commerce raider successfully. 'Heil Hitler,' he said.

'Heil Hitler,' they replied, and their cheers showed Langsdorff that he had struck just the right note and he went back to his cabin well satisfied. He was quite pleased that they were not too keen on the idea he had for fooling the enemy – it showed they were proud of their ship. He had realized, however, that once raiding started it would be impossible to stop the enemy knowing a big German warship was at large, but it would confuse them if her victims gave her conflicting names. From now on, then, the *Admiral Graf Spee* was to become the *Admiral Scheer*.

The second in command, Kay, supervised the painting out of the name *Admiral Graf Spee* on the stern, replacing it with the *Admiral Scheer*, written in the same Gothic lettering. All the names on lifebelts, boats and other equipment were altered; and the crew were given new cap bands which bore the *Admiral Scheer*'s name in gold letters.

Thanks to the *Altmark*, the pocket battleship's fuel tanks were full; if necessary she could carry on for another six weeks without meeting the tanker again. There was plenty of food on board, the ammunition outfit was complete, and apart from the refrigerating plant there were no defects to report. Steadily the pocket battleship moved towards Pernambuco; the noon sights recorded in the log showed her oblique progress towards the Equator – on the 28th she was 15° south of it, and on the 29th, 11° 05′ south.

That evening another signal was received from SKL, and it read:

At the present time England is in need of successes; any gain in prestige by England is therefore undesirable. On the other hand attacks on shipping by the pocket battleship are to be carried out to the fullest extent. Restriction of operations to specified areas is hereby cancelled.

In the North Atlantic battle cruisers and aircraft may be encountered, but not yet in the South Atlantic.

At noon on Saturday, 30 September, Wattenberg took a sun sight and within a few minutes noted in the log the *Graf Spee*'s noon position – 9° 21′ south, 33° 40′ west. The *Graf Spee*, under the guise of the *Admiral Scheer*, was about to make her first kill.

IV

Sinking the Clement

===

1300. Steamer sighted. (From the log of the *Graf Spee*.)

THE WIND was easterly, blowing about Force 4, the sea was moderate, and the British steamer *Clement*, 5,050 tons, was within 200 miles of the end of her voyage from New York to Bahia (Salvador). Stowed in her holds were 20,000 cases of kerosene.

Third officer H.J. Gill was on watch and the master, Captain F.C.P. Harris, was in his cabin, one deck below the bridge. By ship's time it was just after 1115,* and in his report† later Gill said: 'I sighted a battleship four points on the port bow on the horizon. From the time I sighted it, it was making a beeline for us all the way. . .'

Captain Harris reported that the Third Officer called down the speaking tube from the bridge to his cabin. ' "There is a man-o'-war about four points on the port bow, coming in fast." I said, "I expect that is the *Ajax*," which I knew was on the Brazilian coast, "or a Brazilian cruiser," which had left Pernambuco the day before.'

'I could see no flags,' the Captain's report continued, 'only that it was a man-o'-war. It was about four or five miles off with a huge bow wave as if he was coming in at thirty knots.'

1330. Aircraft flown off to stop it. The aircraft signalled to the steamer:
'Stop – no wireless transmitting.' (*Graf Spee*'s log.)

Gill continues: 'Three or four minutes later a plane appeared – more

---

*The *Graf Spee* kept German time but the *Clement* kept local time in common with other British merchantmen and warships.
†Survivors were interrogated for Admiralty Intelligence and records purposes.

on the port quarter. She circled round the *Clement* and flashed a message to the battleship giving the information he wanted – whether we were armed or not, I suppose.

'The seaplane circled round again, then opened fire. She was painted a very dark grey and the black iron cross was just in front of the tail on the port-side fuselage. We stopped engines and the plane kept up his fire until the ship's way was lost, firing at the bridge – the wheelhouse went up in the air . . .'

Captain Harris, who was standing with Gill on the bridge, heard a buzzing sound and saw the aircraft flying past. He continued in his report: 'I was not worried as I knew the *Ajax* had one. We exposed the name board.'

The plane circled and 'came over the ship again, and started firing. I stopped the engines. Just then the Chief Officer looked up and said, "Look, Chief – a German. I can see the markings." I could see that there was some black on the plane but could see no definite markings.

'I could see no flag on the cruiser, which was end on. I said "Swing the boats out, lower them and get the crew in." About five minutes later the ship was stopped.'

He then ordered the confidential books to be thrown over the side in their special weighted canvas bag; and he continues, 'I got the Second Officer to telephone and send out the RRR signal, giving the ship's position. The operator reported that he had got his message through and that it had been picked up by a Brazilian steamer.'

Ship is ss Clement. *Crew took to boats and were left. Captain and Chief Engineer taken off and kept in* Graf Spee. *(Graf Spee's log.)*

As Captain Harris ordered his crew to abandon ship, a picket boat was hoisted out from the *Graf Spee*. On its bows was painted the false name *Admiral Scheer*. All the ratings in the picket boat wore false cap bands bearing the name, and the ruse was successful, as is shown by the following reports.

The picket boat first went to the lifeboat commanded by Third Officer Gill, and a German officer said: 'Proceed to the ship. Where is your Captain?'

As Gill and his men rowed towards the pocket battleship the picket boat went over to the number one lifeboat and took off Captain Harris and the Chief Engineer, Mr W. Bryant. It then went alongside the *Clement* and the two men were taken back on board again.

Mr Bryant reported: 'When I was on board the *Clement* with the boarding party one man with a revolver in his hand took charge and said "Come down to the engine room," and when there he told me to open the sea valves. I immediately opened the tank injection; he did not seem to know much about it. These valves would merely fill the ballast tanks and would not flood the ship. We then came up. While I was with this officer the other men were going round the ship putting bags of bombs around the vessel.'

After the German boarding party had searched all the officers' cabins, wireless room and chart room for any documents, the two British officers were taken in the picket boat to the *Graf Spee*, and Captain Harris's account for the next few hours says: 'The Boarding Officer went and reported to the Captain. We followed an officer up the ladder on to the bridge.

'When there, we met the Captain [Langsdorff] and ten officers. He saluted me and said "I am sorry, Captain, I will have to sink your ship. It is war." Shortly afterwards he said "I believe you have destroyed your confidential papers?" I said "Yes." He answered "I expected it. That is the usual thing." '

Chairs were then brought to the bridge for both Captain Harris and Mr Bryant, and the *Graf Spee* moved closer to the *Clement*. Captain Harris continues: 'Then they said "We are going to fire a torpedo." They fired a torpedo from the starboard quarter aft from the deck tube at about half a mile range, and it passed about fifty feet ahead of the *Clement*. The Captain did not seem at all pleased with this . . .

'Then they fired a second one. It passed about twenty-five feet astern . . .Then they said "We are going to use the guns." They steamed round then under the quarter of the *Clement*. The two ships were then stern to stern and the German ship was 2,500 yards off the *Clement*.

'They started with the 6-inch guns and fired about twenty-five rounds. They were not happy about that either – some were going short and some were hitting. Some of the officers could speak English well, and one said "If we were farther we would hit, but we are too close." They gave us cotton wool during the firing to put in our ears.'

1530. Clement sunk by gunfire. *(Graf Spee's* log.)

Finally, after using heavier guns, they managed to sink the steamer.

Captain Harris was kept on the bridge another hour. Then 'The

Commander [Kay] said to me that the Captain wished to speak to us. The Captain, speaking in good English, said "If you will give me your word not to attempt any sabotage or espionage, and do exactly as we tell you, you will be left free. Otherwise I will have to put a guard on you." I said "You can take my word. Neither the Chief nor I will attempt anything." He said "All right, shake hands." '

Kay took them down to his cabin and offered them cigars and iced beer. He then wrote out in English an order about sabotage, and the two Britons signed it. After that they were given a meal consisting of a large dish of cold meat, tongue and sausage, bread and butter, tea, and some rum put in it. Later some officers came into the cabin and one of them said, 'You may be here a week or a fortnight. Would you like a razor or will you go to the barber's shop? There is a barber's here.'

After the *Clement* had sunk, the *Graf Spee* then continued southward and two and a half hours later sighted another steamer. As they closed, it was seen that she was a neutral, the Greek *Papalemos*. She was ordered to stop and a picket boat took Captain Harris and Mr Bryant across to her. The *Papalemos*, with the two Britons on board, was then allowed to continue her voyage on condition she did not use her wireless within an area of 600 miles of her present position.

Later Langsdorff ordered a signal to be sent to Olinda, the radio station at Pernambuco. Using the call sign DTAR – which belonged to the *Admiral Scheer* – the signal said: *Please save the lifeboats of the* Clement. *0945 south, 3404 west.* Olinda replied: *Thanks. OK Hasta Luego.*

A second signal sent by Langsdorff was addressed to the *Seekriegsleitung* in Berlin. It gave the *Graf Spee*'s position and reported the sinking of the *Clement*, saying that 'because they used their radio the aircraft used machine guns'.

The *Graf Spee* then altered course eastward to pass between Ascension Island and St Helena, as Langsdorff had previously planned.

After narrowly missing the *Graf Spee* and *Altmark* on the 11 September, the *Cumberland* arrived in Rio de Janeiro to find orders from Harwood telling her to start 'out' convoys with the destroyer *Havock*. The destroyer *Hotspur* was due to meet the Commodore in the *Exeter* to start similar convoys from the River Plate. The *Ajax* was in the Falklands investigating the report of the three German merchantmen off the Patagonian coast.

Meanwhile a vast number of reports concerning the coasts of South America were reaching the Operational Intelligence Centre at the Admiralty in London. These reports came from a variety of sources since the Admiralty had set up a worldwide network which not only helped control merchantmen but provided intelligence information as well.

In most parts there were Naval Control Service Officers (NCSO) and in the major ports naval attachés as well. In neutral countries the NCSOs were appointed as additional consular officers, so that they had the right status for carrying out what was really war work on neutral soil. The official task of an NCSO was to interview the captains of Allied merchant ships arriving in port, give them routeing instructions, and report their movements to the nearest Staff Officer, Intelligence, who in turn relayed the information about German ship movements and any other useful intelligence he might discover.

At the Admiralty the movements of merchant ships had been taken over by the Trade Division, while control of warships was handled by the Operations Division. The Plans Division, as its name shows, was responsible for all naval planning, and all three worked closely with the Naval Intelligence Division.

The result was that a complete record of the whereabouts and condition of the larger warships was kept – with almost hourly alterations – on operational plots in the underground rooms at the Admiralty which formed the nerve centre of the Royal Navy at war. Thus, working closely with the Naval Intelligence and Trade Divisions, the Operations Division could switch them about – like a vast and fast-moving game of chess where you do not see your opponent's moves but can only guess them – to meet any eventuality.

Nearby were the trade plots, showing the positions of British merchant ships on the world's sea lanes, and kept up to date by the Trade Division from information arriving hourly from NCSOs, consular officials, intelligence agents, air reconnaissance, naval attachés, shipping companies and their agents.

It was through this complex grapevine that Commodore Harwood received much of his information, and we can resume the narrative with an example. On 10 September, the day before the *Graf Spee*'s Arado sighted the *Cumberland*, intelligence reached the Admiralty that the German merchant ship *Montevideo* was sailing from Rio Grande do Sul for Florianopolis (Brazil). This information was immediately radioed to Commodore Harwood in the *Exeter*, patrolling off the River Plate.

The Admiralty had provided the information; it was up to the Commodore to decide what to do. If he used the *Exeter* to try to intercept her, it meant diverting the cruiser 500 miles from the focal area off the Plate. He had to balance the possible interception of a German merchantman against the possible sinking of several Allied merchantmen if a German raider arrived in the Plate area while the *Exeter* was away. He decided the *Montevideo* would have to be left alone.

These 'What have I to gain compared with what I might lose?' decisions had to be made almost daily by Harwood, although the *Montevideo* is a minor example compared with the one he faced on 24 September, two days before Langsdorff received the order to start operations. The naval attaché at Buenos Aires signalled Harwood that 'according to reliable source' a number of German ships – including two previously reported among those assembling off the Patagonian coast – and a U-boat were to rendezvous south-west of Ascension Island in four days' time.

The position was 1,900 miles from the *Cumberland* at Rio and nearly 3,000 miles from the *Exeter* off the Plate. Harwood promptly signalled the *Cumberland* to steam to the rendezvous at full speed while Captain Woodhouse in the *Ajax* at the Falklands was ordered nearly 2,000 miles north to take the *Cumberland*'s place at Rio de Janeiro. The ships searched, but found nothing, and the *Cumberland* went on to Freetown to refuel.

The first month of the war ended in the South Atlantic with Harwood's two destroyers being recalled to England because of a serious shortage in the Home Fleet. His plan for Plate and Rio convoys was working well, and although some German merchantmen were managing to slip through on their way home to the Fatherland, no British ships had been lost. But, as we have already seen, the *Graf Spee* was on the eve of striking her first blow. Overnight the whole course of the war at sea in the north and south Atlantic was about to change, and we can now view the *Graf Spee*'s activities from the British side.

V

'RRR – Clement *Gunned*'

THE WIRELESS operator in the British cableship *Norseman* was listening in as usual on Saturday, 30 September, with his set tuned to 600 metres. His small cabin was almost lined with grey-finished equipment, and to anyone unused to a wireless office he faced an apparently bewildering number of dials and tuning knobs.

The time was 1452 GMT and suddenly he heard hurried Morse coming through his earphones. The first three letters galvanized him – dot-dash-dot, dot-dash-dot, dot-dash-dot . . .It was the beginning of a raider report, and quickly he wrote on his signal pad:

RRR RRR RRR. . . *3404 W Clement gunned*.

He had not been able to read the middle of the message, but it was clear enough; the steamer *Clement* was being attacked by a raider. He called the Captain and anxiously continued listening in.

Three minutes later, through the crackle of atmospherics, came more Morse, and he automatically wrote it down:

RRR RRR RRR 0908 S 3404 W Clement gunned.

A minute later the same desperate message was again transmitted, and he was able to check the figures in the complete message. By now the Captain was standing beside him in the wireless office, and after four minutes, at 1500, he heard more Morse and noted it down:

PPA DE KIXZ QRT (Amaralina, Bahia, Radio Station from ss Mormacrio – *stop transmitting*).

This was followed a minute later by another signal from the steamer *Mormacrio*, telling Amaralina Radio Station:

If you would listen on 600 metres you would hear ss Clement *in distress.*

The *Norseman*'s operator continued listening; and as he waited for some ship or shore station to acknowledge the call for help, the wireless operator on board the *Clement* reported to Captain Harris that he had got the raider report through.

And while Captain Harris gave the order to abandon ship, and the *Graf Spee* lowered boats to carry a boarding party over to the steamer, the Master of the *Norseman* continued waiting anxiously. When it was obvious to him that no one had answered, he decided he would have to break wireless silence so that the Admiralty could be warned. This was an extremely dangerous thing for him to have to do, since a raider could fix the *Norseman*'s position by direction-finder as she transmitted it; but he realized that far more than the safety of his own ship was involved.

So the *Norseman*'s operator started calling Portishead Radio Station, more than 3,000 miles away in the Bristol Channel. The time was 1512, only seventeen minutes after the last signal from the *Clement*, but the *Norseman* was unlucky; Portishead did not hear her calling-up signal.

There was only one thing for the *Norseman* to do now, and the Captain told his operator to re-broadcast the *Clement*'s raider report on 600 metres, and at 1520 the dramatic signal started crackling out again and again.

But no reply was noted in the *Norseman*'s log; and her Captain decided to try to get a message passed to the British authorities in South America, which was of course much nearer but still out of range of the *Norseman*'s radio. So at 1525 she called up the steamer *Mormacrio*, which was near the coast and whose signals would be powerful enough to reach a shore station.

The operator tapped out:

Will you take a message for re-transmission to Olinda Radio? How are my signals?

The *Mormacrio*'s operator answered:

Go ahead with your transmission.

In the verbal 'shorthand' used by wireless operators the *Norseman* then sent:

CTD CDE Clement *1 10 20 1452 GMT via Western D RM British Consul Pernambuco – RRR 0908 S 3404 W* Clement (secret call sign)* *AR K.*

The *Mormacrio* replied: *R QRA?* (Message received, what is the name of your station?) and continued: *Are U* Clement? *Don't get who from.*

The *Norseman* was not anxious to give her name, since any German raider could – and probably would – be listening and fixing her position; but, providing the *Norseman* did not reveal who she was, there was no reason for any raider to suppose she was not a neutral ship. So she replied:

SRI NO QRA (Sorry, will not give name of my station).

A minute later came another signal from the *Mormacrio*, which, since she was an American vessel, was perhaps understandably rather puzzled:

If you are Clement *why not send direct PPO* (Olinda Radio). *Only 50 miles.*

The *Norseman* answered:

Not Clement. *Too far away to raise.*

By now the *Mormacrio* was extremely suspicious of the whole thing, and at 1536 asked:

Are U DTAR? (Are you *Admiral Scheer*)

No, British, Unable to give QRA (name of station), the *Norseman* replied; and the *Mormacrio* then sent:

Will not take as message, will take as note for PPO (Olinda).

The *Norseman*'s operator then heard the *Mormacrio* calling up Olinda, and as soon as the shore station replied she passed the message to the British Consul at Pernambuco which was to start the opening moves of the greatest hunt ever known up to then.

Three hours later the *Norseman*'s wireless operator heard the following breezy conversation between two ships (probably American) which were working without call signs:

*The secret call sign would identify the *Norseman* to the British Consul.

SA OM WOT QRA OF DT DTAR (Say, old man, what was the name of that German warship?)

Think it's Admiral Scheer, *one of their battlewagons.*

Just before lunch-time on Sunday, 1 October, while people in Britain walked home from church, dug their allotments, had a quiet morning doing nothing, or talked of the disaster in Poland (where Warsaw had fallen to the Germans four days earlier), a wireless signal in code arrived at the Admiralty in Whitehall.

It was one of dozens already received that morning, only it was from the Naval Control Staff Officer at Pernambuco, and it said:

British ship MBBL (Clement) *sunk by surface raider 75 miles southeast of Pernambuco 1400 local time yesterday.*

It took only a second to realize its significance: the Admiralty's suspicion that a pocket battleship was at large might now be confirmed, although the raider that had sunk the *Clement* could be merely an armed merchant ship. Nevertheless a German raider had revealed herself in the Atlantic for the first time; and this was the minute the First Sea Lord, Admiral Pound, had been waiting for. But the most important fact to establish was the identity — and thus the strength — of the raider.

An hour and a half after the first signal from the NCSO at Pernambuco a second arrived at the Admiralty, from the NCSO at Bahia:

W/T message from British ship MBBL (Clement) *received by cable ship GBVS* (Norseman) *and British ship GLTK* (Almanzora) *about 1400 Brazilian time 30September consisted of 'Rs' and possibly 'As' and word 'gunned'. Position 009 degrees 08 minutes south, 034 degrees 08 minutes west. British ship GLTK arrived and suspended sailing pending instructions.*

While plans were drawn up in case the raider was a pocket battleship and not just one of the many German merchant ships which had sneaked out of the sanctuary of a South American port and armed herself, the Admiralty signalled to Admiral Lyon and Commodore Harwood that the order recalling the destroyers was cancelled and they were 'to be retained in the South Atlantic for the present'.

A further signal said that Admiral Lyon's command would be strengthened by the cruisers *Effingham, Emerald, Enterprise, Norfolk* and *Capetown*. The battleships *Resolution* and *Revenge*, and the aircraft carrier *Hermes* would proceed to Freetown or Jamaica.

Meanwhile, just before 0800 that same Sunday morning, the Brazilian steamer *Itatinga* was steaming along the South American coast some miles off Pernambuco when the officer on watch spotted a ship's boat. The steamer stopped and picked up the men in it. They were Third Officer Gill and twelve other survivors from the *Clement*. The master of the *Itatinga* then sent a wireless message to the port he was bound for, Bahia, reporting his find. He also added that he was due at Bahia early on 3 October.

At the same time three other lifeboats from the *Clement*, one of them commanded by the *Clement*'s Chief Officer, were heading for the South American coast; and the Greek ship *Papalemos*, which had been stopped by the *Graf Spee*, was heading for the Cape Verde Islands with Captain Harris and the Chief Engineer on board.

So the first day of October ended with the Admiralty knowing only that there was a raider in the South Atlantic. Whether it was a German cruiser, a pocket battleship or simply an armed merchant ship was a mystery. Mr Churchill and Admiral Pound, as well as the Operations and Planning Divisions, could only wait for more news.

They did not have to wait long. Next day, 2 October, the first signal came shortly after 0900 from the wide-awake Naval Control Service Officer at Bahia:

> *Brazilian ship PUKW* (Itatinga) *expected to arrive Bahia early 3 October with thirteen survivors of British ship MBBL. Immediate report will be sent on arrival.*

This was followed three hours later by a signal from the NCSO at Pernambuco, who reported:

> *British ship MBBL was machine-gunned by seaplanes and Chief Officer slightly wounded. Later sunk by secondary armament. The Captain and Chief Engineer taken prisoner.*

A few minutes after that came a signal from Maceio which gave the first definite news of the identity of the raider (apart from those which referred to the fact that the call sign DTAR used by the enemy was that of the *Admiral Scheer*. That was naturally regarded at the Admiralty as a possible ruse which could be used by any vessel).

The message from Maceio, quickly decoded and taken to Admiral
Pound, said:

> *Ship's lifeboat from British ship MBBL* (Clement) *arrived here today
> Monday with eleven crew including Chief Officer who was slightly
> wounded. Chief Officer confirms name of German armoured ship
> Admiral Scheer *and reports that two other lifeboats following on with
> remainder of crew except Captain and Chief Officer who were taken
> on board German ship.*

The First Sea Lord presided over a meeting of the heads of divisions in
the Upper War Room at the Admiralty later that day to discuss ways of
trapping and sinking the raider. If she was in fact a pocket battleship,
with six 11-inch guns, then each 'killing unit' would have to comprise
one battle-cruiser, or two 8-inch cruisers with, if possible, an aircraft
carrier. It was decided to form 'Force K', the *Renown* and the carrier *Ark
Royal,* and orders were given for them to leave the Home Fleet and make
for the South Atlantic. The French Ministry of Marine was also asked to
provide ships, and they agreed.

While the Admiralty worked out plans for forming hunting groups –
as they were later called – Admiral Lyon at Freetown and Commodore
Harwood in the *Exeter* were doing the best they could with what forces
they had. When the first signals arrived on 1 October, Harwood was far
from sure at that stage that the vessel had been a pocket battleship, and
was reluctant to abandon the River Plate area because of the large
amount of shipping using it – far more than used Rio de Janeiro, the
nearest 'focal area' to the raider's last known position near Pernambuco.

Harwood thought it more likely that the German plan behind the
appearance of a raider off Pernambuco was that they expected him to
move his force northwards, leaving the wide River Plate estuary open to
attack by a second raider waiting in readiness. Given the considerable
number of German merchantmen round the South American coast, and
which could have been carrying guns ready to be fitted when war began,
this was a distinct possibility

He finally signalled to Admiral Lyon that he had decided to
concentrate the *Exeter* and *Ajax* off Rio, send the destroyer *Hotspur* to
cover the Rio–Santos area, and keep the *Havock* patrolling the Plate
area. The NCSOs at Rio and Santos were told to suspend sailings for four
days to give *Hotspur* time to arrive and take over the area which was

being vacated by the *Ajax*. Harwood's signal crossed with orders from Admiral Lyon telling him to concentrate the *Exeter*, *Ajax* and two destroyers in the Rio area. Harwood had in fact already anticipated part of the order.

The *Exeter* fuelled and confirmation arrived that the raider was in fact a pocket battleship. A few hours earlier the Admiralty had sent a welcome signal – Harwood's force was to be reinforced with the cruiser *Achilles*, a sister ship of the *Ajax* and belonging to the New Zealand division of the Royal Navy. She had been operating on her own along the Pacific coast of South America.*

Later in the day Admiral Lyon signalled that when the *Cumberland* rejoined – she was at the time refuelling in Freetown after the abortive search off Ascension Island – the *Ajax*, *Achilles* and the two destroyers should be used for trade protection in the focal area while the two 8-inch cruisers, *Cumberland* and *Exeter*, formed a hunting unit.

Meanwhile plans were being changed at the Admiralty: a meeting presided over by the First Sea Lord cancelled the plan made four days earlier and abandoned the patrolling of focal areas visualized in the War Memorandum. Instead, as a telegram told Admiral Lyon, since a full convoy system in the South Atlantic and Indian Ocean would 'result in unacceptable delay even if escorts could be provided', eight hunting groups were to be formed. These comprised mostly pairs of 8-inch cruisers, some with an aircraft carrier. 'The strength of each hunting group is sufficient to destroy any armoured ship of the *Deutschland* class or armoured cruiser of the *Hipper* class,' the signal said.†

Bearing in mind that at this point the *Graf Spee* had sunk only one merchant ship, the way that a powerful commerce raider can disrupt and disperse the enemy's strength is shown by the composition of the hunting groups:

---

*The *Achilles* joined three weeks later. There was no New Zealand Navy at this time.

†The Admiralty still believed the pocket battleships were within the 10,000-ton treaty limit. They were, of course, bigger, and this led the Admiralty to assume (quite correctly) that it was impossible to pack six 11-inch guns *and* plenty of ammunition *and* powerful engines *and* strong armour into a ship of 10,000 tons – only 1,500 tons larger than the Exeter, which had only six 8-inch guns.

Force	Composition	Area
F	*Berwick, York*	North America and West Indies
G	*Cumberland, Exeter*	East coast of South America
H	*Sussex, Shropshire*	Cape of Good Hope
I	*Cornwall, Dorsetshire* and *Eagle*	Ceylon
K	*Renown, Ark Royal* and one 6-inch cruiser to be detailed by C-in-C South Atlantic	Pernambuco–Freetown
L	*Dunkerque,* three 6-inch cruisers and *Béarn*	Brest [north-west France]
M	Two 8-inch cruisers	Dakar [West Africa]
N	*Strasbourg, Hermes*	West Indies

But the Admiralty were well aware of a raider's vulnerability, and the signal to Admiral Lyon said: 'It is also to be remembered that raiders are vitally dependent on their mobility, being so far from repair facilities. Hence a weaker force, if not able to effect immediate destruction may, by resolute attack, be able to cripple an opponent sufficiently to ensure a certain subsequent location and destruction by other forces.'

The effect of forming the eight groups was immense and world-wide – Force F consisted of ships diverted from Halifax, Nova Scotia; Force H from the Mediterranean; Force I from China and Force K from the Home Fleet. But that was not all – in addition to the hunting groups, the battleships *Resolution* and *Revenge* and cruisers *Enterprise* and *Emerald* were to sail to Halifax to escort homeward-bound Atlantic convoys, and were followed later by *Repulse, Furious* and *Warspite,* while a battleship and aircraft carrier were sent through the Suez Canal to form a ninth hunting group in the Indian Ocean.

VI

Prisoners in the Altmark

AFTER DESTROYING the *Clement*, Captain Langsdorff kept to his plan of withdrawing quickly to the eastward, passing south of Ascension Island and north of St Helena, and by 1 October, the day after the sinking, the *Graf Spee* had already covered a quarter of the distance.

Rapidly the pocket battleship's longitude noted in the log decreased – it was 28° 56′ West on the 1st, 22° 51′ on the 2nd, 16° 42′ on the 3rd and 10° 44′ on the 4th. The crew were cheerful and fit, and as the days passed without the *Graf Spee* being spotted, Langsdorff began to have high hopes for the future.

After passing between the two islands on the 4th, Langsdorff altered course to the north-east, and a sudden call to the bridge at 0630 next morning told Langsdorff that it had probably been a lucky change: smoke had been sighted on the horizon. Alarm bells rang, sending the crew hurrying to their action stations.

Langsdorff decided to steer straight for the smoke, and twelve minutes later two masts and a funnel of a merchant ship could be seen. Rapidly officers and men prepared for action. A group of men assembled under Leutnant zur See Schunemann, and this time it was a prize crew and not a boarding party: Langsdorff had decided that the next ship captured undamaged should be kept as an accommodation vessel for the crews of further victims. So Schunemann had engineers, wireless operators, junior officers capable of standing a bridge watch, and ratings standing by.

Every minute reports came through from the rangefinder, and when the calibrated dials recorded 1,800 metres Langsdorff ordered the 'Heave to' and 'Do not transmit' flag signals to be run up. Still the *Graf Spee* was bows-on to the merchant ship, and at the last moment she swung round, dropped the Tricolour, hoisted the German ensign and

48

hove to. Through glasses Langsdorff and the other officers on the bridge watched the British steamer slowing down and stopping. The *Graf Spee*'s 5.9-inch guns swung round to point menacingly at the merchantman. Would she transmit a distress signal?

As soon as the way was off the *Graf Spee* a launch was lowered to take Schunemann and his prize crew to the victim. As they approached a telephone buzzed on the *Graf Spee*'s bridge. It was a message from the wireless room: the British ship was transmitting a distress signal, but it was very weak.

In a few minutes Schunemann signalled from the steamer's bridge that everything was under control: she was the 4,651-ton *Newton Beech*, and most of her cargo appeared to be maize. He was now sending the British crew over to the *Graf Spee* . . . Within two hours, with the *Newton Beech* in company, the pocket battleship was under way again. This time her speed was governed by the merchantman, and Langsdorff had second thoughts about the distress message her operator had managed to transmit. Finally he shrugged his shoulders. The transmission was weak; it was a hundred-to-one chance against anyone picking it up, especially as it had been sent outside the normal hourly period for ships with only one operator.

Shortly after dawn next day the Arado 196 took off and flew a triangular course of more than 300 miles without sighting more ships, and Langsdorff decided to search farther to the south-east, closing in towards the direct Freetown–Capetown, and Freetown–Lobito trade routes. But daylight on Saturday, 7 October, revealed a clear horizon. The *Graf Spee* was almost in the Gulf of Guinea, and Langsdorff went to his cabin for breakfast, having decided to send up the Arado again later.

He was called at 0824; smoke had been sighted on the horizon to the south-west. Once again on the bridge, with his high spirits restored, Langsdorff went through the now familiar routine: action stations, boarding party stand by, 'Heave to' and 'Do not transmit' signals bent on, the Tricolour hoisted, the 5.9 inch guns loaded, and the German prize crew in the *Newton Beech* warned.

The steamer was the 4,222-ton *Ashlea*, owned by the Cliffside Shipping Company. She was carrying a cargo of 7,200 tons of sugar and was on her way from Durban to Freetown, where she was to pick up a homeward-bound convoy. Like most merchant ships at this time, she was unarmed.

The *Ashlea* had a crew of thirty-five, and this is how her Master, Captain C. Pottinger, later described the next few minutes: 'At about 8 AM GMT* the Second Officer sent down a report that he had sighted a man-of-war on the horizon bearing east-north-east. Our course was about west-north-west and our speed eight-and-a-half knots.

'I went on to the bridge and saw a man-of-war coming towards us on our starboard bow. She seemed to be coming from the direction of the Cameroons. Her fighting top gave me the impression she was either the *Dunkerque* or *Strasbourg* [French battleships] so I carried on.

'She approached very rapidly and kept bows-on all the time she was approaching. She carried on like this until about a quarter of a mile off. It was not possible to see any ensign, and we still thought she was a French warship.

'Suddenly she ran up a signal "Heave to, I am sending a boat across". Then her next signal was "Don't use your radio or we will fire". By that time a launch was already in the water half-way across to us.

'She then altered course to come broadside on to us and then I saw the German ensign. I did not risk putting the Confidenial Books over the side in case they could hook them up with a boathook, so I put them in the furnaces.'

The *Graf Spee*'s boarding party were quick and thorough. They scrambled on board and split up, some men going to the wireless office to make sure no distress signals were transmitted, while Schunemann went to the bridge and others to the Captain's cabin. Schunemann demanded the Confidential Books from Captain Pottinger, but was told they had been destroyed. Pottinger was then told he and his men had ten minutes to leave the ship.

The officer of the watch wrote in the *Graf Spee*'s log:

> *Steamer was ss* Ashlea. *Crew taken off and put on* Newton Beech. *Part of cargo of* Ashlea, *two tons of sugar, taken on board* Graf Spee. Ashlea *sunk by cartridge charges.*

Langsdorff was pleased with himself: in the first place he had been correct in assuming he was somewhere on the wartime trade route from South Africa to Freetown, and his method of approach – keeping bows-on to the victim until the last moment so that his identity would not be discovered – and the boarding had been a complete success, so much so

*The *Graf Spee*'s times were now one hour ahead of GMT.

that the *Ashlea* had not managed to transmit a distress signal.

He decided to move northward again, and the *Graf Spee* moved off, followed by the *Newton Beech*. The steamer was proving rather a nuisance, he decided. Schunemann had already tried her out at her maximum speed and it was not nearly fast enough. She was going to limit the pocket battleship's mobility – her most valuable weapon.

Next day he made up his mind: the *Newton Beech* must be sunk and he would have to risk having the *Graf Spee* overcrowded with prisoners. A signal was passed to Schunemann, and both ships stopped. The pocket battleship's launch took a party across carrying the scuttling charges and then brought over the thirty-five men from the *Ashlea*.

The cartridge charges were set to explode at 1816, and the launch took off the last of the prize crew. Langsdorff and his officers watched the minutes tick by, and exactly on time the charges exploded. But the *Newton Beech* did not sink. All that happened was that she settled in the water a little.

Langsdorff was extremely angry: the farce of sinking the *Clement* was still fresh in his mind, and the *Graf Spee*'s log records the story with understandable reticence:

> *1816*. Newton Beech *sunk by cartridge charges. (Did not sink until 2347 owing to maize cargo.)*

After sinking the *Newton Beech* Langsdorff headed the *Graf Spee* back west-north-westward, turning west on the 9th and south-east on the 10th. Later that day, at 1739, the familiar cry sounded from the lookouts: 'Smoke in sight'.

By the time Langsdorff reached the bridge the ship's masts could be seen, and as the *Graf Spee* approached from her usual bows-on position, he could see through the binoculars that the steamer was bigger than any they had caught up to now.

Once again Schunemann stood by with a boarding party, and when the rangefinders showed the steamer was just under a mile away the *Graf Spee* turned broadside on, stopped and lowered a launch. Within seven minutes Schunemann was climbing on board.

He had a surprise waiting for him: Chief Officer A.M. Thompson recognized him as the former Master of the German coaster *Rudfidgi*, lying in Beira. Schunemann later told Thompson that he had been called back for service in the German Navy and had been appointed to the *Graf*

Spee some days before war broke out. He had been on leave in Hamburg from Beira.

Soon Schunemann was signalling across to the pocket battleship that the steamer was the ss *Huntsman* of 8,196-tons, and with a crew of eighty-four on board. Langsdorff read the signal with mixed feelings. It was one thing to destroy an enemy ship of 8,196 tons, but it was quite another to dispose of eighty-four prisoners. It was certain he could not have them on board the *Graf Spee* – it would impair his fighting efficiency since he had left forty-seven men behind in Wilhemshaven because he had no room for them. Already he had the crews of the *Newton Beech* and *Ashlea* on board . . .

His own wireless operators had warned him that the *Huntsman* had managed to transmit a distress message, but it was in the off-watch period and no one had been heard to reply. So he decided to keep the *Huntsman*, leaving the prisoners on board in the charge of a prize crew. Later they could be transferred to the *Altmark*.

One other point worried Langsdorff. He realised that the presence of his ship in the South Atlantic must now be known – the *Clement*'s lifeboats would have been found, and the *Papalemos* must have landed Captain Harris and his Chief Engineer by now – and that within a very short time the *Newton Beech*, *Ashlea* and *Huntsman* would be reported overdue.*

One way of throwing his pursuers off the scent, he reasoned, would be to make them think the ships had been sunk by U-boats. He therefore ordered a false distress signal, giving a different position and apparently coming from the *Newton Beech,* and using the prefix 'SSS' denoting an attack by a submarine, to be sent out on the *Huntsman*'s wireless.

That afternoon, Tuesday, 10 October, a German operator sat at the *Huntsman*'s wireless and transmitted† on 600 metres:

SSS SSS SSS Position 7 20 S 7 57 W Newton Beech torpedoed.

After laying the false trail, the *Graf Spee*, with the *Huntsman* in company, moved away to the south-westward. Next day the wireless officer reported that they were having rather more success in intercepting

---

*The *Ashlea*'s owners wrote to the Admiralty on 13 November expressing concern over her non-arrival at Freetown on 13 October. The *Ashlea*, *Newton Beech* and *Huntsman* were officially listed as overdue on 22 November.
†Ironically enough, this was never picked up.

British signals and the *B-Dienst* were busy decoding the latest of them. Finally a signal was brought to Langsdorff telling him that the *Ajax* had refuelled at Rio de Janeiro the previous day, 10 October. As Rio was more than 1,800 miles away, he had nothing to fear.

However, the time had come to alter course to meet the *Altmark* at the next rendezvous on the 14th. Langsdorff decided to send the *Huntsman* on alone to a special rendezvous; this would allow the *Graf Spee* to go ahead and meet the *Altmark*, refuel and then return northward with the tanker to find the much slower *Huntsman*. The rendezvous was signalled to Schunemann and at 1600 on the 12th the *Graf Spee* forged ahead, leaving the prize crew feeling rather lonely aboard the merchant ship.

About this time the radar gear broke down once again and the electricians reported it as the old trouble – vibration affecting the power cables. Langsdorff was not unduly worried – the *Graf Spee*'s optical rangefinders were amongst the finest afloat and in good visibility were almost as effective as the *Dt-Geraet*, and certainly a good deal more reliable.

In the evening a long radiogram arrived from the *Seekriegsleitung* giving Langsdorff the latest Intelligence reports of the whereabouts of British warships. The most startling news was that capital ships were moving from the Mediterranean into the Atlantic.

The night was an uneasy one for him, and reports from the monitors in the wireless room next day, the 13th, really worried Langsdorff. They told of a great increase in W/T traffic between the British stations along the African coast.

He now feared that the presence of the *Graf Spee* on the Cape route had been discovered – this could easily be the result of the sinking of the *Newton Beech* and *Ashlea* and the capture of the *Huntsman* – and the British would probably increase protective measures considerably and start sailing their merchant ships in convoy.

Any strengthening of the Cape Town–Freetown trade route, he reasoned in his War Diary, would probably mean the British would use St Helena and Ascension as auxiliary bases as much as Freetown and Cape Town. That would made the *Graf Spee*'s present operational zone an extremely dangerous spot to be in. The time had come, in fact, to change his plans.

Within a short while he had made up his mind and, as usual, described his thoughts, reasonings and decisions at great length in his War Diary:

he would store and refuel from the *Altmark* at the earliest possible moment (they were due to meet next morning), transfer all the prisoners from the pocket battleship to the *Altmark*, and then return with the tanker to the *Huntsman*. The *Altmark* would take off the eighty-five prisoners from the British ship, the *Graf Spee* would retrieve her prize crew, and the *Huntsman* would then be sunk.

The waiting area would be shifted to the westward, clear of the Cape Town–St Helena–Ascension–Freetown route, and once again the pocket battleship would be free to move about at will instead of worrying about a slow merchant ship loaded with prisoners following along astern.

At dawn next day the *Graf Spee* was within a few miles of the rendezvous and at 0824 lookouts reported masts in sight. After the usual brief minutes of anxious doubt over whether it was a merchant ship or a British cruiser, the vessel was identified as *Altmark*.

Soon the two ships were lying stopped within a few hundred yards of each other, and then the *Altmark* manoeuvred so that the hose could be passed across for fuelling to start. At 1000 a launch brought Captain Dau over from the *Altmark* – which was still sailing under the name of *Sogne*.

Dau was not very pleased to hear that Langsdorff proposed to use the *Altmark* as a prison ship, and he pointed out that he had no accommodation to spare. However Langsdorff was quite adamant and impressed upon Dau that the prisoners must be well treated. He had taken four British ships without a life being lost. He told him he was sending across an officer and some men from the *Graf Spee* who would help guard the prisoners (it was unlikely that Dau missed the point of the latter move: he was notorious for his hatred of the British, but the *Graf Spee* officer would ensure that Langsdorff's wishes were carried out).

Oil had been flowing across the pipeline between the two ships since 1105, and it continued for the rest of the day and well into the night. For what Langsdorff had in mind he wanted full tanks, since that would ensure him six weeks' cruising before having to meet the *Altmark* again.

VII

Nice Ships Sunk

RID OF the *Huntsman* and free of the *Altmark*, Langsdorff settled down
with his War Diary and recorded his future programme, starting with
'*Graf Spee* will continue her trade war as long as possible. Its object is not
only disruption of the enemy mercantile marine, but also to force the
enemy to deploy greater forces to protect merchantmen.'

In view of the state of the ship's engines, the food supply and the
refrigeration plant, a refit at a home port was to be aimed at, he added;
and a provisional date for a break-through to Germany would be the
new-moon period in January. Meanwhile, the pocket battleship's
operational zone was to be the Cape route south-east of St Helena . . .

Next day another long radiogram arrived from the SKL and this time it
was welcome news – two German ships were on their way to meet the
Graf Spee with more supplies. They were the motor ship *Dresden*, which
had left Coquimbo the previous day, and the tanker *Emmy Friederich*,
which had sailed from Tampico (Mexico).

The pocket battleship arrived in her new operational zone on 22
October, shortly after midnight, and Langsdorff and Wattenberg had
carefully worked out a search plan. They already knew some of the
courses being used by British steamers from secret route orders found in
one of the captured merchantmen.

Shortly before daylight the crew went, as usual, to Dawn Action
Stations and Langsdorff received his usual call which gave him time to
dress and go to the bridge before the visibility started increasing. But this
morning he was disappointed; there was nothing in sight – only the
endless sea horizon which had circumscribed their little world now for
several weeks. Had the British changed the merchant ship routes? Were

they now sailing their vessels in convoys? Langsdorff ordered the Arado to be catapulted off to make the pre-arranged search, in the hope that an unsuspecting freighter might be steaming along just out of sight of the *Graf Spee*'s lookouts.

Spiering had not been in the air long before he saw smoke on the horizon, and he told the pilot, Bongartds, to approach in a wide sweep. Within a few moments he had identified the vessel as a merchant ship, and noted her course, approximate speed, and her position.

Bongardts then turned the Arado and headed back to the *Graf Spee* at full speed. As soon as she was in sight he put the aircraft into a shallow dive and then circled her while Spiering signalled the news.

More than three hours passed before the steamer was sighted, and then she was rapidly overhauled. The *Graf Spee* approached bows-on as usual, and, when only a few hundred yards away, she turned and ran up the flag signal 'Heave to, I am sending a boat' and then, 'Do not transmit or I will open fire.'

The steamer was the 5,229-ton *Trevanion*, homeward-bound from Port Pirie with a crew of thirty-three and a cargo of 8,000 tons of concentrates. Her Master, Captain Edwards, reacted quickly; he ordered Radio Officer N.C. Martinson to transmit an RRR report. This was picked up immediately by the *Graf Spee*'s monitors and reported to the bridge, and Langsdorff ordered the *Trevanion*'s bridge and upper deck to be sprayed with machine-gun fire.

Captain Edwards wrote later: 'They were about a hundred yards away at the time, and they swept her right the way along. I was on the top bridge, and I blew the signal for the men to come on deck. Then the Wireless Operator stopped sending the message and the battleship stopped firing.

'I ran down to the wireless room and asked if he had got the whole message out, and he said, "No, I have only got half out." I then said that I would stand behind him while he sent the whole message, and I told him not to be nervous about sending it. He then got on with the message and sent the whole of it out from start to finish.

'Immediately the battleship started to machine-gun the ship again and they certainly made a mess of the bridge. They were firing tracer bullets, and one or two of them came on to the table, which knocked the Wireless Operator backwards, and I also fell backwards too. The Wireless

Operator told me that he was positive that he had got the whole of the message out correctly.'*

Captain Edwards then went to the bridge and found that, although it was wrecked, none of his men had been wounded. He just had time to throw the secret papers overboard before the boarding party arrived. Three men, brandishing revolvers, came up to the bridge and announced to Captain Edwards: 'This ship has been captured by the Reich. You have ten minutes to get clothes, etc, before going into the boat.' The Germans then placed cartridge charges, timed to go off in fifteen minutes, round the ship and the crew were taken off. The charges exploded and the ship sank an hour later.

Once on board the *Graf Spee* (Captain Edwards wrote), 'Captain Langsdorff came up to me and said, "I am very sorry to have had to sink your ship. Are you hurt?" I just smiled at him and said nothing. He then said, "Are any of your crew hurt? War is war, Captain." I just stood there and did not bother to speak to him when he reached across me and caught hold of my hand to shake hands with me.'

Next day the aircraft spotted another ship, and the *Graf Spee* altered course to intercept. However, at the time the ship should have been in sight the horizon was clear. Although Langsdorff carried on for another half an hour there was still nothing to see. Positions, courses and speeds were checked with the Arado's observer and the *Graf Spee*'s navigator, but there had been no mistakes. There seemed only one possible explanation – the ship had sighted the Arado and immediately altered course. And the ship might have guessed the aircraft belonged to a German raider and radioed a warning to the British which the *Graf Spee*'s operators had failed to detect . . . even now British hunting groups might be converging on the area . . .

Langsdorff decided to move off to the westward at high speed to get well clear, and within a short time the *Graf Spee*'s engines were turning at full speed for the first time in several weeks while Langsdorff waited anxiously to see if the monitors, their wireless sets automatically combing all wavelengths, noticed any increase in enemy W/T traffic, and he was relieved when they reported it was about the same as usual.

That night Langsdorff sent a signal to the SKL reporting his move and

*Despite the gallantry of these two officers, and others whose ships fell victim to the *Graf Spee*, no awards were ever made. This is in spite of the fact that the sending of an RRR report is an extremely unselfish act which cannot benefit the sender.

asking them to tell the *Altmark* to move the next rendezvous 600 miles to the west. The two ships met on the 28th, and while fuel was transferred the *Trevanion*'s crew were taken over to the *Altmark*.

Langsdorff still had not decided on his new move. For two months he had operated his ship away from a base, and he had sunk five ships, crossing the Atlantic twice in the process. The last four had been intercepted on the Freetown–Cape route, and it was reasonable to suppose the British would be concentrating their search there. The hours Langsdorff spent making his decision were lonely ones. As captain of the pocket battleship he had his duty to perform as a commerce raider, and he was personally responsible for the life and death of more than a thousand men . . .

Six days earlier he had received a signal from the SKL telling him to consider moving unexpectedly into the Indian Ocean if enemy pressure in the Atlantic became stronger. This gave him a lead, showing the SKL were well informed on the problems he faced.

Finally, during the afternoon, he made up his mind: he would take the *Graf Spee* right round the Cape of Good Hopoe into the Indian Ocean. There, he noted in his diary, his course of action would be 'to carry on the trade war south of Madagascar', and 'create alarm there and draw off the British forces'. He would leave the *Altmark* behind in the Atlantic, arranging four provisional rendezvous, the last being for 26 November.

By 8 November the *Graf Spee* was in her new operational area in the Indian Ocean, east of Durban and south of Madagascar, and zig-zagging across the shipping routes. The Arado was launched daily and several hundreds of square miles were searched, but nothing was sighted as the *Graf Spee* worked her way northwards towards Madagascar.

After five days Langsdorff was forced to change his plan: up to now he had been avoiding neutral ships, but it was vital that he made his presence known to the British, otherwise his presence in the Indian Ocean would not cause them to divert their forces as he had planned.

Langsdorff's decision was noted in the *Graf Spee*'s log:

Purpose of operation: to create alarm in Indian Ocean. Only possible if present plans enlarge. Decision: (1) To proceed up the Mozambique Strait and search north-east of Lourenço Marques; (2) Failing that, to attack South African coastal traffic; (3) Possible attack on Durban by Graf Spee's aircraft.

The *Graf Spee* then altered course west-north-west to carry out the first part of Langsdorff's decision, reaching a position close to the coast off Lourenço Marques on 14 November. That night, in heavy seas, they sighted a small ship and identified her by searchlight as a Dutch coaster. Since she was neutral and knowing she would think the *Graf Spee* was a British warship, Langsdorff left her, hoping for better luck after daylight.

And it came soon after noon when a steamer was sighted. The *Graf Spee*'s crew ran to action stations with the prospect of the first bit of excitement for more than three weeks. Again the French Tricolour was hoisted, and the 5.9-inch guns were loaded – after the *Trevanion* incident Langsdorff had decided machine guns were useless in dissuading British wireless operators from transmitting RRR reports.

From the *Graf Spee*'s bridge the approaching steamer looked quite small and was not far off when she suddenly bore away and then headed back the way she had come. Langsdorff ordered more speed and the signal flags were hoisted. Still the merchantman continued steaming away. Langsdorff ordered a warning shot to be fired, and one of the 5.9-inch guns on the port side barked out, to send a shell spinning over towards the little coaster.

The steamer was in fact the *Africa Shell*, 706 tons, bound from Juelimare to Lourenço Marques. She had a crew of twenty-nine and her master was Captain P.G.G. Dove, who later reported* that when a warship was sighted he at first thought it was French. Later, however, he became suspicious and 'I turned my stern on him and ran for it. We kept going and we were about four miles from where we first sighted him when suddenly I saw a flash and a big brown splash about a quarter of a mile astern of me. I realized that the warship meant business and that we had better do something, so I slowed down to half speed. By this time the battleship was about two miles away.'

He and the rest of the crew then saw that the warship was German and he immediately threw the confidential papers over the side. The Second Officer took bearings on Cape Quessico and Cape Zavora and reported to Captain Dove that they were two miles off the beach.†

The *Graf Spee* slowed down and lowered a launch, which immediately made for the *Africa Shell*, and at 1145 a boarding party of nine ratings

---

*In a report to the British Authorities on the sinking.

†i.e. one mile inside Portuguese territorial waters.

and two officers clambered on board the merchantman, revolvers in their hands, and told Captain Dove they were going to sink his ship.

'They said they would give us ten minutes to get ready and we could take all we could collect,' Captain Dove continued. 'They also said we could either go on to the cruiser or go ashore if we liked. I decided to go ashore.

'I called all hands up, we cleared away the boats and lowered them. The Chief Officer got into one of the port side and the Second Officer into the other, with the rest of the crew. The port boat pulled away, the Second Officer's boat waited for me.

'The [German boarding] officer then said he wanted to see our papers, the ship's Register, and the Articles. The Secret Service officer in plain clothes searched the ship. He searched everything. He came across the book for working out salaries, etc, and took that away as there were a lot of figures in it.

'While this search was going on I made my protest that my ship was in territorial waters, and they could not sink it. The officer said, "Oh no, you are not." Apparently the cruiser had meanwhile come round and was between us and the beach, making a complete circle round us.

'He told me that I could make a protest if I liked, so I started to write out that the ship was in territorial waters. I had to dash out to the lifeboat to tell them to wait for me as I was coming in a few minutes. There was an awful commotion going on, and then a man came in and said the Captain of the warship had signalled that I was not to go ashore, but was to go on board the warship, so they rushed me into the waiting launch.

'They took three or four bags of food, typewriting paper, typewriters, torch batteries, all the sextants and the chronometer.

'I protested that I had no clothes, as I only had on a pair of shorts and a shirt. The officer asked me where they were. I said they were in the lifeboat, so we went over to it in the launch and they handed me one small suitcase and half a bottle of whisky to see me through.

'My boats pulled to the shore and I was taken on board the warship. When we left the *Africa Shell* the [German] sailors put a time bomb on the port side of the engine room . . .

'I had left my Ensign up and I saluted it for the benefit of the Germans watching. The last I saw of the ship, she had a heavy list and I understood she turned over and drifted ashore.

'I climbed up a ladder on board the warship and they took me below to the Navigator's cabin. They asked me to have a cigarette saying they thought they had just one left from the *Clement*. Then the cruiser went full speed for another ship which had been sighted . . .'

This vessel turned out to be Japanese, the *Tihuku Maru*, and as she was neutral she was allowed to pass unmolested.

By this time the lifeboats from the *Africa Shell* had reached the shore and Langsdorff decided it was high time the *Graf Spee* made her escape. As it was obvious that they would be under observation from Zavora lighthouse, he ordered the pocket battleship to be steered towards the north-east – as though going through the Mozambique Channel – until they were out of sight of the coast; then he altered to 120 degrees, a course which took them south-eastward and clear of the coast.

Next day, just before noon, another ship was sighted and the *Graf Spee* prepared a boarding party. But they were disappointed – the vessel was the *Mapia*, flying the Dutch flag, and she was left to continue her voyage.

This ended the *Graf Spee*'s operations in the Indian Ocean, and Langsdorff had achieved his objective of diverting the British hunting groups. He headed away south-east on the 16th, altering south-west next day. The log noted '2130 – *journey round Cape begun*'.

Langsdorff knew that the *Africa Shell*'s survivors would by now have been interrogated and, from their descriptions, their attacker would have been identified as a pocket battleship.

Having trailed his red herring, he had now to try to guess what the British would do with their net; and what they did depended on what they guessed his own future actions would be. Would the British expect him to return to the Atlantic after sinking the *Africa Shell*? Or would they think he would go farther into the Indian Ocean, perhaps seeking rich cargoes from the Far East which converged on the Red Sea, making their way through the Suez Canal to Britain?

He decided on the latter; and that meant he would probably fool them if he doubled back into the Atlantic, and the main danger would lie in accidentally meeting any of the forces which would be diverted from the Atlantic round the Cape into the Indian Ocean. These hunting forces, Langsdorff guessed, would be in a hurry and take the shortest route, keeping close inshore. If he rounded the Cape westwards keeping 500 to 600 miles off, he should be fairly safe.

And this is what he did, altering course westward on the 19th and entering the Atlantic the next day. He set a course for the last of the four rendezvous with the *Altmark* – he was too late for the previous three.

The two ships met shortly after dawn on 26 November and once again the pipeline was towed across to the pocket battleship. She had used up a lot of fuel, and pumping started at 0815, by which time several launches were ferrying over tons of stores. Langsdorff wanted the *Graf Spee* to be fuelled and provisioned so that she could operate until February 1940 without meeting a supply ship.

That night the pocket battleship's officers, with some from the *Altmark*, had a big party on board. Perhaps they realized that the operations of their great ship were reaching a climax, or maybe they were pleased at the way they had hoodwinked the British – as they assuredly had, it seemed. They invited Captain Dove, the jovial master of the *Africa Shell*, but he refused. However, Langsdorff and his officers had an admiration for the redoubtable Briton, and during the evening arrived at his cabin with several bottles and noisily drank his health. They told him in all seriousness that he 'would be a prisoner shortly'.

Earlier in the day Langsdorff had written a nine-page review in his War Diary of the situation and the intentions of the *Graf Spee*. The main points were that there were no deficiencies in the ship's main armament, and she had 2,841 tons of fuel on board – enough for her to remain at sea until the end of February – with another 3,600 tons available in the *Altmark*. The marine growth on the ship's bottom had 'increased considerably but in general considering the circumstances, the state of preservation is good'. The ship's machinery required a dockyard overhaul 'in the near future' – in October this had been envisaged for January.

Turning to operations, Langsdorff noted that while the *Graf Spee* would continue attacking enemy shipping for as long as possible, he had to bear in mind instructions from Germany that the enemy must obtain no prestige from the destruction of a pocket battleship. The need for machinery overhaul within two or three months meant that the period of commerce raiding was nearing an end and, Langsdorff wrote, 'in consequence the necessity for avoiding action damage can no longer be so pressing. If the *Graf Spee* were to close the range it could be anticipated that her powerful armament would at least so damage an opponent, with the exception of the *Renown*, as to eliminate her as a pursuer.*

'On the other hand,' he continued, 'it would be difficult to achieve decisive results or shake off fast shadowers in the bright moonlight nights of the South Atlantic.'

This and several previous references in his War Diary during the preceding weeks show that Langsdorff underestimated the problems of night shadowing, even in the clear visibility of the South Atlantic. In the event, as will be described later, the out-gunned British cruisers had difficulty in shadowing the *Graf Spee* at a safe distance even when she was silhouetted against the lights of the city of Montevideo.

Despite the powerful enemy forces disposed against the *Graf Spee*, Langsdorff wrote, no effort had apparently been made to search the area she used for fuelling. In addition, the absence of sinkings in the South Atlantic for the past month had probably led to the enemy relaxing counter-measures. 'This favourable situation must be utilized for further disruption of traffic in the Atlantic before returning to Germany,' Langsdorff noted.

He concluded that, after completing a minor machinery overhaul he would operate again on the Cape–Freetown route in the area where he found the *Travanion* until about 6 December. Then, depending on the state of the machinery, the *Graf Spee* would either return home or operate against the River Plate traffic.

For the next two days Langsdorff kept his men busy altering the appearance of the *Graf Spee* as much as possible. She had a very distinctive shape, quite unlike any British capital ship. Her fighting top was built up solid, instead of the more usual British system of having a platform on top of a tripod; and of course she had only one turret forward and one aft, whereas a British cruiser, battlecruiser or battleship (with the exception of the distinctive *Nelson* and *Rodney*) usually had two turrets forward and two aft.

First of all the crew got busy chipping, scraping and patching up the rusty spots in the hull and upperworks with red lead. After that they started painting the ship with various shades of grey. Langsdorff told

*This reference is the only possible clue to the often-asked question of why Langsdorff, when he found he was engaging three cruisers, did not make an all-out attempt to break off the action right at the beginning of the subsequent Battle of the River Plate.

Captain Dove that he wanted to make the *Graf Spee* look like a British battleship.

Describing what he saw, Captain Dove reported later to the British authorities: 'He rigged up a dummy funnel just aft of his forward turret, even painting a black strip along the top. He also rigged a dummy turret forward, and the Captain and officers went off in a launch four miles away to see the effect.

'He came back and said he was very pleased with the work. He said, "We shall now look like the *Repulse* as shown in *Jane's Fighting Ships*." He told me it was for the benefit of neutrals because when he went back to Germany, if he was sighted by a neutral ship and they were asked by a British ship if they had seen the *Graf Spee*, the neutrals would say they had seen a ship with two funnels and a double turret forward, and then the British ship would think it was the *Repulse* . . .

'He put *Deutschland* on the stern of the ship, painting in letters of gold on tin plate in German script. He said this was also for the benefit of the neutrals. On the other side of the plate was *Von Scheer* . . .'

On 29 November, after being together for three days, the *Graf Spee* left the *Altmark* after giving Captain Dau new positions for meeting in December. Langsdorff steered east-north-east for the position where the *Trevanion* had been sighted, and he had high hopes of sighting a victim almost immediately.

But an empty horizon greeted the men on the pocket battleship's bridge at dawn on the 30th; nor did they have any better luck on 1 December. When nothing was sighted during the rest of the day, Langsdorff ordered the Arado to be ready to fly off early next morning.

Once again the crew were at Dawn Action Stations on 2 December; once again the only people to see anything on the horizon were those whose livers were not in good order. At 0700 the Arado took off to search on either side and ahead of the *Graf Spee*, and it had to return two and a half hours later, because of fuel shortage, to report nothing in sight.

At noon the navigators took their usual sights and they had just finished working them out and were entering the pocket battleship's latest position in the log when a cry came from the tiny lookout position above the rangefinder on the fighting top: 'Smoke in sight'.

The alarm bells sounded, sending the crew to Action Stations; the rangefinders swung round to the bearing given by the lookout; the 3.7-cm guns were manned. As Langsdorff hurried to the bridge, wireless operators switched on the Marconi radio set, which had been taken out of the *Newton Beech* before she was sunk, and tuned it in. The Germans were taking even more precautions, should the unknown ship try to send out an RRR report: the Marconi set would be used to jam any transmission, and the 3.7-cm guns would open fire.

Within a few minutes various reports from all over the ship told Langsdorff that the crew were prepared – gunners, wireless operators, engineers, boarding party and everyone remotely connected with the task in hand. The rangefinder and *Dt-Geraet* operators gave the range as 220 hectometres and as the range stayed the same during the next few minutes it was obvious the vessel was steaming away at high speed.

That could mean only one thing: she was not a warship – that much could be seen even at this range – so she must be a large and fast merchant ship. At last the *Graf Spee* was going to make a worthwhile capture . . .

Langsdorff ordered an increase in speed, and gradually the distances reported by the rangefinders and radar decreased. At 1337, an hour and twelve minutes after the smoke was sighted, Langsdorff ordered a warning shot to be fired and the word 'Stop' to be signalled in plain language by searchlight. The steamer slowed down, but three minutes later the monitors in the *Graf Spee* warned the bridge that she was tuning in her wireless. The British were obviously getting suspicious and Langsdorff ordered 'No wireless' to be flashed by searchlight.

But he was too late. Captain W. Stubbs, the master, had ordered Radio Officer William Comber to transmit a raider report as fast as he could. Immediately the *Graf Spee*'s operators started jamming with the Marconi set from the *Newton Beech* and one of the 3.7-cm guns thundered out another warning shot, which fell very close to the steamer. Langsdorff was told that transmission had now stopped.

Four minutes later, however, Comber started transmitting again. The *Graf Spee*'s operators continued their jamming and reported they thought they were being successful.

Langsdorff did not want to continue shelling the merchantman because she was bigger than anything else he had caught, and she would make a good prize. Through binoculars he could see the steamer's crew swinging out the lifeboats and preparing to abandon ship, and fifteen minutes later the *Graf Spee* turned, less than 500 yards from the steamer, and lowered a boat.

The prize crew were soon on board and signalled across to the pocket battleship that the steamer was the *Doric Star*, 10,086 tons, bound from Auckland to the United Kingdom with a cargo of meat and dairy produce. A further signal, however, upset Langsdorff's plans – the *Doric Star*'s Chief Engineer had damaged the engines, so she could not be got under way . . .

The prize crew were then told to bring off the British, along with some provisions from the steamer's cargo. Scuttling charges were placed and shells and a torpedo were also used to sink her. The *Doric Star* finally submerged at 1710.

Not at all sure that the jamming of the *Doric Star*'s RRR report had been completely successful, Langsdorff lost no time in moving away to the south-west at high speed, and in the meantime the *Graf Spee*'s monitors listened in as their wireless sets combed the wavelengths. The *B-Dienst* group were ready to break down any enemy cipher signals. They had to wait a minute short of two hours after the sinking of the *Doric Star*: at 1909 a powerful signal was picked up from a ship using the British procedure, and within a short while *B-Dienst* reported to Langsdorff that a British warship had just sent a very urgent message to Simonstown naval radio station.

At 1923 the *Graf Spee*'s operators intercepted a signal which dashed Langsdorff's hopes that the Marconi set from the *Newton Beech* had successfully jammed the *Doric Star*'s raider report. It was from Simonstown, addressed to all British warships in the South Atlantic and it said:

1417 RRR 19.15 S, 5.5 E. Doric Star gunned. Battleship.

Langsdorff noted that the position given in the raider report, which Simonstown Radio was now repeating, was five miles farther south than the *Graf Spee*'s navigators had calculated – not that it made any difference in the circumstances. However, the signal told him that his original decision made two hours earlier, that the *Graf Spee* had to get clear quickly, was a correct one.

What he did not know was that the chance meeting with the *Doric Star* at 1225 that day – which resulted in him sinking his biggest capture up to date – also meant the beginning of the end for the *Graf Spee*. It meant the death of thirty-seven of his men, the wounding of fifty-four more, and it meant his own suicide a short while after. Yet Langsdorff did not know that death was near when he took his pocket battleship away to the south-west at full speed; and in any case the *Graf Spee* still had more victims to claim.

Next morning, shortly before daybreak, the crew went as usual to Dawn Action Stations; and, just as they had done every morning since the voyage had begun back in August, the officers on watch waited anxiously for dawn to light up the horizon and reveal if there was a victim – or a hunter – nearby.

This time, on 3 December, they were not disappointed: at 0518 they sighted a steamer on the port quarter, and the *Graf Spee* swung round towards her. As the crew were already at Action Stations it was only a question of having a prize crew standing by.

By 0551 the *Graf Spee* was close enough to the steamer to run up flags ordering her to 'Heave to, I am sending a boat', and 'Do not transmit or I will shoot'.

Within a few minutes – as soon as the flags had been read by the men on the bridge of the steamer – she began to slow down. Suddenly a warning reached the *Graf Spee*'s bridge from the wireless monitors that the steamer was transmitting, and Langsdorff ordered the 3.7-cm guns to open fire at the bridge. For two minutes the guns kept up a rapid fire, shells bursting on the chart house. Then the monitors reported that transmission had ceased, and the guns stopped firing. Two minutes later, while the smoke of the shell bursts was still clearing, the steamer started transmitting again, and again the 3.7s opened fire, shells exploding on the bridge. The wheel and binnacle were smashed and transmission finally ceased altogether.

As the shelling started Captain Starr, the steamer's master, ordered all hands to the boats. As the men ran to their positions shells were still bursting, wounding three of them. By this time the *Graf Spee* had stopped and her prize crew – for Langsdorff intended using the steamer as a tender – were in the launch. Six minutes after the shooting had stopped they had boarded her and were soon reporting details to the *Graf Spee* by signal lamp: the steamer was the *Tairoa*, of 7,983 tons, bound from Melbourne to Freetown to join a convoy for the rest of the voyage home. She was carrying a cargo of meat, wool and lead. She had heard the *Doric Star*'s raider report when four days out from Cape Town; and Captain Starr had promptly altered course to keep clear of the position.

The boarding officer ordered Captain Starr to get under way; but he told the German the wheel had been smashed. Semaphore messages were sent across to the *Graf Spee* and Langsdorff decided he would have to sink her instead, and take the crew of eighty-one on board the pocket battleship. That meant his ship was getting very crowded again, since he already had the *Doric Star*'s crew on board.

At 0920 the *Tairoa* was sunk by torpedo, and a tribute to her gallant wireless operator was written in the *Graf Spee*'s log: 'The first 3.7-cm shells hit the chart house and radio cabin. At the end the radio operator was lying on deck attempting to transmit his report until finally shrapnel [sic] put the transmitter out of order.'*

The *Graf Spee* moved off at twenty-two knots, heading across the Atlantic towards South America, 2,000 miles to the westward. Langsdorff planned to refuel from the *Altmark* on 6 December and then continue to an area between Rio de Janeiro and the River Plate. After sinking any ships he found, he would go south to the River Plate and stop a neutral ship so that the British would think he was going south round Cape Horn and into the Pacific. Instead he would double back and start the long voyage back to Germany.

On 4 December he received a far from cheering signal from SKL giving the latest estimated enemy positions. The *Ajax*, *Achilles*, *Exeter* and *Cumberland* were in the Rio–Plate area, a powerful British and French force, including an aircraft carrier, was on the West African coast, and two cruisers were at the Cape.

The *Graf Spee* met the *Altmark* as planned on the 6th and refuelled. All the prisoners, with the exception of a few British officers, were transferred to the *Altmark*, and Captain Dau was given new positions for a rendezvous after the River Plate foray and for the journey home. At 0800 next day, 7 December, the two ships parted. Although no one on board either ship realized it, they would never see each other again. Their hunting days as a team were over, and the notorious Dau had the crews of six British ships on board. He talked a good deal of how he was eventually going to take them back to Germany, but instead they were to be rescued by the British destroyer *Cossack* as the *Altmark* hid in a snow-rimmed Norwegian fjord.

After leaving the *Altmark*, the *Graf Spee* continued to the westward and later that day, at 1746, smoke was sighted. A few minutes afterwards the lookouts identified a small merchant ship and once again the pocket battleship closed for the kill.

* As in the case of the *Trevanion* and *Doric Star*, no award was made by the British Government.

The steamer was the *Streonshalh*, of 3,895 tons, bound from Montevideo to Freetown, where she was to join a convoy for England. She was owned by the Marwood Steamship Company, of Whitby, and was carrying a cargo of 5,654 tons of wheat. The crew numbered thirty-two and her master, Captain J.R. Robinson, later told the British authorities:

'I was sitting on the lower bridge reading. The Chief Officer came down and said he thought he had seen a sailing ship on the horizon. I went up to the top bridge and put my telescope on her and made her out to be the fighting* top of a cruiser.

'I had heard the *Doric Star*'s distress signal recently and knew that there was a raider in the vicinity. However, in this case I thought it was a British cruiser but took no chances regarding this.

'I got all hands on deck, and had the boats swung out and had provisions put in them. I kept the ship going on her course.

'The cruiser approached us, bows-on all the time. She was not camouflaged but had some signals flying. I could not make out what they were as she was stern on to us, until she was about two ships' lengths away on my starboard side.

'She steamed right round on to my course and then at last I observed she was German. The signals read: "If you transmit on your wireless I will open fire immediately." '

A boarding party came over and with it was the usual man in civilian clothes who ransacked the bridge and cabins in the usual fruitless search for secret papers or anything else he thought might be of use.

Captain Robinson and his crew were then taken over to the pocket battleship, and he continued in his report: 'We were taken to the Navigator's cabin, where two officers, one of whom was Lt Hertzberg, gave us a glass of beer, and tried to find out about the routes from the Plate to Freetown.

'We had, it is true, been routed from the Plate, but we were miles off the ordinary route. I told him that I did not know anything about routes at all as we were not following any special route.'

Unable to get any help from Captain Robinson, Langsdorff had to guess at where the wartime steamship lane ran from Buenos Aires and Montevideo to Freetown. The course the *Streonshalh* was steering when

---

* 'Flying' in the verbatim report

sighted was plotted on a chart to see if that gave any indication, and Langsdorff altered course to the south-west.

He stayed on this course until midnight and then came round more to the south, but nothing was sighted on the 8th. Next day he came round further to the westward, headed in directly towards the River Plate, so that by noon he was some 1,200 miles off Montevideo.

Later in the day he received a signal from Berlin which told him that the British cruiser *Achilles* was reported to be at Montevideo. It also gave him some far more important news – the movements of some big British merchant ships.

The 14,000-ton Royal Mail lines *Highland Monarch*, said the Berlin signal, had left the Plate on about 5 December, and the *Andalusia Star* (owned by the Blue Star Line, which also owned the *Doric Star*) had sailed from Buenos Aires on the 8th. After estimating their speeds and carefully plotting their possible courses on his chart, Langsdorff estimated that if they were bound for the north-east (i.e. towards Freetown) they would be in his vicinity the next day.

However, nothing was sighted on the 10th; and on the 11th and 12th the *Graf Spee* continued on a south-westerly course towards the Plate estuary. By the 12th Langsdorff reached what he estimated would be the shipping lane and he took the *Graf Spee* along it with the intention of patrolling to and fro across it during the night. If by the following day, 13 December, nothing had been sighted, he intended to turn right round and cross the South Atlantic again to an area off the West African coast near the Gulf of Lagos. There he would search along and on either side of the peacetime shipping lanes.

So it came about that shortly before dawn on Wednesday, 13 December, 1939, the *panzerschiff Admiral Graf Spee* was cruising at fifteen knots on a course of 155 degrees in a position 34° 27' south, 49° 55' west. She had destroyed nine British ships, totalling 50,089 tons, without the loss of a single life. The man who made that proud claim, Kapitän zur See Hans Langsdorff, was at that moment in his sea cabin on the bridge, his tasks as a commerce raider nearly finished and his life, at the age of forty-two, almost over.

VIII

Achilles *Joins the Party*

WE LEFT Commodore Harwood's force of the *Ajax*, *Exeter*, and the destroyers *Havock* and *Hotspur* off Rio, waiting for the *Cumberland* to join them from Freetown. The Admiralty had formed the hunting groups; interrogation of the *Clement*'s survivors had established beyond all doubt that the raider was a pocket battleship – apparently, thanks to Langsdorff's subterfuge, the *Admiral Scheer*; and the real search of the South Atlantic trade routes was about to start.

The Commodore's first orders from Admiral Lyon were that as soon as the *Cumberland* arrived, she and the *Exeter* would form a hunting group and carry out a sweep northwards from Rio towards Pernambuco, off which the *Clement* had been sunk. The *Ajax*, *Achilles* (when she arrived from the west coast of South America) and the two destroyers would patrol the focal areas protecting the merchant shipping.

The Commodore's plan was that if he met a pocket battleship in daylight he would shadow until dusk – he had the advantage of speed and would be able to keep out of range. After darkness had fallen he would then go into action. If, however, he found the enemy at night his destroyers would immediately attack her with torpedoes.

The position therefore on 5 October (the *Clement* had been sunk on 30 September) was that Harwood's force was concentrated off Rio de Janeiro ready to engage the pocket battleship should she come south from Pernambuco, and that the *Achilles* was passing through the Magellan Straits on her way to join him.

On that day the British steamer *Martand* intercepted a raider report from a British merchant ship saying that she was being attacked by a German armed raider. The *Martand* had not managed to get the whole signal and did not know the name of the vessel. [She was in fact the

Newton Beech which the *Graf Spee* had sighted at dawn 900 miles away on the Cape–Freetown route.]

Later that day the *Martand* met the *Cumberland*, which had left Freetown two days earlier and was due to rendezvous with Commodore Harwood on the 9th; and while Leutnant zur See Schunemann and his prize crew aboard the *Newton Beech* steamed along with the *Graf Spee*, the captain of the *Martand* told the *Cumberland* of the distress message his radio operator had picked up.

The *Cumberland* was then 700 miles from Freetown and her captain assumed that the message would be intercepted by the other merchant ships much nearer on the Cape–Freetown route and passed on to Admiral Lyon at Freetown, even if it was not intercepted by shore stations. He also considered wireless silence particularly important and decided against breaking it.

However, the *Newton Beech*'s distress signal – reported by the *Graf Spee* as having been weak – does not appear to have been picked up by any other British ship, and the Admiralty remained in ignorance of the fact that shortly after dawn that morning the position of the *Graf Spee* was 9° 20′ south, 6° 19′ west. Admiral Lyon, in a subsequent official report* said that in his opinion this information, if acted upon, might have led to the early destruction of *Graf Spee* and the *Altmark*. (As it was, he knew nothing of it until 21 January 1940.)

Meanwhile many conflicting reports continued to arrive at the Admiralty, giving the alleged positions of German ships and U-boats; and it was the task of the Director of Naval Intelligence to assess them. The *Admiral Scheer* is in the St Helena area . . . two German cruisers and six U-boats along the South American coast . . . German merchantmen sailing from various South Atlantic ports on a variety of likely and unlikely operations . . . so the reports flowed in.

During the first half of October the Commodore's force protected various convoys leaving Rio and the Plate, and steamed here and there following up Intelligence reports on German shipping. They were busy days with little rest for the officers and men of the British warships; and on the 13th Harwood told Admiral Lyon that as the *Exeter* needed certain repairs he proposed taking her to the Falklands on the 17th, returning on the 27th.

Admiral Lyon, however, said that he would prefer the *Exeter* to stay

* Given in an Admiralty account: *The Chase and Destruction of the* Graf Spee.

until the Commodore transferred to the *Ajax* on the 27th, when the *Achilles* was also due to arrive. Then she and the *Cumberland* could operate as Force G until the *Exeter*'s return. It had previously been agreed that the Commodore should transfer from the *Exeter* to the *Ajax* because Force G would have to maintain wireless silence. Thus Harwood could continue patrolling the focal areas and still keep in touch with Admiral Lyon. At the same time the Commodore pointed out the endurance differences of the *Exeter* and *Cumberland*, and suggested that the former should be replaced by a 10,000-ton cruiser as soon as possible.

On 26 October the *Cumberland* entered Montevideo and an hour later the *Achilles* joined the *Exeter* off the Plate. She was the first British warship the New Zealand cruiser had sighted since before the war.

The *Achilles* had returned to Auckland, New Zealand, on 18 August from a typical peacetime cruise of the Pacific Islands, and the following week had been spent carrying out exercises with the cruiser *Leander*. On 25 August both ships were ordered to prepare for war. Two days later they were stored and provisioned and at twelve hours' notice to sail for any part of the world . . .

The New Zealand Government had decided they would retain only one of their two cruisers, and the *Achilles* was chosen to go. Captain W.E. Parry, her commanding officer, received his sailing orders at 0900 on 29 August. During the morning fifty extra ratings from HMS *Philomel* and two RNR officers from the *Leander* joined the ship.

Groups of relatives appeared at the dockside to say goodbye – including Captain Parry's wife, who had just arrived in New Zealand: they had only been able to spend two weekends together before being parted again. At 1330 the *Achilles* left her berth, bound for a secret destination. One officer scrambled aboard as the last hawsers were being cast off: he was another doctor, Surgeon-Lieutenant Pittar. He had been warned only one and a half hours earlier and immediately dropped a flourishing ophthalmic practice to join the *Achilles*.

As soon as the cruiser cleared Rangitoto the bugle sounded 'Everybody aft', and Captain Parry briefly told his crew the plans for the *Achilles*: they were bound for the West Indies, via the Panama Canal, and they would come under the orders of the C-in-C, America and West Indies Station.

So the *Achilles* headed for Panama, 6,500 miles away. The northerly winds made her roll, and there was an air of excitement in the ship. The BBC news bulletins became gloomier and gloomier; and warning telegrams from the Admiralty in London and the Navy Office in New Zealand arrived thick and fast.

On 2 September Captain Parry's new C-in-C ordered *Achilles* to Valparaiso, where he was to meet the Naval Attaché and 'in the event of hostilities to take such immediate action as is considered necessary'.

Late the next evening a signal was received on board. It consisted of two words: '*TOTAL GERMANY*'.

Captain Parry wrote later: 'As in 1914, when I was in the *Grasshopper* at Malta, I heard this news from my bed; and it did not cause me a sleepless night, for which I was grateful . . . I think we all felt rather pleased to be going on a lone job, away from fleets and squadrons. Certainly it is much more interesting for me.'

For the next six weeks the *Achilles*'s task was to protect Allied shipping and stop enemy trade on the west coast of South America. That meant covering the 4,100 miles between Panama and Cape Horn alone . . .

At the beginning of October orders arrived from the Admiralty telling Captain Parry to take the *Achilles* through the Magellan Strait to the South Atlantic, where he would come under the orders of Admiral Lyon. The cruiser left Valparaiso on 13 October, passed through the Magellan Strait on the 19th, and arrived at Port Stanley, in the Falkland Islands, on 22 October. The islands are large and bleak, consisting mainly of sparse moorland intersected by ridges of rocky hills, and the Sailing Directions describe the climate as 'stormy, and a day without wind is unusual. Sudden and severe squalls may occur at any time, or gales which blow heavily.'

The islands' strategic value was proved in the First World War, although in 1939 they had not been developed as a naval base. There were no stores, except fuel, and no repair facilities. As often as not ships had to keep steam on the main engines because of the danger of dragging anchors. In fact it was a base only in name.

After the *Achilles* met the *Exeter* on 26 October, the two ships carried out manoeuvres together and then the *Achilles* went to oil from the *Olwen*. Meanwhile Captain Parry went on board the *Exeter* to meet

Commodore Harwood. They were both torpedo specialists but had met only once previously – in HMS *Vernon*, the torpedo establishment at Portsmouth.

The position which the Commodore outlined to Captain Parry during their two-hour talk was not a very cheering one: he was suffering to some extent from divided control since – as mentioned earlier – Admiral Lyon could override his plans,* particularly with regard to Force G. If he could not allocate this force to one of the focal areas he could not compete . . . The Admiralty were insistent over not accepting any benevolence from neutrals which might also be useful to the Germans if granted to them. For instance he had to stop keeping his oiler at Montevideo when she was not being used, since we did not want the Germans to be allowed a similar privilege.

The *Achilles* sailed the same day to meet the *Cumberland* off Lobos with orders for both ships to cover the Rio–Santos area as Force G. The *Ajax* arrived from the Rio area and took all the fuel remaining in the *Olwen*, which was going north to the West Indies. Next morning Commodore Harwood and his staff transferred to her and his Broad Pendant was hoisted. Captain Bell then sailed the *Exeter* to the Falkland Islands, where his crew could rest and repairs be effected.

Meanwhile the *Cumberland* and *Achilles* went on patrol. As the captain of the *Cumberland* was three years' senior to Captain Parry, *Achilles* had to 'Follow Father' which, as he commented at the time, 'at least gave our watch-keeping officers some badly needed practice in station keeping'.

As Force G now comprised only an 8-inch and a 6-inch cruiser (instead of two 8-inch cruisers), it was not considered strong enough to tackle a pocket battleship in daylight; and Commodore Harwood gave them definite instructions that if they made contact they were to shadow by day but attack by night.

Captain Fallowfield, of the *Cumberland*, planned that the two ships would work out to the eastward of the enemy in daylight so that they could close in at dusk and have her silhouetted against the afterglow of the sunset. That would enable the cruisers to see her at a greater range than she could see them. The *Achilles* would steam ahead of *Cumberland* in an attempt to fire torpedoes (the *Cumberland* had none) but of course the two ships would stay within supporting distance of each other. As

*In practice this rarely if ever happened, and their relationship was a cordial one.

Captain Parry rather wryly commented, 'I am not sure that the prospect is altogether a pleasant one, though I take some comfort from the possibility that the enemy is likely to put his main armament on *Cumberland* and only his secondary armament on us . . .'

IX

Casting the Net

―――

By 21 October the Admiralty knew for certain that the *Deutschland* was at large because of reports from her victims, and the whereabouts of the raider which sank the *Clement* on 30 September became even more of a mystery. In fact, despite the reports of the survivors who landed in South America on 3 October, and the Master and Chief Engineer who had been transferred to the Greek steamer *Papalemos* by the *Graf Spee* and landed at St Vincent, Cape Verde Island on 9 October* (when they were interrogated by two naval officers and the British Vice-Consul), there was doubt in the minds of some people as to the identity of the raider.

The mystery was partially solved the very next day, 22 October, when in the afternoon the British liner *Llanstephan Castle* intercepted a garbled signal from an unknown ship which said:

Gunned in 16°south, 4° 3' † east at 1400 GMT.

But unfortunately there was no confirmation of the report. [The victim was the *Trevanion*, which had been ordered to heave-to by the *Graf Spee* at 1420. As described earlier, her bridge had twice been machine-gunned as her wireless operator transmitted an RRR report.]

So apart from the brief and incomplete signal intercepted by the liner, the Admiralty were no wiser: they did not know the identity of either attacker or victim. The message could have been a hoax, transmitted in the first instance by a U-boat or a German armed merchantman.

Although the southern half of the Cape–Freetown route had been swept by Force H (*Sussex* and *Shropshire*) between 14–22 October,

*Not 9 November, as mentioned in certain official reports.

†The *Graf Spee* logged the position as 19° 40' south, 4° 2' east.

Admiral Lyon decided, in view of the *Llanstephan Castle*'s signal, on a new and complete sweep along the whole route. The two cruisers were ordered to search up to St Helena while Force K (*Ark Royal* and *Renown*) with the *Neptune* and four destroyers, sailed from Freetown to cover the northern end.

Both searches were unsuccessful – although the German steamer *Uhenfels*, which had escaped from Lourenço Marques, was spotted by one of the *Ark Royal*'s aircraft and taken in prize by the destroyer *Hereward*.

The first half of November was, as far as the British were concerned, comparatively quiet on both sides of the Atlantic; and on the 3rd the Admiralty told Admiral Lyon that all German capital ships were apparently in home waters. It appeared, therefore, that the pocket battleship – still thought to be the *Admiral Scheer*, thanks to Langsdorff's ruse – had returned home, and the raider reported by the *Llanstephan Castle* was only an armed merchantman.*

Here, then, was a good opportunity for resting the hunting groups, and at the same time the Admiralty ordered that Force G (*Cumberland* and *Exeter*) should change places with Force H (*Sussex* and *Shropshire*), so that Commodore Harwood should have the balanced and long-endurance hunting group he so greatly desired.

Admiral Lyon had planned that the *Sussex* and *Shropshire*, which had arrived at the Cape on 7 November, should sweep towards Durban, arriving there on the 11th. This would have taken them within 160 miles – five hours' steaming – of the *Graf Spee* when she sank the *Africa Shell* on 15 November.

But on the 5th, however, he ordered the two cruisers to sail on the 11th for a position off St Helena to change over with the *Cumberland* and *Exeter*. Despite the fact that on the 8th the Admiralty cancelled their signal about the German capital ships being in home waters, and said that the *Admiral Scheer* was now believed to be in the Indian Ocean, Admiral Lyon still sailed the two cruisers for St Helena, away from the Indian Ocean.

Bad weather delayed the departure of the *Cumberland* and *Exeter* from the Plate, where the latter had been damaged when her oiler cast off in a heavy sea. Before the exchange could take place it was cancelled.

* Unfortunately the Admiralty could not have been more wrong: the *Graf Spee* was then 400 miles south of Cape Town, and the *Deutschland* was off Greenland.

The reason was not hard to guess: the *Graf Spee* had, under the guise of the *Admiral Scheer*, struck again. The Naval Officer-in-Charge, Simonstown, signalled to the Admiralty on the 16th that the *Africa Shell* had been attacked off Lourenço Marques the previous day and sunk by time bombs. The crew 'believed a battleship was responsible'. After that, messages poured in. The crew, shown photographs, identified their attacker as either the *Graf Spee* or the *Admiral Scheer*. From Intelligence sources, incidentally, the Naval Attaché in Buenos Aires reported that the ship was the *Graf Spee*, the only person to identify her correctly until after the battle.

Immediately the presence of an enemy raider in the Indian Ocean was confirmed, the Admiralty's Operations Division in Whitehall started a wholesale movement of warships to hunt and destroy her. Unfortunately all the hunting groups were badly placed for an immediate search, and valuable days were bound to be lost.

The First Sea Lord and his staff, meeting in the Upper War Room at 2200 on the 16th, had to put themselves in the position of the captain of the German raider and of the German Naval War Staff. They would know the British were by now aware the raider had struck more than twenty-four hours earlier. The question was – which way round would the raider move? Or, more correctly, which way had she moved, since she had the vital twenty-four-hour lead?

She had plenty of ocean to choose from. She could double back into the Atlantic and then either go northward or stay in the south, down towards the Antarctic ice barrier; stay in the Indian Ocean and go northward between Madagascar and the African mainland, and strike at shipping always converging on the Red Sea; cross the Indian Ocean diagonally towards Ceylon, and play havoc with the trade routes there; move towards the Dutch East Indies and Bay of Bengal, focal points for the Far East sea traffic; or steam along the open wastes of the Southern Indian Ocean to attack the vulnerable shipping round Australia and New Zealand.

Every alternative – with the exception of lying in wait off the Antarctic – would provide her with plenty of merchant ships to sink or capture; any move she chose to make would achieve one of her main tasks – drawing off powerful British warships from other theatres where they were badly needed. She could pick any one of four oceans as her hunting ground.

It was late that evening before the meeting finished, having decided that the battleship *Malaya* was to stay with Force J (in the East Indies); the battleship *Ramillies* to be placed at the disposal of the C-in-C, East Indies (in whose waters the raider, by moving towards Madagascar, was now apparently operating); the cruiser *Kent* and the French *Suffren* would form Force M at Dakar, if the French agreed; Force H (*Sussex* and *Shropshire*) would return to the Cape; and Force G (*Exeter* and *Cumberland*) were to remain on their station. They also suggested that the *Renown* and *Ark Royal* should steam direct to Mauritius to fuel, thus avoiding Cape Town where their presence might be reported to the Germans. Shortly after midnight signals started going out from the Director of Operations Division (Foreign), Captain R.H. Bevan, to start the movements of these ships.

Next morning, 17 November, two German merchant ships, the *Adolph Woermann* and *Windhuk*, were reported to have sailed the previous day from Lobito, and Admiral Lyon decided that the *Sussex* and *Shropshire*, now heading for the Cape, were in a good position to intercept them. He therefore signalled them to close Lobito 'at best possible speed'. Both ships swung eastwards, and increased to more than thirty knots. The destroyers from Force K were also ordered to join in the hunt, but they were unsuccessful. However, a British merchant ship found the *Adolph Woermann* and shadowed her until the *Neptune* had time to get to the position. The Germans, however, scuttled their ship.

As the search for the German merchantman had taken Force K nearly 200 miles to the eastward of the original course from Freetown, Vice-Admiral Wells decided to steam towards the Cape by the route inside St Helena to save fuel. This may have resulted, according to Admiral Lyon, in the escape of the *Altmark*, which was waiting in the unfrequented areas west of the Cape–Freetown shipping route. The *Ark Royal* and *Renown* would have swept through these areas had they not been diverted.

The day after the scuttling of the *Adolph Woermann*, 23 November, the hunting groups were in the following positions:

Force
F   *Berwick:* in dock at Portsmouth.
      York: at Bermuda.
G   *Cumberland, Exeter:* patrolling off S America.

H   *Ajax:* off Montevideo.
    Achilles: off Rio de Janeiro.
I   *Cornwall, Eagle:* at Colombo.
    Dorsetshire: in Ceylon area.
J   *Malaya, Glorious:* Aden area.
    Ramillies: off Aden.
K   *Ark Royal, Renown:* on way to Madagascar.
L   *Furious, Repulse:* covering Atlantic convoys.
M   *Kent, Suffren:* patrolling off Sumatra.
X   *Hermes* and 2 French cruisers with
Y   *Strasbourg, Algérie:* patrolling between Pernambuco and Freetown.]

From this it will be seen exactly what Langsdorff had achieved in his efforts to draw off Allied warships. [On that day the *Graf Spee* was already back in the Atlantic, having returned round the Cape, and was more than 600 miles west of Simonstown. She was due to meet the *Altmark* on the 26th south-west of St Helena.]

New orders went out from the Admirtalty to the *Ark Royal* and *Renown*, and the *Sussex* and *Shropshire* on 27 November to patrol south of the Cape. The plan was that they should prevent a raider passing from the Indian Ocean to the Atlantic or vice versa and, according to Admiral Lyon, 'was a good one in theory' but found to be unsuitable in practice because of local weather. This allowed aircraft to fly off from the *Ark Royal* only once in five or six days, so the patrol could not be extended far enough south to intercept a raider 'bent on evasion'.

When the *Exeter* and *Cumberland* returned to the South American coast they were sent to patrol off Rio de Janeiro while the *Achilles* fuelled from the *Olynthus* on the 22nd, ready to relieve them. It was the *Ajax*'s turn to go to the Falkland Islands for a rest and repairs, so the *Exeter* and *Cumberland* were told that at the end of their patrol they were to refuel and then take over the Plate area. Before he sailed, the Commodore told Captain Parry to move a further 800 miles to the north of Rio, and make sure the German ships in Pernambuco, reported to be ready to sail, knew that he was around. He was to return to Rio at once if any raiders were reported in the South Atlantic.

By the beginning of December the *Graf Spee*, as we have already seen, was about to strike again. Nothing had been heard of her since she sank the *Africa Shell* on 15 November; and on 22 November four British ships had been reported overdue at Freetown – the *Newton Beech* and the *Ashlea* which should have arrived on 13 October, the *Huntsman*, due on the 17th, and the *Trevanion* on 1 November.

There had, in the meantime, been plenty of rumours and conflicting reports arriving at the Admiralty, and the Director of Naval Intelligence was kept busy weeding out the crop. Again the majority originated in South America, where there was a fairly complete network of British agents and where, of course, so many German ships were waiting for an opportunity to escape back to the Fatherland.

X

Sums on a Signal Pad

ON SATURDAY, 2 December, the British steamer *Port Chalmers* was steering a north-westerly course at fifteen knots. Many miles ahead lay the island of St Helena, where the exiled Napoleon had dragged out the last, bitter years of his life.

No one aboard the steamer realized that their own radio operator was shortly to play an anonymous but vital part in the destruction of the *Graf Spee*. But at 1245 he intercepted a signal, the first three letters of which revealed its urgency:

> *RRR RRR RRR 19° 15' south, 05° 05' east,* Doric Star *gunned battleship.*

The *Port Chalmers*'s master, Captain Higgs, was immediately called, and four minutes later the same signal again flashed out from the *Doric Star*.

Then there was silence until 1300 when the *Doric Star* started transmitting a long dash which suddenly ceased. For many anxious minutes Captain Higgs and the wireless operator listened for any messages which would show that shore stations had received the raider report or reveal why the steamer had broken off signal.

But none came, and at 1313 Captain Higgs ordered the *Doric Star*'s raider report to be repeated and signed with the *Port Chalmers*'s signal letters, EADG. This was done, and once again the operator listened in vain for a reply.

Then at 1349 a station with the call sign GOTA was heard repeating the signal – but that was all. Once again, at 1416, the *Port Chalmers* transmitted the message and a minute later a weak station using no call sign signalled *RRR Received*.

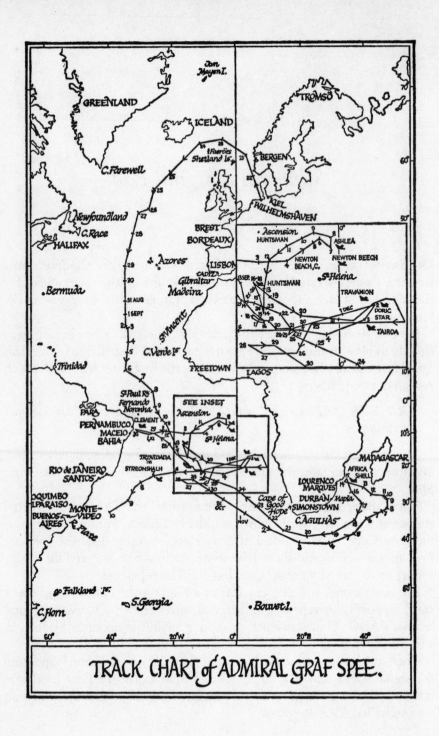

TRACK CHART of ADMIRAL GRAF SPEE.

Nothing more was picked up until seven minutes after midnight, when they were relieved to hear Walvis Bay Radio Station (in South Africa) transmitting the *Doric Star*'s raider report as repeated by the *Port Chalmers*. Six minutes later they heard Slangkop Radio, also on the South African coast, sending it. Captain Higgs was now satisfied he had done his duty: shortly the signal would be in the Admiralty and appropriate action would be taken.

But within five hours the *Port Chalmers* was again helping in the hunt for the German raider: at 0501 her wireless operator once more heard a signal being transmitted,* beginning with the fateful letters 'RRR'. This time the Morse as received was jumbled up and the words were run together. The message he managed to write down on his pad was incomplete, but said:

RRR 21° 20' south 310 battleship Von Scheer.

Two minutes later the ship started transmitting 'RRR' and then stopped. Nothing more was heard. No shore station acknowledged the raider report: no ship repeated it. Captain Higgs had been called and he decided at 0529 to repeat the signal. This was done . . . but no one replied. It was repeated again.

Several hours later Simonstown was heard to signal a reference to aircraft from a raider attacking a ship, and as this seemed to refer to the message *Port Chalmers* was repeating† Captain Higgs ordered it to be re-broadcast with an explanation.

Early that Saturday, before the *Doric Star* was attacked, the First Sea Lord had signalled to Admiral Lyon that on Force I (*Cornwall, Dorsetshire* and the carrier *Eagle*) approaching the Madagascar area from Ceylon, it was possible that any raider operating there would move into the Atlantic; and because of this Force H (*Sussex* and *Shropshire*) and Force K (*Ark Royal* and *Renown*) should fuel immediately and then return to their present area. This was south of the Cape on a patrol line which should prevent a raider slipping through. Admiral Lyon, as soon as he received this order, signalled it to the two hunting groups and they immediately altered course for the Cape.

Then at 1530 that day Admiral Lyon at Freetown and the First Sea

---

*This was from the *Tairoa*.

†The Morse letter 'R', standing for raider attack, is dot dash dot, and could be confused with 'A' referring to aircraft attack, which is dot dash.

Lord in Whitehall received the dramatic signal they had been waiting for since the *Africa Shell* was sunk on 16 November. It was from the Naval Officer-in-Charge at Simonstown and said a raider report from the *Doric Star* (re-broadcast by *Port Chalmers*) had been picked up by Slangkop and Alexander Bay radio stations.

So once again the mystery of the whereabouts of the raider was partially solved, thanks – as already described – to the bravery of the *Doric Star*'s captain and her wireless officer, who stayed at his Morse key despite gunfire from the *Graf Spee*, and the alertness of the operator of the *Port Chalmers*.

Speed was now vital if the raider was to be trapped. Which way would she go? Westward into the vast wastes of the South Atlantic, north to break through into the North Atlantic, or round the Cape into the Indian Ocean? (It must be borne in mind that the Admiralty did not know the identity or possible speed of the raider, nor where she had come from.)

To the *Ark Royal, Renown, Sussex,* and *Shropshire*, Admiral Lyon immediately signalled: *Force K, H to proceed with all dispatch to the Cape fuelling ports.* The ships were already on their way and the signal said nothing of the sinking of the *Doric Star*; yet it told the four ships that something dramatic had happened. The wording of naval signals follows a time-honoured tradition: no ship is ordered to 'go' from one place to another – it is always instructed to 'proceed'. And 'proceed' means steaming at an economical speed – economical from both the oil fuel and Treasury point of view. But the phrase 'proceed with all dispatch' is a discreet and dignified way of conveying the need to go flat out because there is something in the wind.

Four minutes later a further signal from Admiral Lyon gave them rather more scope for speculation. It said briefly that the *Sussex* and *Shropshire*, without waiting for the *Ark Royal* and *Renown*, were to proceed immediately after fuelling to cover the trade route between the Cape and the latitude of St Helena.

It was too late for the *Ark Royal* and *Renown* to reach the area between Freetown and Pernambuco and 'seal the gap' in order to intercept a raider breaking out into the North Atlantic. Instead, Admiral Lyon wanted them to steam from the Cape to a position west of where the *Doric Star* had been sunk.

In a signal to the Admiralty he said: *Believe appearing from previous experience that raiders after tip and run attack on trade routes disappear*

*to unfrequented areas, and if the raider is proceeding south and east, she
will probably proceed well clear of trade routes.*

It seems from this that Admiral Lyon thought the raider was perhaps
on her way to the Indian Ocean, and that she was not responsible for the
previous attacks (i.e. the *Clement* and *Africa Shell*, since they were the
only ones known to the Admiralty). Anyway, Admiral Pound, the First
Sea Lord, did not agree, and signalled: *It should be assumed that raider
will not repetition not proceed round the Cape.*

On 3 December the *Sussex* and *Shropshire* reached Simonstown three
quarters of an hour before the *Ark Royal* and *Renown* arrived at Cape
Town. The Vice-Admiral Aircraft Carriers, Vice-Admiral Wells, was
then ordered by Admiral Lyon to make for a position south-west of St
Helena. At Vice-Admiral Wells' request this was changed to a point 500
miles farther south so that he would be in a more central position to go to
Freetown, the Falklands or Rio de Janeiro.

But early next morning, while oil fuel was being pumped into the ships
of the two hunting groups and mechanics aboard the *Ark Royal* worked
hard to get her aircraft serviceable, the *Graf Spee* struck again and for
several hours the *Port Chalmers* struggled to get the raider report from
the *Tairoa* (for that was the ship) through to a shore station.

Once again Admiral Lyon received the news from the Naval
Officer-in-Charge at Simonstown. At 1030 the signal arrived in
Freetown saying that Slangkop had intercepted the following garbled
message from an unknown ship, assumed to be the *Tairoa*:

> *AAA Von Scheer de Madn. 0501. LOtt 21° 20' south, 3° 10' (?)
> datarshpt?*

This was followed later by a further signal saying that a full raider
report, re-broadcast by the *Port Chalmers* had been intercepted at 0530.

At 1700 that afternoon the *Sussex* and *Shropshire* left Simonstown at
twenty knots and headed north-westward. The hunt for the elusive *Graf
Spee* across the broad waters of the Atlantic was once more in full swing.
Had long-range Coastal Command aircraft of the type that swept the
North Atlantic later in the war been available, the hunting groups might
have had a chance; as it was, the search for a proverbial needle in a
haystack was, by comparison, an easy task. The two cruisers were
followed next day by the *Ark Royal* and *Renown*.

Although Admiral Lyon had been told to assume that the raider would not go round the Cape into the Indian Ocean and as there were clear indications from the positions radioed by the *Doric Star* and *Tairoa* that she was moving westward, the First Sea Lord was taking no chances, and the Admiralty ordered the *Cornwall* and *Gloucester* and the carrier *Eagle*, in the Indian Ocean, to establish a new patrol off the Cape.

More than ever before it was now necessary for the British to put themselves in the position of a lone raider and try to guess which way she would go next. Admiral Lyon estimated that if the enemy went northward at fifteen knots she would cross the Freetown–Pernambuco line between 9–10 December.

He therefore arranged with Vice-Admiral Duplat, the French Senior Officer of the new Force X (the cruisers *Dupleix* and *Foch*, the British carrier *Hermes* and two French destroyers, *Milan* and *Cassard*) that he should take the *Neptune* and her destroyers under his command and patrol the gap between Freetown and Pernambuco from 10 to 13 December.

Meanwhile the *Sussex* and *Shropshire* searched the area where the *Graf Spee* had been operating, but the pocket battleship was already a thousand miles away to the westward. The *Ark Royal* and *Renown* had no better luck, crossing her track on 9 December, four days too late to intercept her.

The sequence of events during the next few days, leading up to the Battle of the River Plate, are necessarily rather complicated, so it is proposed to separate the actual hunt from the rest of the story.

Once again contradictory reports started arriving at the Admiralty to confuse the issue even more. On 4 December, for instance, the French reported that the *Deutschland* had been off Pernambuco on the 2nd. This was quite feasible if the raider which sank the *Doric Star* and *Tairoa* was the *Admiral Scheer*; and the possibility of having two pocket battleships marauding in the South Atlantic was an alarming one. Fortunately the men most likely to be immediately affected – those manning the merchant ships steaming in that area – were in a state of ignorance, even if not bliss.

In the meantime the *Ashlea*, *Newton Beech*, *Trevanion* and *Huntsman*, previously reported overdue, were officially considered lost. It seemed certain they had been sunk by a raider. On 7 December the *Graf Spee* sank her last victim, the *Streonshalh*; fortunately she managed to send out a raider report, part of which was received by the Admiralty, although not enough to reveal her name.

At the beginning of December, Commodore Harwood's ships were scattered along South America's Atlantic seaboard. The *Ajax* and *Exeter* were at Port Stanley in the extreme south for a much-needed rest and self-refit; the *Cumberland* was in the River Plate. The *Achilles* was a good deal farther north patrolling the Rio de Janeiro area.

On Saturday, 2 December, Commodore Harwood took the *Ajax* north from the Falkland Islands, bound for the River Plate. The whole ship's company had benefited from the rest, despite the fact that there was little social life ashore in Port Stanley. However, almost anything was a relief from the almost constant steaming of the past months, even if the Falklands were a particularly windy place and the only entertainment ashore was drinking beer out of tins.

Before leaving the islands Commodore Harwood had made certain plans. December 8 was the 25th anniversary of the Battle of the Falklands, and thinking the enemy might attempt to try to avenge the defeat, he had ordered the *Cumberland* – which was also in need of an urgent refit – to join the *Exeter* there on the 7th and patrol the islands for two days before entering Port Stanley.

Then on the same afternoon that the *Ajax* sailed a coded signal arrived in the *Ajax*'s wireless office addressed to the Commodore Commanding South America Division and marked 'Immediate'. It told Commodore Harwood that the *Doric Star* had been attacked by a pocket battleship in 19° 15′ south, 5° 5′ east. The *Ajax* continued moving northward and before dawn the Commodore was handed another 'Immediate' signal: an unknown ship had been attacked by a pocket battleship 170 miles south-west of the *Doric Star*'s position at 0500.

What was the enemy's next move to be? At present the pocket battleship was more than 3,000 miles from any of the South American focal areas. And 3,000 miles was a great distance. Yet Harwood recognized that the enemy's next objective might well be the valuable shipping off the South American coast, since it was there he could do the most damage.

In the *Ajax*'s chart room Harwood and his staff worked over a small-scale chart of the South Atlantic, and the raider's last known position was plotted. Using a cruising speed of fifteen knots, a remarkably accurate estimate, as captured German documents subsequently proved, Harwood worked out in pencil on a signal pad how long it would take the *Admiral Scheer* (for this was still the supposed name of the raider) to reach the focal areas, and how quickly the *Exeter* could come north.

The *Admiral Scheer*, he estimated, could be at Rio de Janeiro on the morning of 12 December; or the River Plate by the morning of the next day; or the Falkland Islands by the morning of the 14th. Which would she choose? It was 1,000 miles from the Falklands to the Plate, and a further 1,000 to Rio. If Harwood made a mistake in his choice the raider would escape again; if he was correct it could mean its destruction . . .

Admiral Lyon had concluded that the *Admiral Scheer* would go north; but Harwood subsequently wrote: 'I decided that the Plate, with its larger number of ships and its very valuable grain and meat trade, was the vital area to defend. I therefore arranged to concentrate there my available forces in advance of the time at which it was anticipated the raider might start operations in that area.

'In order to bring this about, I made the following signal to the South America Division timed 1315 of 3 December 1939:

> *In view of report pocket battleship, amend previous dispositions,* Cumberland *self-refit at Falkland Islands as previously arranged but keep at short notice on two shafts.* Achilles *leave Rio de Janeiro so as to arrive and fuel Montevideo 0600 (Zone plus 2) 8th December,* Exeter *leave Falkland Islands for Plate* AM *9th December, covering ss* Lafonia *with returning volunteers.* Ajax, Achilles, *concentrate in position 35° south, 50° west at 1600 (Zone plus 2) 10th December.* Exeter *to pass through position 090° Medanos Light 150 miles at 0700 12th December. If concentration with* Ajax *and* Achilles *not effected by that time further instructions will be issued to* Exeter . . .'

His decision was now made. He had ten days to wait before he would know whether it was the right one – ten days in which the raider could round the Cape and circle Madagascar in the Indian Ocean, reach up north-westward to strike round the West Indies, go up to the Canaries, off North Africa, move down to the ice limits of the Antarctic – or make for Rio, the Falklands, or the Plate . . .

The *Achilles* had been having a busy but not unenjoyable time in the north, rattling the bars outside Pernambuco and Cabadello, where

German ships were caged. 'Our appearance so far north was un-expected,' Captain Parry wrote later, 'and we were reported by the Brazilian Air Force as a pocket battleship, which caused a flutter until C-in-C, South Atlantic, heard the truth.'

During this trip the crew passed the time with competitions – including an obstacle race which started off with twenty yards in diving boots, standing long jump, and an original item, a singing relay, in which each team ran right round the ship and then sang a popular song. For them, war seemed a long way off, but Captain Parry wrote: 'I remember thinking how fit and well and happy they all seemed; and how damnable it would be, if we got into action with the enemy, to face heavy casualties amongst such a fine lot of men.'

Then Commodore Harwood's signal arrived and the *Achilles* turned south for Montevideo, increasing speed to 19½ knots in order to arrive on time. Once at Montevideo they had a great reception, and the Uruguayan authorities berthed the New Zealand cruiser alongside and instituted a very thorough guard to prevent possible sabotage. Mean-while the *Ajax* was steaming northward. Admiral Lyon signalled the Commodore on the 5th that the cruiser *Dorsetshire* would arrive in Port Stanley on 23 December to relieve the *Exeter*, which would then cross the South Atlantic and refit at Simonstown where there were plenty of dockyard facilities.

On the same day the British Naval Attaché at Buenos Aires signalled that the 7,800-ton German steamer *Ussukuma* had left Bahia Blanca at 1900 the previous evening. The Commodore promptly ordered the *Cumberland*, which was by now on her way south to the Falklands, to search the southern arcs of the *Ussukuma*'s possible course, and at the same time he headed the *Ajax* southward at twenty-two knots in case the German ship, which was known to be short of fuel, should try to reach Montevideo inside territorial waters.

At 1910 that day smoke from a steamer was sighted and within a short time the vessel was identified as the *Ussukuma*. She was orderd to heave to and a boarding party from the *Ajax* was put aboard. But they were too late – the Germans had started scuttling. By the time they reached the engine room, sea water was covering the valves. Captain Woodhouse recalled them when the ship took on a dangerous list and the ship sank during the night. Her crew were made prisoners, and they were transferred to the *Cumberland* when she arrived shortly after dawn the next day and the *Ajax* went in to refuel from the *Olynthus* in San Borombon Bay.

On 10 December at 1000 the *Achilles* joined the *Ajax* in a position 230 miles east of Montevideo, and at 0700 two days later the *Exeter* joined them. It was the first time three of Commodore Harwood's ships had ever worked together.

He wrote: 'I then proceeded towards position 32° south, 47° west. The position was chosen from my Shipping Plot as being at that time the most congested part of the diverted shipping routes, i.e. the point where I estimated a raider could do most damage to British shipping.'

At noon Commodore Harwood made a signal to Captain Parry in the *Achilles* and Captain Bell in the *Exeter*, which gave, in a few words, his plan for battle. It was brief and it was clear. In Nelson's time the two captains would have joined him and Captain Woodhouse for dinner aboard the *Ajax* and he would have discussed it with them over a bottle of good port.*

The three captains would then have talked over every eventuality with him; and they would have gone back to their ships knowing exactly what move to make at a given flag signal. In that way signalling would be kept down to a minimum, and in an emergency each captain could act on his own initiative knowing exactly what Nelson had in mind and what he would have ordered them to do. But in 1939, more than a century later, it was not necessary.

Modern weapons had not, at this stage, complicated the tactical issue; they only increased the number of specialist officers and ratings carried on board. Harwood had had many weeks to consider the tactics he would use: since the attack on the *Clement*, which revealed a raider's presence, any one or two of his cruisers might have happened on a pocket battleship.

Now, on 12 December, if his assessment was correct, he would be employing those tactics within a few hours. And in a few more hours, if he was still alive, he would know whether they had been the correct ones.

In most men's lives there comes a time when the whole future is precariously balanced. For Nelson it had been the few hours before the Battle of the Nile, which for him could have ended in disaster but in fact

---

* It has been variously reported that before the battle the captains did in fact meet on board the *Ajax*; but this was not the case, and the suggestion detracts from Commodore Harwood's feat.

resulted in fame, further opportunities, and the final victory at Trafalgar.

Now Henry Harwood, a month short of his fifty-second birthday and hardly known outside the Royal Navy and his own circle of friends, had also reached that point. Nelson had won at the Nile by brilliant, daring and totally unexpected tactics. Had they failed his enemies and the politicians would have had him sent home in disgrace. That was the price for losing when gambling with high stakes.

Harwood's small force, which would be outgunned from the start, could only sink or cripple a pocket battleship by superior tactics. There would be no scope for the unexpected move which would take the enemy unawares that Nelson had employed at the Nile; but there was just as much scope for mistakes.

So at noon, as the signal giving his plan was sent, Harwood had reached the crisis for which thirty-six years of naval training had prepared him. Britannia Naval College in 1903 as a cadet; service as a midshipman in the *London* and *Bulwark*; Torpedo Officer in the cruiser *Sutlej* in the Atlantic and the *Royal Sovereign* in the Grand Fleet during the First World War; the cruiser *Southampton*; Plans Division at Admiralty; the Third Battle Squadron; Commander in the *Cumberland*; the Imperial Defence College; command of the cruiser *London* as Flag Captain and Chief Staff Officer, First Cruiser Squadron; on the staff of the RN War College between 1934 and 1936; and then, in September 1936, the proud moment when he hoisted his Broad Pendant in the *Exeter* as Commodore Commanding the South America Division.

The future held what? Bitter disappointment or death after failing to destroy the pocket battleship, a task most senior officers in the Navy would give up a pension to attempt? Or victory, promotion, and all that goes with it? Or was his deduction wrong in any case, and the pocket battleship now hundreds of miles away, steaming in a different direction?

Supposing the enemy was steaming for Rio de Janeiro when he had placed his three cruisers off the Plate? Supposing the pocket battleship was approaching the Falkland Islands, to attack and slip into the broad waters of the Pacific? Supposing . . .

There were plenty of questions that day; but there were no answers.

The Commodore planned to attack immediately by day or by night, and he would split his force into two divisions – the *Exeter*, with her heavier 8-inch guns forming one, and the *Ajax* and *Achilles*, with their less effective and shorter-ranged 6-inch guns, forming the other. Both divisions would attack from slightly different directions so that each could spot the other's fall of shot (flank marking) and also force the enemy to divide his attention. This splitting of his main force was unorthodox – it would have been more usual to keep the three ships concentrated – but it might keep the enemy guessing.

As mentioned earlier, Harwood's signal to his captains was a masterpiece of brevity; and as Captain Parry wrote later, 'His intentions were so clear that practically no signals were made during the action, because we all knew exactly what to do.'

The signal said:

My policy with three cruisers in company versus one pocket battle-ship. Attack at once by day or night. By day act as two units. 1st Division (Ajax and Achilles) and Exeter diverged to permit flank marking. First Division will concentrate gunfire. By night ships will normally remain in company in open order. Be prepared for the signal ZMM, which is to have the same meaning as MM* except that for Division read single ship.

He amplified this signal later as follows:

My object in the signal ZMM is to avoid torpedoes and take the enemy by surprise and cross his stern. Without further orders ships are to clear the line of fire by hauling astern of the new leading ship. The new leading ship is to lead the line without further orders so as to maintain decisive gun range.

That evening the three ships practised the manoeuvre and also carried out concentration and flank marking exercises. Concentration of gunfire means that two or more ships act as one – the *Ajax* and *Achilles* in this instance. The *Ajax* would pass all the necessary orders, ranges, deflection and firing signals to the *Achilles*, which would apply correction for her distance and bearing from the *Ajax*.

Concentration increases the hitting rate and prevents confusion in spotting the fall of shot since theoretically all the shells from both ships would fall simultaneously and in much the same piece of water. The two ships therefore spent some time testing the communication procedure.

* MM – 'Commanders of Divisions are to turn their Divisions to course . . . starting with the rear Division.'

The flank-marking exercises were for much the same purpose. If the two Divisions, *Exeter*, and *Ajax* and *Achilles*, could keep the enemy so that their individual lines of fire were roughly at right angles, then each could report how far 'short' or 'over' the other Division's shells were falling.

Otherwise all that the gunnery control officer in each of the three ships could do was to correct the salvoes which fell in line with the enemy. So the three cruisers passed imaginary spotting signals to each other and exercised using this information on the gunnery fire control equipment.

While they were doing that, the rest of the hunting groups were in the following positions:

Force H (*Sussex* and *Shropshire*) sweeping off the West African coast, more than 4,000 miles away:

Force I (*Eagle*, *Cornwall*, and *Gloucester*) were at Durban, more than 4,100 miles away, short of fuel after a wild goose chase into the Indian Ocean;

Force K (*Ark Royal* and *Renown*) the most powerful hunting group in the South Atlantic, were off Pernambuco, 2,000 miles northwards;

Force X (*Hermes* and the French cruisers *Dupleix* and *Foch*) with the *Neptune*, *Hardy*, *Hostile* and *Hero*, were still farther north, off St Paul Rocks.

The *Cumberland* was at the Falkland Islands; and the *Dorsetshire* was on the eve of sailing from Simonstown to relieve the *Exeter*. The submarine *Severn* was half-way between St Helena and Bahia, on her way to the Falklands, and the submarine *Clyde* was approaching Dakar.

That, then, was the scene in the South Atlantic on 12 December 1939, the eve of the Battle of the River Plate.

XI

Graf Spee *is Trapped*

THE TIME was 0552 on the 13 December. In four minutes the upper margin of the deep-red orb that was the sun would edge above the horizon; and it would find a clear sky and a south-easterly breeze from the trade winds ruffling the low swell into lazy wavelets.

While Kapitän zur See Hans Langsdorff rested in his bridge cabin the great pocket battleship *Admiral Graf Spee* slipped through the water at fifteen knots, seeming graceful as the bow wave curved up and outwards with geometric precision from her stem; yet the easy light of early dawn could not soften the harsh shape of the six 11-inch guns jutting aggressively from the curved armour plating of their turrets.

The quartermaster at the wheel was having an easy watch – it was no trouble for him to keep the ship on her course of 155 degrees, and he was lost in his own thoughts. In eight minutes' time he would receive a curt order to come round to 335 degrees, north-westward, the next course laid out by the Navigator to ensure a thorough search of the area.

There had been something of an anti-climax at first light: Langsdorff's hopes of finding a British merchantman in sight – for visibility was soon twenty miles, somewhat reduced by mirages – were dashed. He half-expected to find a liner, the *Highland Monarch*; and today, just when he wanted it, the Arado float-plane was out of action. An engine block had cracked the day before and that had meant dismantling the whole engine. The wings too, had been dismantled, so that the aircraft looked like a trussed turkey waiting to be put in an oven.

Four minutes to sunrise on 13 December 1939 . . . lookouts leisurely swung their binoculars through their allocated arcs, each watching a segment of a circle of which the *Graf Spee* formed the centre. Each searched his sector with the ease of precision which comes only with long practice.

96

With the first light it was always a tense job since the rolling back of darkness could reveal a powerful enemy within gunshot; but now, with the whole sky becoming blue and the sun soon to rise, confidence came back as usual and barely comprehended fears slid back into the limbo of the men's spirits.

Then suddenly one man perched high up above the bridge saw, fine on the starboard bow, two thin masts on the horizon, looking like pins stuck on the far edge of a vast grey-green pin cushion. The curvature of the earth hid the ship to which they belonged; but a lone raider has no friends. All masts, all smoke, all aircraft – all belong to the enemy.

A quick check on the bearing, a harsh call to the bridge: two masts in sight. Then binoculars back on the bearing with eyes straining to see if they belong to a merchantman or a warship . . .

The officer of the watch rapidly passed the word for the Captain; and that was hardly done before lookouts were reporting four more thin masts. Langsdorff reached the bridge just as the first estimated ranges arrived – about seventeen miles. Someone passed him a pair of binoculars.

'Maintain course and speed,' he said. 'Action Stations.'

Alarm rattlers clattered throughout the ship to startle hundreds of men from sleep. Pulling on clothing with the near-conditioned reflexes of trained but sleepy seamen, they started running to their action stations – to the guns, to rangefinders, to magazines and damage control centres, to first-aid stations and a dozen other positions. Water-tight doors clanged shut, hatches slammed down and were secured with clips. In a few seconds the ship became a honeycomb of water-tight compartments.

Fregattenkapitän Ascher, the Chief Gunnery Officer, went to the Director Control Tower with his team of spotting observers, layers and trainers, and the great rangefinder high above the bridge moved a few degrees until the nearest masts appeared in the eyepieces. Ranges were called into telephones and Ascher waited . . .

Korvettenkapitän (Ing) Klepp, the Chief Engineer, was soon in the engine room reporting all was well with the great diesels; Kapitän-leutnant Brutzer, was standing by his beloved torpedo tubes; all over the ship fifty-four officers and 1,080 petty-officers and ratings waited for orders from Langsdorff: orders which could lead to the destruction of another British merchantman, or – and nine 'kills' without trouble were making them over-confident – the remote possibility of action against a

97

British warship. In any case, hadn't they been told the *Graf Spee* was almost invincible?

As Langsdorff made his way to the flying bridge an officer reported to him that the pocket battleship was cleared for action. The time was 0600, four minutes after sunrise.

By now more than a dozen powerful binoculars, as well as the main rangefinder on the fighting top, and the smaller one on the foretop, were trained on the ships ahead.

What were they? Merchantmen? If so, what size? Any sign of an escort? What was their course? Where were they bound? In a few moments an excited lookout reported he could identify the one farthest to the right: she was the British cruiser *Exeter*. . .

An officer hurriedly grabbed a reference book, leafed through the pages and started reading out details of her guns, armour and speed. The photograph showing her very tall masts was compared with the vague silhouette on the horizon. There was no doubt about it – she was the *Exeter*, with six 8-inch guns . . .

Then more reports from lookouts: the two ships to the left had low-lying superstructure. Two destroyers, Langsdorff noted. They would be screening the cruiser in case there were any U-boats about.

Briefly he summed up his views to his officers gathered round him on the bridge: the *Exeter* and the destroyers were obviously protecting a convoy which at the moment was out of sight. He would attack immediately – the *Graf Spee* had not much to fear from the *Exeter* – and close to an effective fighting range before the *Exeter* had raised enough steam to make her best speed. Then the *Exeter* and her attendant destroyers disposed of, the *Graf Spee* could finish off the convoy.

The bridge telegraphs were altered and in the engine room corresponding indicators pointed to full speed, and the pocket battleship's diesels increased their thundering power. On deck, ratings clawed at halyards and her Battle Ensigns ran up to flap in the wind, now increased to almost gale force by the ship's forward speed. At the same time a masthead flag was reported to have been run up by the *Exeter*.

Five minutes later an officer turned to Langsdorff: the two smaller ships, he said, were not destroyers. They were cruisers of the *Ajax* class. He added – quite unnecessarily, since Langsdorff knew the details by heart – that they mounted eight 6-inch guns and had a designed speed of thirty-two knots . . .

Thus, in a few seconds, the whole situtaion had changed alarmingly
. . . and while Langsdorff thought, the *Graf Spee* raced at twenty-four
knots towards the cruisers crossing her bow. Each couple of minutes'
thought brought the ships nearly a mile closer . . . A lucky hit by an 8-
inch shell from the *Exeter* and nowhere to repair the *Graf Spee* . . . These
British cruisers could make at least thirty knots compared with his
twenty-four . . . If he could not sink them could he shake them off in
daylight – darkness was more than fifteen hours away? . . . Or would
they dog him like terriers round a slower, snarling badger, their yelps
bringing up more powerful reinforcements?

Rapidly Langsdorff made up his mind and changed his original plan.

From the Graf Spee's *Action Report: At 0612 course was changed to
115 for a running fight to starboard. The enemy steered an easterly
course. The light cruisers pulled ahead to the east at high speed so that
their distance from the* Exeter *quickly increased . . .*

At 0617 at 197 hectometres [21,000 yards] the Graf Spee *opened
fire with its main battery on the* Exeter. *Four salvoes of each turret
shot at first base-fused shells for better observation purposes,
afterwards impact fuses (Kz) were ordered in order to obtain the
greatest possible damage to the lightly-armoured turrets and superstructure and through hits on its hull to reduce the ship's speed . . .*

XII

'Open Fire. G 25'

IF YOUR name was Henry Harwood Harwood, Commodore, Royal Navy, then at 0610, as the *Graf Spee* identified* the two smaller cruisers, you were having a well-earned rest in your bunk in the *Ajax*, which was steaming at fourteen knots and zig-zagging about a mean course of 060 degrees, followed by the *Achilles* and *Exeter*.

From 0450 to 0540 the crews of all three cruisers had been at Dawn Action Stations as usual. Night had almost imperceptibly merged into the grey of dawn; and then it had been daylight, with visibility quickly lifting from a few hundred yards to twenty miles.

And there was no sign of the German raider – or indeed, any ships at all. The whole 360 degrees of the horizon was empty. For Harwood there was a moment of disappointment and the thought that his conclusion that the enemy raider would be lured to the Plate area might be wrong: that while he was waiting here more merchant ships 1,000 miles away might already have been sunk without being able to send out RRR reports . . .

But he had made his decision and acted: there was no going back on it now. He could wait – wait until his lookouts spotted something, or his wireless operators picked up a signal addressed *To CCSAD: IMMEDI-ATE* . . . which would give him news.

With the last of the dawn, he had exercised his three ships, using the signal *ZMM*, in the manoeuvres they would use in action against a pocket battleship. A practice shoot together, since the *Ajax* and *Achilles* would concentrate their gunfire, was planned for later in the day.

Finally, at 0540, the crews went from Dawn Action Stations to Day

* Her much taller fighting top gave her a far greater visibility range than the cruisers.

Defence Stations. Only one gun in each turret was left manned and certain of the ships' boilers were shut off to save fuel.

If your name was Edgar Duncan Lewin, Lieutenant, and pilot of the *Ajax*'s Seafox aircraft, you were the officer of the watch and standing on the cruiser's bridge talking to Lt-Cdr Richard Pennefather. You had control of a vessel which cost £1,480,097 to build and needed another £133,000 a year to maintain. Yet if she went into battle your Action Station would be in the Seafox, spotting the fall of shot.

If your name was Charles Woodhouse, Captain and Commanding Officer of the *Ajax*, ultimately responsible for everything connected with the cruiser and the thirty-nine officers and 554 men who made up her crew, you were in your sea cabin after spending the previous hours on the bridge, manoeuvring under the command of Commodore Harwood.

But if you were one of five officers and forty-eight ratings in the *Exeter*, or four ratings in the *Achilles*, or seven ratings in the *Ajax*, you had less than two hours to live.

Lt Richard Washbourn, a New Zealander, was the Principal Control Officer in the *Achilles*, and at the first sign of dawn he had gone to Action Stations – as every warship had done each morning since 28 August. Captain Parry had climbed up to the bridge and taken over from Washbourn, who had then scrambled up to the Director Control Tower. After the usual testing of electrical circuits and communications he had reported to Captain Parry 'Main armament closed up and cleared away', using the voicepipe to the bridge. Then had come the usual exercises, which had stopped as night slowly changed into the grey of dawn. While visibility increased, he and his men in the DCT used their powerful binoculars and telescopes to watch the diffuse and indeterminate line where the sea merged with the sky.

There had been nothing on the horizon and as broad daylight brought maximum visibility Washbourn had reported to the Captain, 'Horizon clear, Sir. May I fall the quarters out?' With the order 'Sound the disperse. Close up the cruising watch', Washbourn had climbed down to the bridge where Captain Parry was standing with the Navigator, Lt Cowburn.

Normally Captain Parry went straight down to his cabin to shave and have a bath; but this morning he stayed on the bridge longer than usual, talking to Washbourn about the gunnery exercises planned for later in the day. He was on the point of going to his cabin when the bridge lookout reported 'Smoke bearing Red one double oh, Sir.'*

The smoke had been sighted a minute earlier in the *Ajax*, at 0610. It was a vague blur just above the horizon on the port beam when Leading Signalman Swanston reported it to Lewin. It was probably from a British or neutral merchantman bound for the Plate. But today all smoke had to be regarded with a certain amount of suspicion. It might be caused by best-quality Welsh steaming coal shovelled into a furnace by perspiring Scots stokers, or by the oil-fired engines of a neutral liner. Or by a German pocket battleship.

Still, it was unlikely that an enemy raider would advertise her presence with a lot of funnel smoke; and in any case they were in fact due to meet a particular merchantman. The Commodore had previously given a coded signal to the *Exeter* so that she could pass it to a British steamer, which would, on arriving at Montevideo, pass it on to the British Consul. In this way the cruisers could avoid breaking wireless silence.

So Lewin went to the voicepipes and told first Captain Woodhouse of the sighting, and then Commodore Harwood. The Commodore told him to order the *Exeter* to investigate and, if it was a British ship, pass the signal. In the meantime the *Exeter* had sighted the smoke and ran up a flag signal *Smoke bearing 320 degrees*.

A few seconds later Leading Signalman Swanston was sending the Commodore's order to Captain Bell:

Investigate smoke bearing 324 degrees. If this is a British merchant-man bound for the Plate due to get into harbour soon, transfer your signal to her.

The time was 0614. The *Exeter* acknowledged the order and hauled round to port out of the line, towards the smoke lying to the north-west.

A few moments later Swanston reported to Lt Lewin that he thought there was a pocket battleship under the smoke. Lewin and Pennefather both had a good look with their binoculars and decided

*For lookout purposes the horizon is divided into two 180-degrees arcs – from o degrees (dead ahead) to 180 (astern) on either side. 'Red' signifies the port side, green the starboard. Thus 'Red one double-oh' is 100 degrees on the left side – 10 degrees abaft the beam.

that what looked like a warship's fighting top was in fact a plume of black smoke.

Very soon, however, Lewin became converted to Swanston's point of view, and sounded the alarm rattlers. He would face a good deal of leg-pulling if he was wrong, but precious minutes would be saved if he was right.

Captain Woodhouse came to the bridge and Lewin explained the position. Pennefather, who was still rather doubtful about the identity of the strange ship, was sent aloft, where he would have a better field of view.

By now the *Exeter* and the *Graf Spee* were approaching each other at a mean speed of forty miles an hour. Every second found them climbing towards each other over the curvature of the earth. In the *Graf Spee* 1,134 men prepared to meet an enemy; in the *Exeter* everyone was alert, waiting to see if they would find a friend.

The *Graf Spee* had the advantage of height: from the lookout position high on her fighting top she could see farther over the curve of the earth than the smaller cruisers. This, plus the fact that she knew she had no friendly ships at hand, was giving her nearly twenty-four minutes start* in the battle for her life which was to be called The River Plate.

Less than two minutes after the *Exeter* turned towards the smoke the fighting top of a warship was seen and at 0616 Captain Bell ordered the following signal to be flashed to Commodore Harwood in the *Ajax*:

> *I think it is a pocket battleship.*

The Torpedo Officer, Lt-Cdr C.J. Smith, then definitely identified her as a pocket battleship of the *Admiral Scheer* class.

Immediately flag 'N', a yellow triangle with a blue tongue, followed by the numerals 322, was run up: *Enemy in sight bearing 322.*

The *Graf Spee* would be opening fire any minute . . . Action Stations was sounded, the main wireless office in the *Exeter* was warned, and all depth charges in the traps were released – there was no point in having high explosive lying around waiting for an enemy shell to detonate it.

Then her Battle Ensigns were run up. They were White Ensigns which streamed at the fore- and main-mastheads, from the yardarm and from

---

*On the assumption that the times given in the German report are correct.

the gaff. There were four in case one was shot away; and they would only be hauled down at the end of the battle. If they were hauled down before then it would mean only one thing – the *Exeter* had surrendered.

Now, with her crew at Action Stations, her guns loaded, aimed and ready to fire, her boilers rapidly increasing to full power, and Battle Ensigns flying, the *Exeter* was ready for the unequal fight.

In the *Ajax*, while Pennefather was beginning his laborious climb, Captain Woodhouse called to the Director Control Tower above and behind the bridge to see if they could see anything; but apart from the smoke they had nothing to report.

Then Pennefather, from his vantage point up the mast, shouted down to the bridge. What was he saying? The wind and the noise carried his voice away. Captain Woodhouse, straining his ears, was conscious of a signalman reading a message coming from the *Exeter*. Pennefather shouted again: 'It's a pocket battleship!' At that moment the signalman reported the *Exeter*'s message.

The Commodore had been right.

After the alarm rattlers had sounded earlier throughout the cruiser the Commodore had come up to the compass platform. On the port beam his enemy appeared as a blur of smoke stemming from a small, dark and vague shape on the horizon; the *Achilles* was astern; and on the port quarter the *Exeter* headed towards it, her Battle Ensigns being run up.

His three ships were already in the formation he wanted them – the *Exeter* hauled out of the line and preparing to attack from one direction, and the *Ajax* and *Achilles* forming another division to attack from another direction. There was no need to hoist ZMM.

Now he had the *Graf Spee* within range; but she might wipe out his small force by the sheer weight of her 11-inch shells,* or keep them at arm's length and escape at night. He had first to send an enemy report – which would also bring reinforcements – as soon as possible, and within a few minutes his wireless operators were transmitting his signals. To the *Cumberland* 1,000 miles to the south, waiting at Port Stanley, to the Senior Officer of Force K (*Renown* and *Ark Royal*) 2,000 miles to the

---

*A broadside of the *Graf Spee*'s 11-inch guns weighed roughly 4,140 lbs against the 900 lbs of each of the 6-inch cruisers and the 1,600 lbs of the *Exeter*. The *Graf Spee*'s secondary armament of 5·9-inch was, of course, only a fraction smaller than the smaller cruisers' 6-inch guns.

northward, off Pernambuco; and to the Senior Officer of Force X (the French cruisers *Dupleix* and *Foch* and the British carrier *Hermes*) and the *Neptune* and three destroyers stilll further north of St Paul Rocks, went the signal:

IMMEDIATE. One pocket battleship 034° south 049° west, course 275 degrees.

By this time Harwood could see the *Graf Spee*'s shells falling round the *Exeter*: the splashes showed she was shooting fairly accurately. Then, through binoculars, he saw the *Exeter*'s guns belching smoke. The time was 0618.

Suddenly shells from the *Graf Spee* threw up gouts of water near the *Ajax*: she had turned one 11-inch turret on to the First Division.

'It appeared at this stage as if the enemy was undecided as to her gunnery policy,' Harwood wrote later. 'Her turrets were working under different controls, and she shifted target several times before eventually concentrating both turrets on the *Exeter*.'

Then, as the *Exeter*'s shells fell near the *Graf Spee*, Harwood saw the pocket battleship begin to turn to port, away from the *Exeter* and on to a course parallel with the *Ajax* and *Achilles*. Was she going to keep the cruiser in range of her 11-inch but far enough away to be out of range of the 8-inch and 6-inch guns?

As Rate Officers in the three cruisers rapidly passed the *Graf Spee*'s new course to the transmitting stations and Director Layers trained their sights round further to starboard, the turrets followed obediently. In accordance with his plans Harwood's first order, after seeing that the 'enemy report' had been sent, was to alter course towards the *Graf Spee*.

A brief order and within seconds a signal was being sent to the *Achilles*:

Alter course together to 340 degrees.

The time was 0620.
Then a second order was sent to the *Achilles*:

Open fire. G 25.*

Captain Langsdorff noted: 'The first salvo was observed to be short. The following ranging salvo located the target and about four minutes

*G 25 – speed 25 knots.

after opening fire the first hit was observed on the *Exeter*'s fo'c'sle. *Exeter* returned the fire about two minutes later. Her first salvoes were short.'

The Battle of the River Plate had begun.

XIII

'Broadsides . . . Shoot'

When the lookout in the *Achilles* had called out 'Smoke bearing Red one double-oh, Sir,' Captain Parry and Lt Washbourn had walked unhurriedly over to the port wing of the bridge. Both of them had heard scores of similar reports before, and each time a merchant ship had come into sight. There was no tension, only boredom . . .

Captain Parry levelled his binoculars at the smoke and Washbourn looked through the Principal Control Officer's sight – powerful binoculars mounted on a moveable arm.

There was, however, no mistaking what they saw. There was a thin feather of orange-brown smoke hanging low on the horizon. Beneath it they could see a gunnery control tower and a mast; but it was a gunnery control tower and a mast of a peculiar and unmistakable design.

They both turned to each other.

'My God,' said Captain Parry, 'it's a pocket battleship. Sound the alarm, Pilot. Warn the engine room that we will be going on to full speed shortly, and are going into action.'

He wrote later: 'I remember a rather sickening feeling in the pit of my tummy as I realized we were in for an action in which the odds were hardly on our side. Luckily there wasn't much time to think about that.'

As Washbourn started to climb back to the DCT the Chief Yeoman of Signals, Lincoln Martinson, reported: '*Exeter* has hoisted Flag N, Sir . . ."Enemy in sight".'

On the bridge Cowburn had automatically taken over from Washbourn as officer of the watch and from now on would give all helm and engine orders (Captain Parry would give him all the instructions, addressing him as 'Pilot').

The first order had come very promptly.

'Open out to about three or four cables from the *Ajax*, Pilot, and keep loose formation. Weave when the pocket battleship fires at us, but don't use too much rudder.'

By that time the ship's company were racing to their Action Stations. Having fallen out at 0550, almost every one of them not at Defence Stations had turned in again. Sleep was very precious in wartime, and the forty minutes before 'Call the hands' at 0630 was not to be missed.

As the alarm rattlers had sounded, followed by a bugle's urgent doh soh-soh, doh soh-soh calling them to 'Action' (which was not preceded and followed by the 'G' indicating 'exercise'), they tumbled out of their hammocks and ran to their quarters in all sorts of garb – pyjamas, underclothes, shorts or anything they could grab on the way.

Down in the engine room Lt Jasper Abbott, a small, precise man with a neatly-trimmed black beard, worked under the Commander (E) in the ever-present task of using sluggish fuel oil to turn water into super-heated steam – a transformation undreamt of by ancient alchemists intent on changing base metals into gold, but far more valuable. It was steam which at 700 degrees Fahrenheit was invisible, yet three times hotter than boiling water; steam which could strip the flesh from a man's body within seconds.

Each pair of the *Achilles*'s six boilers supplied steam to an engine room, forming a self-contained unit. If one unit was damaged and flooded, another could keep the ship moving at a reasonable speed.

While the men in the engine room were hard at work providing more steam for the ever-hungry turbines, the guns' crews were getting ready. Lt Washbourn had climbed into his seat in the Director Control Tower and pulled on headphones and the microphone transmitter. In a moment he would be in communication with all the gun turrets and the Transmitting Station. He was preparing to unleash more destructive power in one minute than a medieval emperor dreamt of in a lifetime.

He switched on the microphone.

'Control, TS. Testing communications . . . Report when closed up . . . Enemy in sight bearing Red nine oh . . . All quarters with CPBC* and full charges load!'

These orders, repeated with loud shouts in the gun turrets, caused an

* Common Pointed Ballistic Capped: the then latest six-inch armour-piercing shell. The 'ballistic cap' was a light steel nose fitted on the shell to streamline it and so increase the range for a given charge.

exchange of meaning glances: the men, in their hurried dash to their positions, had had no time to glean any news. Now they realized something was very definitely in the wind.

By this time the whole Director Control Tower had trained round towards the enemy, like an owl with many eyes. Washbourn was looking through stereoscopic binoculars at the *Graf Spee* on the horizon. Between his knees was the gun-ready lamp box with eight indicators on its face. Each of these would glow red as the gun it represented was loaded and ready to fire.

Sitting on Washbourn's right was the Spotting Officer, Sergeant Samuel Trimble. This big, red-faced Ulsterman was better known as 'Baggy' Trimble, and his job was spotting the fall of the *Achilles*'s shells and reporting them to the Transmitting Station.

On Washbourn's left was the Rate Officer, Mr Eric Watts. Rotund, placid and very competent, he was the Gunner. He had the difficult job of estimating the *Graf Spee*'s course and speed, and any alterations she might make, and reporting constantly to the Transmitting Station.

Behind these three men were Telegraphist Frank Stennett, who would be the link with the *Ajax* when the two ships' gunfire was concentrated, Telegraphist Neville Milburn, who would pass on flank-marking reports from the *Exeter*, and Boy Dorsett, a young New Zealand lad who operated the telephones to the turrets.

Above the telegraphists, was the Position-in-Line (PIL) Rangetaker, Able Seaman Shirley, a New Zealander. Using a special instrument, and with his head stuck out of the DCT, he was taking the range of the *Ajax* to get the correction for the position in line when gunfire was concentrated and the *Achilles* was using the *Ajax*'s fire orders.

In the forward section of the DCT, sitting lower than the others were four more men. Two of them operated the Director Sight, the master eye by which all the ship's guns were aimed. And they were men hand-picked by Washbourn: men who had keen eyes and keen minds, who would not get flustered or frightened, and who could be relied on, whether the ship was rolling or pitching in a heavy sea, zig-zagging, burning or sinking, to go on turning the hand wheels which would keep the Director Sight, and, in turn, the guns aimed at the chosen enemy.

Working at the left side of the sight, an eye glued to a stabilized telescope, was the Director Layer, Petty Officer Alfred Maycock. He was responsible for laying the guns vertically on the enemy (elevation) and, when ordered, pressing the trigger which would fire them simultaneously. On his right was the Director Trainer, Petty Officer William Headon. Using his special telescope, he trained the guns horizontally.

The other two men with them were the Range to Elevation and Deflection Unit Operator, Able Seaman Shaw, and the Cross-Level Operator, Ordinary Seaman Rogers.

Below the DCT was the rangefinder. It worked like a pair of vast human eyes except that Chief Petty Officer William Bonniface and a New Zealander, Able Seaman Gould, focused them; and instead of a brain to register the range, there were dials which were repeated in various parts of the ship.

But although the DCT and the rangefinder were the ship's eyes and the kingdom of the Gunnery Officer, a mechanical 'brain' several decks below, protected by armour, worked out all the complicated mathematics which would ensure that the shells, if Headon and Maycock aimed the Director Sight correctly, arrived on the target.

This 'brain' was officially called the Admiralty Fire Control Table and it was situated in the Transmitting Station. It was a fantastic product of scientific designing, and when it had certain information fed into it, it transmitted a series of answers, or corrections, to the guns.

When the enemy position (from Director Sight), range (from the rangefinders), speed and course (from the Rate Officer), and fall of shot (from the Spotting Officer), were fed in, it –

Indicated how much the guns had to be trained left or right;

Gave the correct angle of elevation for them;

Worked out precisely where the *Achilles'* shells had to fall, allowing for the problem that she and the *Graf Spee* would each be going in different directions at upwards of twenty-five knots, and the shells would be in the air for almost a minute, and applied the necessary correction;

Allowed for the fact that the right-handed spin given to the shell by the rifling of the gun made it wander to the right;

Allowed for the effect of wind on the shell while it was in flight, and for the temperature and barometric pressure;

Caused the aim of each gun to converge on the target (if the guns were aimed in the same direction they would shoot parallel lines and the shells would fall the same distance apart as the guns were in the ship. This spread would be far too great);

Allowed for the fact that, when firing over the bow, each gun would be at different distances from the enemy and would require slightly different elevations.

Thus, as Maycock and Headon aimed the Director Sight at the *Graf Spee*, the enemy's elevation and bearing were transmitted to the 'Table' and also to the guns, which trained round in the same direction.

But the Director Sight was aimed directly at the enemy. Since the shells would be in the air for a minute, the guns would have to be aimed at where the *Graf Spee* would be in a minute's time. This 'aim off', called 'deflection', was worked out by the Table and sent electrically to the guns.

But in far less time than it took you to read this, Washbourn was giving his next order:

'Broadsides.'

Every gun in A and B turrets forward and X and Y turrets aft was now loaded with a 112-lb shell and a 30-lb cordite charge. Breeches were closed, and in each breech was placed a small tube like a rifle cartridge with the bullet removed. In the base of the tube – which was filled with explosive – was a thin iridio-platinum wire, and when the Director Layer pressed the trigger an electric current would flow across and fuse it, firing the explosive which would in turn explode the cordite charge.

Quickly the gun-ready lamps in the box between Washbourn's knees flickered on – one, two (X turret, manned by the Royal Marines, was the first to be ready), three, four, five . . .

Washbourn leaned over and spoke into the voicepipe to the bridge.

'Captain, Sir.'

'Yes, Guns?' replied Captain Parry.

'Ready to open fire.'

'Open fire.'

Washbourn glanced at the gun-ready box: all eight lamps were glowing.

He spoke into the microphone:

'Shoot!'

The fire gong in the DCT sounded its 'ting ting' and Petty Officer Headon, his left hand automatically spinning the elevating hand wheel to keep the Director Sight aimed at the base of the *Graf Spee*'s foremast, squeezed the trigger and completed the circuit.

Electricity flowed across the iridio-platinum bridges – far more than their resistance of o·9 ohm could take – and fused them. Spurts of flame leapt out to explode the 30-lb charges of cordite, packed like long strings of macaroni in silk bags, and turn it into gas – far more than the chambers could hold without bursting. Something had to give way – and it was the shells.

They were thrust up the barrels, spinning one and a half times as they engaged in the thirty-six grooves of the rifling, and leaving at more than 2,000 miles an hour. They would rise nearly 19,000 feet into the atmosphere before plunging down 60·89 seconds later; and they would burst between twenty-two and twenty-seven millionths of a second after striking with a velocity of 1,500 feet per second.

But once the shells left the barrels the guns' crews were concerned with the next broadside. Each gun, weighing six-and-three-quarter tons was flung back by the enormous power of the cordite and stopped after thirty-and-a-half inches by the recoil cylinder, and then thrust into position again by the run-out springs.

Another shell and another charge came up the hoists to each gun from the magazines, which were hidden behind armour well below the waterline; the breeches were flung open and blasts of compressed air automatically cleared the cordite chambers of any burning residue; soaking-wet rammers – better known as 'woolly 'eaded bastards' – were thrust up the chambers to clean them and cool the mushroom head of the breech block; shells were swung into the chambers and rammed home; charges were slid in after them; the tubes were changed and the breeches closed.

One after another the eight gun-ready lamps in front of Washbourn flicked on again.

Maycock and Headon were still keeping the Director Sight on the *Graf Spee*; Sergeant Trimble was still waiting for the shells to land and Watts was reporting on the pocket battleship's course and bearing. The Deflection had come up from the Table to train the guns round slightly.

'Shoot!' said Lt Washbourn in the *Achilles*.

'Shoot!' said Lt Desmond Dreyer in the *Ajax*.

'Shoot!' said Lt-Cdr Richard Jennings in the *Exeter*.

The *Achilles* had opened fire at 0622, and the *Ajax* at 0623. The range was just over 19,000 yards. The *Ajax*'s first broadside fell short. This was signalled to the Transmitting Station, and the Table did many more calculations so that the next salvo would fall where the *Graf Spee* should be sixty seconds after the shells left the guns.

When Lt Dreyer, the Control Officer, ordered 'Up ladder, shoot', the elevation of the guns was adjusted up the scale and the guns fired again. The shells burst over. The range was corrected and a zig-zag group – the guns being so elevated that the salvoes would fall in a zig-zag pattern – fired.

A rapid group was being fired when suddenly the *Ajax* was straddled by a salvo of 11-inch shells from the *Graf Spee*. Immediately Commodore Harwood ordered a thirty-degree turn to starboard to dodge the next salvo and the *Ajax*, steaming at twenty-five knots, heeled as she swung round, followed by the *Achilles*.

The guns of both the cruisers were thrown out by this sudden alteration of course; but rapidly the DCTs and Transmitting Stations brought the turrets round again. Two minutes later the Commodore altered back to the original course, and Captain Parry, whose orders were to conform loosely with the *Ajax*'s movements, brought the *Achilles* round again.

From the *Graf Spee*'s log: 'The light cruisers pulled rapidly ahead so that at 0625 from their twenty-eight-degree to twenty-five-degree relative bearing there was a danger of torpedo attack. The Captain decided . . . to slowly turn away on to a northerly course. At the same time he ordered a change of target on to the left, light cruiser . . .

'At 0631 the main batteries had another target change to the *Exeter*. At the same time* the light cruisers opened fire against the *Graf Spee* without at first scoring any hits.

'The *Exeter* turned to starboard on to a westerly course [and] *Graf Spee* turned with rudder hard to port to a course of 270 degrees. The light cruisers were now quartering off to port and turning slowly to port.

'About 0634 the *Exeter* turned sharply away after heavy hits – only Turret C was still firing – making heavy smoke and for the time being was out of sight.

'The light cruisers were travelling at full speed off the starboard quarter. They could be brought under fire with B turret and secondary

*In fact the *Achilles* opened fire at 0622 and the *Ajax* at 0623.

batteries several times, but only for short periods because of their use of smoke and fog.'*

As soon as he saw the *Graf Spee* swinging round to port at 0637, Commodore Harwood ordered Captain Woodhouse to steer first north and then west to close the range again. As she moved north-westward, away from the three British ships, the pocket battleship started making smoke. Billowing black and brown clouds soon hid the ship for long periods.

The rate officers could see she was zig-zagging violently to avoid the salvoes of the three cruisers; and there was the satisfaction that it threw off the *Graf Spee*'s gunners more than it did the British.

Lt Lewin, the pilot of the *Ajax*'s Seafox, was anxious to get into the air. After the *Graf Spee* had opened fire he asked Captain Woodhouse: 'Can I take off?'

The aircraft would be useful for spotting; but X and Y turrets were firing within a few feet of the aircraft as it stood in its catapult. At this stage Captain Woodhouse was more concerned with the rate of fire. 'If you can,' he said, 'but I'm not going to hold fire for you.'

That was enough for Lewin. With Kearney, his observer, he went aft to the Seafox which had been prepared for catapulting by Pennefather and Warrant Engineer Arthur Monk. Blast from the muzzles of the guns in X and Y turrets was shaking the aircraft as the two men climbed into their seats. The catapult was trained round and, with her engine at full throttle the tiny Seafox was flung into the air.

Just before this, Kearney discovered that the Seafox's wireless was tuned into the reconnaissance wave of 230 kcs instead of the spotting wave of 3800 kcs. To save time he decided to use 230 kcs instead of re-tuning the set, and made a visual signal to the flagdeck telling them to warn the W/T office. This message was never passed on, and the omission was to have a serious result in the early part of the action.

While Lewin climbed to 3,000 feet, the *Achilles* was concentrating her gunfire with the *Ajax* and after thirteen broadsides a salvo of 11-inch shells from the *Graf Spee* erupted in the sea along her port side. Hundreds of splinters spun into the air, several of them cutting through the light plating round the bridge. Six sliced through the 1-inch armour of the DCT, making it look like a tin savaged by a large tin opener.

*The cruisers were not deliberately making smoke at this stage.

Captain Parry woke up to find himself prostrate on the deck with Martinson, the Chief Yeoman of Signals, lying nearby and moaning.

He stood up, conscious that all the *Achilles* guns had stopped firing. Then he saw that they were pointing in the wrong direction . . . Previously, when the *Graf Spee*'s gunfire had been getting unpleasantly close, he had told Cowburn: 'Alter *towards* the splashes, Pilot. That will probably upset his gunnery more than anything else we can do.'

Cowburn had been playing this game very skilfully – Captain Parry was later to attribute the *Achilles*' apparent invulnerability to this – and as soon as the salvo had landed along the port side Cowburn had ordered a high-speed turn to port.

The idea behind this was that the *Graf Spee*, spotting her own salvoes, would make an 'up' correction for 'shorts' and a 'down' correction for 'overs'. By steering the *Achilles* towards the splashes, Captain Parry would always be steering away from where the second (and corrected) salvo would fall.

Realizing the Gunnery Control was not functioning Captain Parry went to the voicepipe and called up to the Director Control Tower. There was no reply.

At that moment someone said: 'Look at your legs!' Captain Parry glanced down. Blood was streaming down the back of one of his calves. He sat down on the edge of the monkey island, the platform round the two compasses, and within a few moments the first-aid party arrived.

They found that Martinson's left leg had been hit with splinters and he had a compound fracture of the tibia. Splints were tied on and he was taken away on a stretcher – still asking whether 'my boys' were all right.

The Sick Berth Petty Officer bandaged one of Captain Parry's legs and then said, 'Now the other leg, please, Sir.' Preoccupied with the battle, Captain Parry said, 'Oh, what's wrong with that?' Looking down he saw that it, too, had been badly cut with splinters.

Up in the DCT the situation was far worse. Washbourn – in his official report he wrote 'I was conscious of a hellish noise and a thump on the head' – came round to find the tiny compartment in a shambles. There were several jagged holes in the armour and the wind whistled in.

Behind him both the telegraphists, Milburn and Stennett, had collapsed, killed outright. One of the bodies had fallen through into the tiny rangefinder compartment below (CPO Bonniface was later to report 'A good bit of vibration was set up inside the rangefinder by our own speed and gunfire. Ranging was otherwise comfortable bar the fact of having a corpse at the back of the neck most of the time made it unpleasant. AB Gould kept calm during the action and did not take any notice of the extra ventilation we were getting. He got a bit peeved over a foot sticking in his ear, but soon settled down after it was removed . . .')

The Concentration Link Rangetaker, Edgar Shirley, had dropped off his stool and was bleeding badly from wounds in his thighs and face. Sergeant Trimble had been severely wounded in the back but he said nothing and carried on with his job so that no one would know he had been hit.

Shaw, the R to ED Unit Operator, was dead from multiple wounds in his chest; but he had slumped over his instrument in such a way that no one knew he had been hit. Washbourn saw that both Headon and Maycock were still all right at the Director Sight, and Boy Dorsett was still alive.

Mr Watts, the Rate Officer, spoke quickly into his microphone: 'DCT has been hit. After Control take over.'

Then he stood up and said to Washbourn:

'Come on, Sir. Running repairs.'

Washbourn, still rather dazed, did not understand. 'What's up? I'm all right.'

He put his hand to his head, and it came away sticky. He climbed off his stool as Watts took down a first-aid bag, extracted a large bandage, and tied up the scalp wounds.

Climbing back into his seat, Washbourn called down the voicepipe:

'Control: bridge.'

Cowburn answered almost immediately.

'Tell the Captain that the DCT has been hit and the After Control is now controlling. Send up first-aid parties.'

That dealt with, he called out to the surviving DCT crew: 'What's out of action?'

Headon turned from his telescope to say: 'Director seems all right, Sir.'

Meanwhile the *Achilles* started shooting again, but the gunfire was extremely ragged because the After Control position was very in-effective. The two men manning it had been experiencing the continuous blast from the muzzles of X turret guns and were completely deafened and nearly stupid from concussion. Although they were also being sick from time to time they carried on as best they could.

Washbourn, realizing it was essential that the DCT started operating again as soon as possible, said:

'We'll see what happens. Switch to DCT controlling.'

Everything seemed to work all right, and while Watts deftly tied a tourniquet on Shirley's leg to stop some of the bleeding, Washbourn went to work.

'DCT controlling,' he said into the microphone. 'Broadsides . . . Shoot!'

Nearly a dozen broadsides had been loosed off before Petty Officer Maycock turned round from the Director Sight and reported: 'Archie's had it, Sir.'

Washbourn stooped in his seat and looked down into the forward part of the DCT. He saw that Shaw, sitting at his instrument in a natural position, was in fact dead.

He called to the cross-level operator: 'Rogers, take over Shaw's job.'

It was fortunate that Washbourn, in the previous weeks of practice, had made sure that all the men in the DCT could do every job. Rogers, who took over his new task without a word, could not move Shaw's body; and he had to sit on it to operate the instrument until later in the action.

It was about this time that Boy Dorsett, who had escaped unscathed, could be heard talking angrily into the telephone to the turrets. Somehow the rumour had got round that he had been killed.

'I'm *not* dead,' he said. 'I tell you I'm not *dead*. It's me who's speaking to you.'

When the DCT was hit all wireless communication with the *Ajax* failed and concentrated gunfire was impossible. It is unlikely that Washbourn was very upset by this – no self-respecting Gunnery Officer likes to have the control of his guns taken away from him.

XIV

Seven Hits on Exeter

From Captain Bell's report: '. . . At 0620 A and B turrets opened fire at a range of 18,700 yards, Y turret joining in 2½ minutes later, having been given permission to disregard the aircraft. At this time the ship was being straddled. At 0623 a shell bursting just short amidships killed a tube's crew, damaged communications, and splinters riddled the searchlight, funnels and starboard aircraft . . .'

The *Exeter* had been steaming with four boilers in B boiler room, and as the alarm was sounded all the boilers in A boiler room were flashed up and connected. At 0620 Captain Bell ordered full speed, and by that time the Damage Control Headquarters in the Engineer's Workshop was closed up and the majority of the outlying parties had reported correct.

The Gunnery Officer, Lt-Cdr Jennings, had straddled the *Graf Spee* with his third salvo of 8-inch shells. The prospects looked promising and he ordered a zig-zag group.

At that moment one of the six 11-inch shells from a broadside fired by the *Graf Spee* landed in the water close alongside the *Exeter*, just short of amidships. A shower of splinters spattered the ship like a handful of rubble flung at a window.

Some spun aft, cutting down and killing most of the crew of the starboard torpedo tubes; others pierced the thin steel plating of the ship's side and killed two of the decontamination party waiting in the Chief Stoker's bathroom and started a small fire among clothing and towels.

Still more sprayed the searchlights, the two funnels and the starboard aircraft. Electric leads were cut and holes pierced in the upper deck. All the gun-ready lamp circuits and the fall of shot hooter went out of action, making Lt-Cdr Jennings' job as Gunnery Officer doubly difficult. Now he was unable to tell when all his guns were loaded, how many splashes to look for, or when his salvoes were falling.

Immediately reports started coming into the Damage Control Head-quarters and parties were sent to start repairing the damage. Men began to douse the fires, plug the holes in the ship's side and upper deck, and shore down hatches in the compartments below. The bodies were dragged away from the torpedo tubes and fresh men took over. Wounded were led or carried to the Medical Stations.

A few moments later the *Graf Spee* scored her first direct hit on the cruiser. An 11-inch shell smashed through the embarkation hatch on deck abaft B turret, ploughed into the Sick Bay, and went outwards through the ship's side into the sea without bursting.

A Sick Berth Chief Petty Officer was walking back from the fore part of the Sick Bay with bottles of morphine sulphate solution when the shell came through and sent splinters flying through the bulkhead. He was knocked unconscious and the precious bottles fell from his hands and smashed. Men in agony from wounds were waiting for the relief that morphine would give them . . .

When he came round he realized what had happened and stumbled back through the smoke and fumes to get more solution. Coughing and half suffocated, he could not find any bottles so he brought back morphine ampoules. But his troubles were only just starting – the task of helping the wounded had to alternate with dealing with the water flooding through the splinter-ridden deckhead, and the *Exeter* was still to be struck by another six 11-inch shells.

But within a minute of this hit the *Graf Spee* was to deliver an almost decisive blow.

> From Captain Bell's report: '. . . *After the eighth salvo B turret received a direct hit from an 11-inch shell and was put out of action. The splinters also killed or wounded all the bridge personnel with the exception of the Captain, Torpedo Control and Firing Officers, and wrecked the wheelhouse communications . . .*'

As mentioned earlier, the *Graf Spee*, after firing four salvoes of base-fused shells, switched over to impact fuses 'in order to obtain the greatest possible damage to the lightly-armoured turrets and superstructure and through hits on its hull to reduce the ship's speed'.*

*Later in the action she reverted to base-fused shells.

One of these shells landed on B turret just between the two guns, ripping off the front armour plate and killing eight men at the front of the gunhouse.

They had fired seven broadsides and the Number Ones of the two guns were just about to ram home the next rounds when the shell burst. All the lights went out, leaving the gunhouse in darkness, and dense, acrid fumes started to burn the nostrils and throats of the stunned survivors.

Sergeant Arthur Wilde, RM, groped for the Number Ones who should have been either side of him, but they were not in their seats. Then he saw daylight coming in through the left rear door of the gunhouse, which had been blown open, and he made his way out on deck.

'As I was going aft,' Wilde reported later, 'Marine Attwood called for me to assist him with Marine W.A. Russell. I turned and saw Russell had lost a forearm and was badly hurt in the other arm.

'Attwood and I assisted Russell down to the port 4-inch gundeck and as we reached it there was another violent explosion which seemed to be in the vicinity of B turret. I dropped to the deck, pulling Russell with me.

'After the splinters had stopped, I cut off two lengths of signal halyard, which were hanging loose, and put a clove hitch for a tourniquet around both of Russell's arms above the elbows.

'I went to the Sick Bay and told someone that I had left Russell sitting against the funnel casing, port side. I proceeded down to the waist and turned forward, intending to go to B magazine and shell room, but was ordered back as the gangway was blocked by CPO Evans who was attending to a man who was seriously injured around the legs . . .

'Sometime later I collected Marines Camp, Attwood and Thomas and we went back to B turret to see what could be done. I observed several small fires, some of which were put out by sand, the fire hydrants being dry.

'Marine Thomas drew my attention to a small fire near the left elevating standard, and I sent him for water and sand. Then, remembering I had seen water in the starboard waist, I went down for some. When I returned Lt Toase, assisted by Marine Thomas, had extinguished the fire and we proceeded to take the cordite from both rammers and pass it overboard . . .'

While this was being done, the badly-wounded Russell, his clothing bloodstained and his arms still bound with signal halyard, walked round making cheering remarks and, in the words of Captain Bell, 'encouraging all by his fortitude'. (He stayed on deck until after the action, when he collapsed.)

While the guns' crews were handling the dangerous cordite charges, Sergeant Puddifoot was dealing with the magazine and shell room below. When the shell burst, 'We heard a violent crash and felt a shock from above, and simultaneously the turret pump stopped', Puddifoot wrote later.

He called the gunhouse several times but there was no reply. Two men just above then told him they were sure it had gone. He ordered two ratings to continue calling the gunhouse, opened the escape hatch to the magazine, and then told everyone to abandon it.

'When this had been done,' Puddifoot wrote, 'I once more challenged the gunhouse and still having no reply I decided to abandon and ordered everybody on the Boys' and Torpedo messdecks to await further orders . . . When I reached the messdeck the Sergeant Major informed me that he had reported by phone to Damage Control Headquarters and that we were to await further orders, and acting on instructions from SPO Knight, in command of Fire and Repair Parties in that sector, we lay down clear of the gangways.

'Shortly after this the ship was struck by the shell which damaged the CPOs' flat and I told SPO Knight to use my people as he liked, and I tried to get aft to ascertain the proximity of the fire with reference to the magazine. Owing to the intense heat and glare it was impossible at that time to enter the CPOs' flat and in view of the fact that the magazine was immediately below I decided to flood, and went below to the handling room.

'The lights were out but ERA Bond, equipped with a torch, followed me down, and together we unshipped the hopper guards, battened down the doors, flung what cordite we could find through the escape door, battened that, and then opened up the flood and seacock . . .'

But although the shell had hit B turret, the worst damage was done on the bridge just above: a withering shower of splinters, like spray from a big sea, had been flung up at more than the speed of sound and cut through the thin armour and window openings, ricocheted down from the metal roof and killed or wounded nearly every man standing on the bridge.

Within a fraction of a second the *Exeter* was changed from a perfectly-handled fighting ship to an uncontrolled machine. The wheelhouse was wrecked; all communications to the engine room and Lower Steering Position were cut. Captain Bell had been wounded in the face. Among the dead were the Navigating Officer, plotting staff and the men standing either side of Captain Bell.

It took Captain Bell only a few seconds to realize that, with all controls gone, he could not fight the ship from the bridge any longer, and he would have to take over from the After Conning Position. He gave his orders and with the survivors made his way aft as quickly as possible.

The *Exeter*'s guns – with the exception of B turret – were still firing; but with no one on the bridge to con the ship she was slowly turning to starboard.

Just after Captain Bell and the rest of the survivors had left the bridge to hurry aft, Sub-Lieutenant Clyde Morse, who was in the Air Defence Officer's Position, happened to look down at the bridge and saw no one there – except for dead and badly-wounded men lying about in grotesque attitudes among the wreckage.

Realizing the ship was out of control and seeing the wheelhouse was wrecked, yet not knowing quite what had happened, he jumped down and ran to the buckled voicepipe communicating with the Lower Steering Position. Above the thunder of A and Y turrets' guns and the cries of the wounded he managed to shout 'Steer 275 degrees.'

In the meantime the Torpedo Officer, Lt-Cdr Charles J. Smith, who had been knocked down by the blast of the bursting shell, was on his way aft to join Captain Bell. He had not gone far before he saw that the *Exeter* was turning to starboard, away from the enemy: in a minute or two, he realized, she would be so far round that the 'A arcs'* would close and A turret would not be able to fire.

Running back to the bridge he found Morse had managed to get one message through to the Lower Steering Position, and he was able to pass the order 'Port 25' to bring her round again.

Captain Bell, wounded in the face, arrived at the Aft Conning Position to find the steering-order transmitter and the telephone had been put out of action, so that the whole position was isolated. Midshipman Bonham, whose action station was the After Control Position, ran down to the After Steering Position with helm orders while a chain of ratings was being formed to repeat Captain Bell's orders.

As soon as this was done, Captain Bell sent Bonham forward to the

* The bearings on which the main armament could fire.

bridge to hoist the Not-under-control balls.* He reached the bridge safely despite splinters flying up from near misses, and with the help of Yeoman Harben, who was wounded in the thigh, hoisted them on one of the few remaining halyards. They had been up only a few seconds when the halyard parted.

Stoker John Minhinnet had previously been ordered by Captain Bell to go to the engine room and tell them to change over to the After Steering Position. He made his way down to the control platform and, above the din of the turbines, now spinning at full speed, passed the message.

He was told to go on to the After Steering Position and give the order direct to the Engine Room Artificer in charge; but on the way there a shell bursting close alongside wounded him. A first aid party took him to the after medical station, but Minhinnet refused any treatment until he was sure his message was delivered.

But the *Exeter* was hitting back at the *Graf Spee*. Mr Cook, the Director Gunner, reported: 'I think it was with our fifth or sixth salvo that we straddled and obtained a hit† near the funnel. In different salvoes after this I saw several hits, while the whole of one salvo appeared to burst just along the waterline. The Control ordered an up correction, having taken this as a short. Soon after the fall of this salvo the enemy made smoke and altered course.'

About this time the Chief Quartermaster, Petty Officer William Green, was seriously wounded. Green was at the Upper Steering Position when the bridge was wrecked, and at once went below to make sure that the Lower Steering Position was undamaged and fully manned. Finding everything all right there he started to make his way aft when he was hit.

Meanwhile the two aircraft had been riddled with splinters and twisted by blast. The one on the port side had been fuelled at dawn and petrol was by now spurting from the tanks and blowing aft over the deck and the After Conning Position.

The triatic stay linking the two masts had been cut by blast or splinters, and the heavy wire had fallen across the starboard aircraft. But Leading Seaman Shoesmith realized that both planes would have to be jettisoned very shortly.

Without waiting for orders, and despite the fact that the blast from Y

* Two black balls which, when hoisted vertically, indicate that a vessel is not under control.

†See page 143.

turret's guns and the enemy shells dropping round the ship might set alight to his petrol-soaked clothes or explode the fuel in the tanks, he climbed up on to the wing and dragged the heavy wire clear.

The Gunner, Mr Shorten, had been round to try and help the men wounded at the torpedo tubes when he met Cdr Graham, who had already been wounded. He ordered Shorten to get the charges for firing the catapults to get rid of the two damaged aircraft. The Gunner had already made them up the night before and he collected them and took them along to the catapults. But the catapults had been damaged and were not yet ready.

Less than five minutes had elapsed since the hit on B turret. Captain Bell was successfully conning the ship from aft, using a chain of messengers, and heading north-west at high speed. The *Graf Spee* was by now about 13,000 yards away on the starboard bow heading on a parallel but opposite course.

From Captain Bell's report: '. . . The ship had received two more hits forward and some damage from splinters sent up by shells bursting short. . .'

The first of these two shells burst on the sheet anchor, tearing a hole six feet by eight feet in the *Exeter*'s side above the waterline. Splinters ripped into the paint store – where a fire started – and Bosun's store and riddled No. 10 watertight bulkhead.

Stoker Petty Officer Albert Jones had immediately started taking his No. 1 Fire Party forward to deal with the damage, but more shells from the *Graf Spee* burst in the water nearby. A splinter hit him and he collapsed; but he realized the next salvo would probably be even nearer, and his men were in a dangerously exposed position. He shouted to them to shelter behind A turret. It was his last order before he died, and it saved their lives. A few seconds later a shell burst on the deck ahead of them, ripping open a twelve-feet-square hole abaft the cable-holder. Again splinters did a great deal of damage, and soon fires were burning.

The Fire Party then ran forward, avoiding the blast from the two guns of A turret, to plug up the holes with hammocks, deal with fires, and examine the watertight bulkheads.

Engine Room Artificer Frank McGarry had been up forward since the beginning of the action, and without waiting for orders he had flooded the petrol compartment – where one spark, let alone a flash from a shellburst, would cause an explosion.

Then the shell had hit the anchor, only a few feet from him. Dense fumes from the explosion had streamed in; men had fallen, killed or wounded by splinters. He was trying to see how much damage had been done when the other shell burst on deck abaft the cable-holder and the blast flung him against a bulkhead and temporarily stunned him. Then, half suffocated by the acrid smoke of the shell bursts, he set about getting shipwrights to investigate the damage, organize stretcher parties and deal with fires.

Sub-Lieutenant Morse, who had jumped down to the bridge when he had realized it was deserted, now saw a fire burning on the fo'c'sle after the shell bursts, and ran down to organize a party of men to deal with it. He quickly realized he had too few men to tackle it and ran aft to collect more. He found Midshipman Cameron, who was in charge of the 4-inch guns. Cameron, since his guns were not wanted at the moment, had used his men for rigging hoses to the forward part of the ship, but after B turret was hit it had been reported to him that there was no water coming through them and a fire was burning on the fo'c'sle.

Cameron had immediately sent half his guns' crews forward to help while most of the remainder struggled to get the hoses patched up and the water flowing. At that moment Morse arrived, asking for more men and water. Cameron told him that all the men he could spare had already gone forward, and the others were doing the best they could with the hoses.

Morse hurried back to the fo'c'sle to supervise the men. Then the second shell exploded very close to him. He was never seen again, and it is believed his body was blown over the side.

By now the forward part of the ship was slowly flooding. Water streamed out of a shattered fire main and from hoses pouring water on to the fo'c'sle fire; and the sea was spurting in through splinter holes caused by the hit on the anchor and the many near misses. The flow was increased by the forward thrust of the ship, which was now steaming at full speed.

From Captain Bell's report: '. . . At 0631 the order to fire torpedoes was correctly anticipated by the Torpedo Officer and he fired the starboard torpedoes in local control. . .'

After passing the order to the Lower Steering Position which brought the *Exeter* round to starboard again, Lt-Cdr Smith, the torpedo officer, realized that the *Graf Spee*, on her present course, would very soon be a good torpedo target. But there was no time for him to wait for orders from Captain Bell.

Many of the torpedo tubes' crew had been wounded by the near miss at the beginning of the action. Among them was the Torpedo Gunner's mate, Petty Officer Charles Hallas. However, he was in charge of the tubes and as soon as they were trained he stood by waiting for the order from Lt-Cdr Smith.

Smith waited as the ship slowly swung round; then he gave the order to fire. Compressed air thrust the torpedoes over the side into the sea, and gyroscopes inside took over to keep them on a straight course as they sped at more than forty knots towards the pocket battleship.

But the *Exeter*'s luck was out: they had been running only two minutes when the *Graf Spee* suddenly swung round 150 degrees to port, away from the three British cruisers – and away from where she was to have had a rendezvous with the torpedoes. At the same time she started laying a thick smoke screen to hide her movements and confuse the British gunners.

Immediately Captain Bell, passing his orders through the chain of messengers, swung the *Exeter* round to starboard towards the *Graf Spee* so that the port torpedoes could be fired; but as she turned, the pocket battleship struck twice more.

From Captain Bell's report: '. . .Two more 11-inch hits were received, one on A turret putting it out of action, and one which penetrated the Chief Petty Officers' flat where it burst, causing extensive damage . . .'

Just before the Chief Petty Officers' flat was hit another shell, not mentioned in the above report, hit the Navigating Officer's cabin, passed through the Armament Office, killed five telegraphists and went on for sixty feet before bursting on the barrel of 'S–one' (Starboard one) 4-inch gun, killing or wounding several more men.

The foremost ready-use locker, containing 4-inch shells, immediately caught fire and the ammunition started bursting, sending up showers of debris and splinters. At that moment a man ran up to Midshipman Cameron, in command of the 4-inch guns, and warned him that the fore topmast was just about to fall down.

'I gave the order to clear the fire end of the gun deck,' Cameron reported later. 'As it did not appear to be coming down immediately I started the crews working again.'

The men in A turret had fired between forty and fifty rounds when, at this moment, an 11-inch shell hit the right gun. Once again the explosion tore at the armour plate on the front of the turret. Inside all the lights were put out and fumes streamed in.

Petty Officer Pierce tried to get through to the bridge by telephone, but it was wrecked. Ordering the telegraphists to stay at their posts, he climbed out of the gunhouse to go up to warn the bridge, but finding it had already been wrecked he went back to the gunhouse to tell the men to abandon it.

By this time an 11-inch shell had burst in the Chief Petty Officers' flat and started a bad fire above the 4-inch magazine. After checking that it was being dealt with, Midshipman Cameron returned with Ordinary Seaman Gwilliam to find the 4-inch ready-use ammunition locker still burning from the earlier hit.

'There were still several live shells in the bottom of the locker. Without any hesitation Gwilliam removed his greatcoat and attempted to smother the flames with it,' Cameron reported later. 'At the same time somebody else threw a bucket of sand over it. The flames extinguished and we proceeded to throw over the side what was left in the locker.

'Gwilliam reported to me that there were still several cans of petrol underneath the port catapult. These we threw overboard.

'As the fire on the messdecks was still raging I got more hands on to the job of carrying buckets to it. At the same time Lt Kemball and I kept the remainder occupied in breaking up blocks of holystone in an effort to make sand out of them . . .

'At this time an effort, which subsequently proved to be successful, was being made to get the planes over the side, they having been badly holed and showering out quantities of petrol.'

The shell which burst in the CPOs' flat did so much damage that the *Exeter* later had to discontinue the action. It penetrated the light plating of the ship's side amidships, as if it were cardboard, cut through three bulkheads and then burst on the lower deck above the 4-inch magazine and the torpedo gunner's store, blasting a hole measuring sixteen feet by fourteen feet.

The explosion was felt all through the ship, as though she had been punched in her solar plexus. Blast and fumes thrust back along the starboard passage; one bulkhead door was blocked with debris and bodies, and another with the wreckage of kit lockers; the Chief Petty Officers' flat was in darkness and filled with dense fumes and steam escaping from a punctured heating pipe.

A fierce fire broke out in the lower servery flat, and the crews of the switchboard and forward dynamo rooms were trapped, the whole place filling with fumes, steam and water spraying out from a burst fire main.

Splinters from the shell cut a large number of electric leads, among them vital ones supplying power to the Transmitting Station, the main armament's 'brain'. Because the Fire Control Table could work no longer, the Transmitting Station was abandoned.

More splinters pierced the lower deck and slashed the fire hoses. Water poured into the Lower Steering Position and the Number One low-power room below. Generators and compass alternators were flooded and this put the compass repeaters out of action.

Other splinters sliced through a bulkhead into A boiler room; but fortunately the boilers were saved by spare firebricks which had been stacked up out of the way – otherwise it is probable that every man in the boiler room would have been killed by superheated steam.

The immediate task for the Damage Control parties was to get at the men trapped in the forward dynamo room and the switch-board.

Number Four Fire Party were the first to try. Smoke and fumes would have suffocated any man along the starboard passage in a few moments, so they pulled on their anti-gas respirators and started dragging their hoses towards the fire. But debris and the bodies of seamen killed by the explosion blocked their way.

It seemed impossible to force an entrance into the Chief Petty Officers' flat to see exactly what had happened and what was on fire, so another party was sent up on deck to try to break in from forward: every minute counted now because the trapped men were being badly affected by the fumes.

In the meantime, however, Stoker Patrick O'Brien was trying to break through alone to the main switchboard. In darkness, tripping over twisted metal, bodies and smashed equipment, and almost suffocating from the high-explosive fumes and steam, he managed to clamber and crawl through the apparently impenetrable Chief Petty Officers' flat and shout a message down the main switchboard hatch, which was blocked by debris.

After that he crawled to the hatch over the dynamo room. This, too, was blocked by twisted metal and all sorts of debris; but O'Brien managed to call to the Engine Room Artificer, Thomas Phillips, who was in charge of the trapped party.

Phillips had been struggling in the thick fumes and smoke to get a dynamo going. It had stopped as the shell burst above, and the exhaust fan had broken down. Having made contact with the trapped men, O'Brien then crawled and scrambled out on to the upper deck, and ran back to his fire party and led them into the reeking flat.

In the meantime Petty Officer Herbert Chalkley, who had also been in the forward dynamo room, had managed to force open the door in the escape trunk and crawl over the wreckage to the switchboard hatch. It was jammed, with a good deal of wreckage piled on top of it.

Amid the swirling smoke and barely able to see what he was doing, Chalkley pulled and pushed at the wreckage, trying to lever pieces off to free the hatch. But he could not move it.

Realizing he would not be needed again in the dynamo room, he guessed his best move would be to get out on to the upper deck so that he could then guide fire parties to his trapped shipmates. He carefully made his way back through the smoke and steam to the escape trunk and climbed up it. Once in the open air again he found the fire parties and went back to help fight the fires in the servery and CPOs' flats.

By now the blaze in the servery flat was raging fiercely and almost out of control. The 4-inch magazine, bomb room, and the magazine of B turret were in danger from the heat and fumes.

The 50-ton pump supplying water for the hoses forward had failed four or five times and it was at this point that, as mentioned earlier, Sergeant George Puddifoot, in B magazine, realized the fire overhead was getting out of hand and, with ERA Frank Bond, decided to flood the magazine.

Bond then went to the main centre of the fire to check up how much damage had been done – and found that the flooding valve spindle had been shot away and the fire main shattered. However, there was sufficient water from the burst mains pouring into the magazine through shell and splinter holes, so he went on to help fight the fires.

This was proving a difficult task: the ship was so badly riddled with splinters by this time that many hoses and fire mains had burst. Midshipman Robert Don, for instance, was having great difficulty in running hoses to the burning Marines Barracks and also in fighting the fire over the Lower Steering Position. He was one of several men searching for the wounded lying amid the smoke and debris, and dragging them to safety.

The *Exeter*'s tall topmasts were still in danger. Flying splinters had cut through many of the wire shrouds supporting them, and when finally the triatic stay joining the heads of the two masts was severed they had started to whip so violently that all the main aerials parted and the ship's wireless link with the Commodore was cut. As soon as the sets had gone dead, Chief Petty Officer Telegraphist Harold Newman began the dangerous and laborious job of rigging jury aerials.

The topmasts were so tall that they undoubtedly helped the *Graf Spee*'s gunners in finding the range, and had the weather not been exceptionally calm they almost certainly would have toppled down.

As mentioned earlier, the Transmitting Station and the Fire Control Table were out of action. Mr Dallaway, the TS Officer, reported that when communications with B Turret ceased he did not know it was because it had been hit. 'Thinking B turret may have some mechanical trouble,' he wrote, 'I decided to send the Ordnance Artificer from the RS to 'B' to see if he could be of assistance, realizing that he would not have far to go, and also that while everything was running smoothly in the TS he was wasting his talent.

'With that object in view I ordered the TS hatch to be opened so that he could get out of the TS. Before I had time to tell him what to do there was a slight blast effect felt and the TS started to fill with dust and fumes. The TS crew, with the exception of the TS Officer and Communications Number, put on their gasmasks and carried on with their jobs.

'Lights in the TS then went off with the exception of two which remained burning dimly . . . The effect was that the TS was practically in darkness, and combined with the dust it was hardly possible to see anything.

'Everything appeared to happen at once . . .' he added. 'A turret reported they were going on to "local" firing, the range receiver unit stopped working, and then the compressed air working the Fire Control Table failed.

'I did manage to see the Ordnance Artificer playing around with the air valves, but still no air was available on the Table. To work hunters by hand in the existing light was impossible, and that combined with the report from A turret that pointers were not working forced me to the conclusion that the TS was useless. I reported this fact to the Gunnery Officer and then the order to go into local control was passed. Communication to A turret was then lost.

'I then asked permission for the TS crew to go on the Marines' messdeck in order to use them for work. This was agreed to by the Gunnery Officer.

'The crew could not get out of the TS as they were told that the upper hatch was closed. I went up to investigate the possibility of opening the hatch and found it open. The crew then came up. Everywhere was in complete darkness, but I tried to get into the servery flat, which I soon discovered to be in a shambles.

'Realizing that a gangway through there was impossible, I shouted back to the remainder to work their way forward, which they did. For some reason or other I could not get out of the flat by the same way that I had entered, and I have recollections of being lost among the debris. Eventually I managed to make the starboard waist where I found the TS crew and other ratings.'

Despite all the bitter punishment the *Exeter* had taken in forty minutes, she was still in action: Y turret, right aft, was still firing in local control. Lt-Cdr Richard Jennings, the Gunnery Officer, had gone aft to see what was happening, and while standing outside the After Control Position talking to the After Control Officer, Y turret trained round on to an extreme forward bearing and fired. Both men were badly shaken by the blast. Jennings then sent Sub-Lt Wickham, the After Control Officer, to take charge of Y turret while he stationed himself on the roof of the turret, where he could see better, and, ignoring the blast of flying splinters, shouted spotting corrections down through a manhole.

The position at 0700, therefore, was that:

  1. A and B turrets were out of action from direct hits;
  2. Y turret was still firing in local control;
  3. The bridge, DCT and Transmitting Station were out of action;
  4. A fierce fire was raging in the CPOs' and servery flats;
  5. Minor fires were burning on the Marines' messdeck and in the paint shop;

6. There were no telephone communications – orders could be passed only by messengers;

7. The ship was down by the bows by about three feet because of flooding forward, and had a list of from seven to ten degrees to starboard – due to about 650 tons of water, which had flooded in;

8. Only one 4-inch gun could still be fired;

9. Both aircraft had been jettisoned;

10. Wireless communications had completely broken down.

But mercifully the engine room was undamaged and the ship was steaming at full speed. The heat was so great in the furnaces that the floors were becoming almost fluid, and because of the list molten brickwork had run over the starboard side.

Many gallant actions in those forty minutes went almost unnoticed: it needed bravery to carry out even normal duties in the ravaged cruiser. An order to take a message to a position twenty yards away could mean sudden death from an invisible rain of shell splinters; young ratings were making split-second decisions which meant life or death to many of their shipmates. But fortunately months of drill under keen and able officers paid dividends.

Already more than fifty officers and men had been killed and others were so seriously wounded they would die before the day ended; more than twenty others had been badly hurt.

There was, for instance, the cold-blooded gallantry of Captain Bell, one of the few men left alive in the ship who knew all the facts and dangers. Despite the damage caused by the almost undivided attention of a pocket battleship which could match each of his 8-inch shells with an 11-inch shell at the beginning of the action, and now still had six 11-inch guns firing to his two 8-inch (and one of them had stopped firing for a short while), the *Exeter*'s Battle Ensigns were still flying and the ship continued in action against the *Graf Spee*.

From the After Conning Position Captain Bell was having to steer the ship with the help of a compass taken from a whaler – the compass repeaters had been damaged some time earlier. But the compass needle was so badly affected by the magnetism of the steel all round that it did almost everything except spin round like a catherine wheel.

There was the gallantry of Chief Shipwright Anthony Collings, who, although seriously wounded and badly burned, continued to supervise and direct the work of the shipwrights repairing damage in the forward part of the ship. He only stopped when he fell unconscious. A few moments before that he had been asking for a report on the condition of a damaged hatch.

There was Commander Robert Graham, who was wounded in the face and leg early in the action. Yet despite that he cheerfully carried on walking round the ship seeing what was damaged or on fire and giving orders to deal with it.

There was Midshipman Bonham. After hoisting the 'not under control' balls he had been ordered to find some flexible voicepipe so that Captain Bell could communicate with the engine room.

He took two ratings and unrigged the flexible lead from the bridge to the armament office, and while doing this he found a man lying outside Captain Bell's sea cabin. He had both legs blown off but was still alive, so Bonham sent a rating to warn the sick bay.

After searching various places in the ship for more voicepipe he went back to the After Conning Position. He saw that some more had been found and was being rigged, and he was sent forward to the fire still raging amidships.

'I went down through the sick bay flat into the Marines' messdeck where I met Midshipman Don,' he reported later, 'and together we got a hose in, and we were getting it down through the hatch outside the bookstall when he fell through the hatch and vanished. I heard voices below so assumed he was all right, and continued getting more hose and switching on the water.

'I had to go outside several times as the smoke was very bad . . .

From the *Exeter*'s log: '. . .0729, Y turret ceased firing owing to failure of electricity supply. 0730, broke off action, 0750, Enemy disappeared to westward pursued by Ajax *and* Achilles . . .'

Strangely enough, it was not the *Graf Spee*'s hits which forced Captain Bell to break off the action, but her near misses. As long as he had a gun which worked Captain Bell was determined to keep the *Graf Spee* under fire, but at last water flooding in through splinter holes in the *Exeter*'s side abreast of No 216 bulkhead stopped the power supply.

With his last turret out of action, and only a boat compass to steer by, Captain Bell was now able to devote all his attention to keeping his ship afloat.

XV

Shells and Snowballs

From Commodore Harwood's dispatch: '. . . Ajax and Achilles hauled round to the north-westward at 0656 to open their A arcs. Graf Spee made frequent alterations of course to throw out our gunfire and from 0700 onwards she made great use of smoke; she appeared to have some form of chloro-sulphuric apparatus aft and used this as well as smoke floats . . .'

THE *Graf Spee* was now heading away to the north-westward at full speed with the two cruisers pursuing on her starboard quarter. The *Achilles* had recovered from the damage to the Director Control Tower, her four turrets were in action again, and Lt Lewin and Lt Kearney were spotting the fall of shot from the Seafox aircraft.

At first their reports were not picked up in the *Ajax* because, as mentioned earlier, they were using the reconnaissance wavelength and Kearney's message to the flag deck before taking off had not been passed on to the main wireless office. It was not until 0649 that their first report was received.

Shortly before this, after the *Achilles*'s DCT had been hit and the wireless link for concentration firing broken, Lt Washbourn had begun firing in individual control.

However, neither Kearney in the Seafox not the *Ajax*'s Gunnery Officer, Lt Dreyer, knew this, and it led to the *Achilles*'s salvoes being reported to the *Ajax* by the aircraft and Dreyer naturally regarded them as referring to his own and corrected accordingly. The *Ajax*'s salvoes, as a result of this, were falling well over the *Graf Spee* for a short while.

The two men in the Seafox had a fine view of the battle although there was not time to sit around and appreciate the grandeur of the scene.

Lewin had climbed to 3,000 feet, where there was slight cloud, because he knew the enemy had two aircraft, each of which had forward-firing machine guns, and if they came up after him it might well be convenient to dodge into a cloud to escape their attention.

He took the Seafox to a position a mile off the *Ajax*'s disengaged bow and Kearney started passing his spotting reports. It was quite easy for him to see the splashes of the near misses, but hits on the *Graf Spee* were more difficult to discern, mainly because of the smoke from the pocket battleship's 11-inch guns.

On one occasion Lewin took the aircraft too close to the pocket battleship, which immediately opened fire from her anti-aircraft guns. The first few rounds burst short but the German gunners quickly corrected and for two minutes the shells were bursting far too near for either Lewin or Kearney to have an easy mind. A splinter from one shell went right through both the starboard wings, and Lewin turned the aircraft and climbed up into a cloud for a few moments to give the German gunners a rest.

The position at 0707, when the *Exeter* had only one turret left in action, was that the *Graf Spee* was eight and three-quarter miles from the *Ajax* and *Achilles*, constantly zig-zagging to throw the British gunners off their aim, and streaming out funnel smoke and dropping smoke floats.

Thus in the first phase, from 0618 when the *Graf Spee* opened fire until 0638 when she put down a smoke screen and hid behind it, the *Exeter* had suffered considerably and the other two ships had escaped unharmed. In the second phase the enemy had scored several times on the *Exeter* and damaged the *Achilles*. Her smoke screen was hampering the British gunners, and later on, although the *Ajax* and *Achilles* were shooting fast, their fire was inaccurate because of the spotting mix-up.

In other words, the gunfire of the three British ships had deteriorated badly, giving Lansdorff, had he known it, a golden opportunity. But unfortunately he did not take it. Instead he swung the *Graf Spee* round in a big alteration of course to port, away from the First Division.

For the last half an hour the battle had been indecisive. Although the range was just right for the *Graf Spee*'s 11-inch guns, it was still high for Commodore Harwood's 6-inch guns. So he decided to close the *Graf Spee* as quickly as possible even though it meant halving the number of guns which he could bring to bear. It was a bold decision and one reached amid the brain-numbing crash of his own ship's broadsides and while the *Graf Spee*'s shells were bursting close. It could mean victory at a terrible cost for the *Ajax* and *Achilles*, or it could mean annihilation.

While the message was passed to the *Ajax*'s engine room his order was also signalled to the *Achilles*: *Proceed at utmost speed.*

The *Ajax* came round to port, followed by the *Achilles*, and now, the spotting sorted out, their shooting was fast and accurate. On an average, the 'gun ready' lamps flickered on three times a minute in each DCT, and Dreyer and Washbourn ordered 'Shoot'; and all the while each Director Sight was being skilfully trained round to keep the guns aimed at the *Graf Spee*, with the Fire Control Tables supplying the bearing and elevation.

> *From Commodore Harwood's dispatch: '... At 0716 Graf Spee made a drastic alteration of course to port under cover of smoke, but four minutes later she turned to the north-west and opened her A arcs on the First Division.* Ajax *was immediately straddled three times by 11-inch at a range of 11,000 yards, but the enemy's secondary armament was firing raggedly, and appeared to be going consistently over, between* Ajax *and* Achilles ...'

As the *Graf Spee* made this sudden turn to port, Commodore Harwood immediately concluded she was moving down to finish off the crippled *Exeter* – now steaming in a pall of smoke only eight miles to the south – and would then concentrate all her guns on the First Division.

He promptly ordered the *Ajax* and *Achilles* to turn to starboard at once so that all their guns would bear on the enemy; his only chance of rescuing the *Exeter* was to provoke the pocket battleship to shift all her gunfire on to the First Division.

And their shooting was magnificent: Kearney, up in the Seafox aircraft, signalled 'Good shot', and a few moments later the red glow of a 6-inch hit was seen amidships in the *Graf Spee*, followed by a fire which burned fiercely.*

This determined attack seemed to do the trick, and Harwood saw the *Graf Spee* turn to the north-west so that she could bring both her 11-inch turrets to bear on the *Ajax* and *Achilles*. It soon appeared to the Commodore that she had taken the bait and now intended to neglect the *Exeter* and give the First Division her undivided attention.

Harwood was, however, not a torpedo expert for nothing: guessing

*This was in fact the Arado aircraft blazing.

that she would hold her present course, at 0724 he ordered the *Ajax* to fire a salvo of torpedoes. She turned to starboard to bring her port tubes to bear, and at 0727 four torpedoes were loosed off at the *Graf Spee*, 9,000 yards away to the westwards.

Unfortunately all four broke surface after being launched, and from the splashes it must have been obvious to wide-awake lookouts in the *Graf Spee* that they were on their way. Anxiously the Commodore, Captain Woodhouse and the Torpedo Officer waited and waited.

Then they saw the great pocket battleship start swinging round to port, away from them – 10 . . . 20 . . . 50 . . . 60 . . . 100 . . . and finally 130 degrees. Although the chance of hitting with torpedoes at 9,000 yards was never very rosy, there was none at all now; and three minutes later, the danger passed, the *Graf Spee* came back on to her original course, still laying a smoke screen.

A few moments later there was a sudden explosion aft in the *Ajax* and the whole cruiser shuddered: an 11-inch shell had burst somewhere inside the ship. Almost immediately Lt Dreyer reported from the DCT that both X and Y turrets were out of action.

But neither the Commodore nor Captain Woodhouse had a moment to spare, apart from seeing that the ship was still afloat and steaming at full speed. Almost before the shaking of the explosion had stopped, Kearney, in the Seafox aircraft, signalled: *Torpedoes approaching; they will pass ahead of you.*

Harwood, however, was taking no chances and ordered an eighty-degree turn to port and, so as to blank her fire for as little time as possible, signalled to the *Achilles: Cross my stern.**

Now the *Graf Spee* was on the *Ajax*'s starboard side and rapidly A and B turrets swung right round, obediently following the Director Sight. Both the two cruisers were now hitting the pocket battleship frequently and the range was closing rapidly; by 0738 it was only four miles – close range for the *Graf Spee*'s 11-inch guns. Yet despite the number of times the two cruisers were scoring hits, there was very little apparent damage. The pocket battleship's vitals were protected by a belt of armour five and a half inches thick, and even at four miles' range a 6-inch shell had very little chance of penetrating it.

Nevertheless, the hits were worrying the *Graf Spee* because she turned

---

*Apart from 'Open fire' and speed signals, this was the Commodore's first order to *Achilles* and is an indication of how well the two ships worked together.

south-west and once again brought all her guns to bear – 11-inch, 5·9-inch and anti-aircraft guns firing time-fused shells.

> *From Commodore Harwood's dispatch:* '. . . *By 0738 the range was down to 8,000 yards. At this time I received a report that* Ajax *had only 20 per cent of ammunition left and had only three guns in action, as one of the hoists had failed in B turret and X and Y turrets were both out of action.*
>
> '*Graf Spee's shooting was still very accurate and she did not appear to have suffered much damage.*
>
> '*I therefore decided to break off the day action and try to close in again after dark. Accordingly at 0740* Ajax *and* Achilles *turned away to the east under cover of smoke . . .*'

By this time a messenger had reached the *Ajax*'s bridge to report to Captain Woodhouse the extent of the damage. The 11-inch shell had hit the upper deck at an angle of thirty-five degrees, ploughed through three cabins – belonging to Captain Woodhouse, his secretary, and the Commander – and struck X turret ammunition lobby. There the splinters it ripped from the deck and bulkheads killed four men, and wounded five more. It then hit the horizontal angle irons and shot upwards through the working chamber killing two more men, finally bursting in Commodore Harwood's sleeping cabin.

The heavy base plug of the shell was blown straight aft, denting the armoured ring and jamming Y turret. Splinters cut through the upper deck, slicing through the power main* and causing flooding.

X turret had naturally received the worst damage. The gunhouse crew were all flung into the back of the turret, and when the Officer of the Quarters, Lt Ian de'Ath, picked himself up he saw smoke and sparks pouring up the hatch from the lobby below, and smoke was coming from the cordite hoists. Each of the buckets of the hoist had a 30-lb charge in it. Realizing the whole lot might explode any second, he ordered the hoists to be drenched with water.

Sergeant Raymond Cook, at the left gun, dragged a hose to the hatch, but no water came out when the valve was turned on – the main had been smashed below.

---

*About 150 electrical cables were cut during the action. Twenty per cent were destroyed by the 11-inch shell before it burst, fifteen per cent by the explosion, fifty per cent by splinter from the same shell, and fifteen per cent by other splinters.

De'Ath then ordered the cordite charges to be taken out of the top buckets of the hoist and flung over the side. Then he had a look down the hatch. Clouds of smoke were pouring out and flames could be seen below, but all the lighting was out of action and it was impossible to see exactly what was going on.

Another hose was dragged in from the quarter-deck, but this was found to have been pierced by splinters. A third hose was brought along by a fire party, and fortunately this worked. It was thrust down the hatch, where Stoker Bertram Wood, who had broken into the lobby, was tackling the blaze single-handed.

In the flat below the turret the explosion had flung men across the deck, several being killed or hurt by splinters. All the lights were put out and the whole flat filled with fumes and smoke. Visibility was cut down to less than arm's length so torches were useless, and while men struggled to find their way round, small electrical fires were started.

Then the atmosphere began to clear – helped by compressed air escaping from a bottle in X lobby – but water and oil started flooding in from burst fire mains and fuel pipes. It swilled from side to side as the ship rolled and greatly hindered the fire and repair parties.

It was about this time that Commodore Harwood, worried by the possibility of running out of ammunition, asked Captain Woodhouse to see how much was left in the *Ajax*. This was passed on and the answer came back that there were fifty rounds a gun left.

This meant that each turret had fired about 300 rounds – 150 broadsides in an hour's action . . . But if there were only enough for another fifty broadsides the Commodore realized he was dangerously short.* It was this knowledge, plus the apparent lack of damage to the *Graf Spee*, which made him break off the action. He commented: 'we might just as well be bombarding her with a lot of bloody snowballs . . .'

Just as the *Ajax* was about to turn away she was damaged again: 11-inch shells straddled her and one of them hit the main topmast and cut it in two. The shell was not seen to burst, but all the wireless aerials were brought down and the Commodore could not pass any more wireless signals until jury aerials were rigged.

So with the *Ajax* turning away and signalling to the *Achilles: Make smoke*, the third phase of the Battle of the River Plate ended.

*In fact the report was wrong: it referred only to A turret which had fired far more than the other three turrets, but at the time was thought to refer to all the turrets.

XVI

Graf Spee *Runs Away*

THE *Graf Spee*, however, had not escaped as lightly as Commodore Harwood thought. At 0631* when the *Exeter* had turned to fire her first salvo of torpedoes, the *Graf Spee* was using her two 11-inch turrets against her, and the Torpedo Officer had just passed a message to Langsdorff warning him that there was also danger of torpedo attacks from the other two cruisers.

At this time the *Ajax* and *Achilles* were not scoring hits, and when Langsdorff saw the *Exeter* moving off to the west he turned hard a port, away from the two light cruisers.

But at 0634 he could see the *Exeter* was being hit hard by his own guns, and suddenly she turned away, making heavy smoke and with only Y turret firing.

The *Ajax* and *Achillles* were now moving up fast on the *Graf Spee*'s starboard quarter. Only B turret, aft, and the 5·9-inch batteries could fire at them; and since both British ships were hidden in smoke the German gunners had to break off from time to time.

At 0700 the *Exeter* came in sight again. From the flying bridge Langsdorff could see that her A turret guns were trained fore and aft, whille B turret pointed to starboard. Only Y turret was firing at him.

The *Graf Spee* opened fire with her B turret and soon the Germans saw the *Exeter* being hit again, and once more she turned away under thick black smoke.

In the meantime the *Ajax* and *Achilles* had closed the range, as Commodore Harwood intended, and since the *Graf Spee*'s B turret was firing at the *Exeter*, only the 6-inch guns could engage them.

*All German times are approximate and must be taken only as a general indication.

1. The end of the *Admiral Graf Spee:* she blew up at sunset on 17 December 1939

2. Commodore (later Rear-Admiral) Harwood (*right*) and
Captain Parry aboard the *Achilles* after the battle

3. Sinking the German steamer *Olinda:* the first British shells fired in the war

4. Kapitän zur See Hans Langsdorff, commanding officer of the *Admiral Graf Spee*

5. (*Above*) The *Exeter* after the battle: note the armour torn off the front of both turrets and splinter damage to the bridge

6. Splinter damage to the front of the *Exeter*'s bridge

7. The CPO's flat in the *Exeter* after an 11-inch shell had exploded

8. The *Ajax* after the battle: note the remains of the main-mast

9. On the *Achilles*'s bridge during the battle: Captain Parry (*sitting*) after being wounded in the legs; Lt Cowburn next to him

10. (*Below*) During the battle: the smoke on the left is coming from the *Graf Spee*. The ship in the centre is the *Ajax*, manoevouring to avoid torpedoes. The smoke on the right is from an 11-inch shell burst

11. The men killed in the *Ajax* during the battle are buried at sea while the cruiser still pursues the pocket battleship

12. The damaged *Graf Spee* in Montevideo: note the burnt-out Arado aircraft and the hit on the hull directly below the mast

13. (*Below*) The damaged *Graf Spee* at anchor. This photograph was sent by Commodore Harwood to his eldest son, then aged 13, after he had marked in some of the hits. Note the false bow wave painted on the ship's side

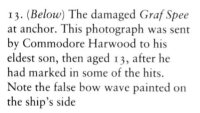

14. The *Achilles*'s Director Control Tower: note the splinter holes

15. Lt Richard Washbourn, the *Achilles*'s Gunnery Officer, has 'breakfast' during a lull in the action after being wounded in the head when the DCT was hit

16. Lt Lewin lands the *Ajax*'s Seafox at the Falklands. The *Exeter* (note the tall masts) is in the background

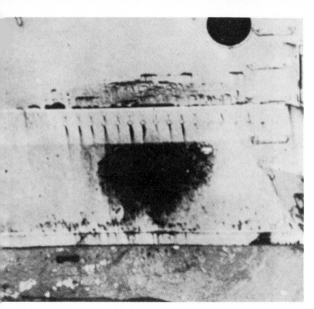

17. One of the *Achilles's* 6-inch shells which failed to get through the *Graf Spee's* armour plate

18. Captain Langsdorff (*centre*) on the quayside at Montevideo talks to Dr Otto Langmann (*in trilby hat*), the German Ambassador

19. (*Below*) At the funeral of the *Graf Spee's* dead. Only Langsdorff gives a naval instead of a Nazi salute, closely watched by the German Ambassador standing behind his left shoulder

20. The *Graf Spee* blazes after explosions had torn her hull

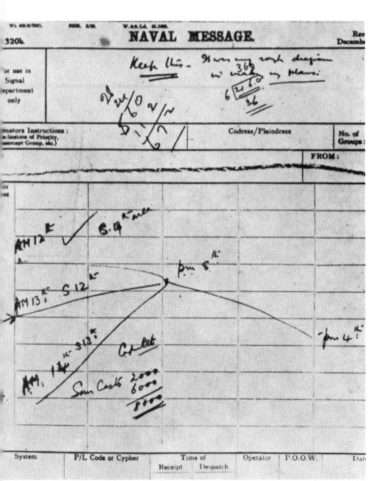

21. Commodore Harwood's rough diagram in which he worked out the *Graf Spee*'s possible future moves. 'R AM 12th' refers to Rio de Janeiro, 'P' below it to the Plate, and 'F' to the Falklands; 'pm 4th' and the lines leading from it refer to the *Graf Spee*'s possible courses. As the Commodore deduced, she arrived off the Plate 'AM 13th'

From Captain Langsdorff's log: '. . . They fired very fast, their fire being at times very effective, the ship receiving in this part of the action a large number of hits . . .'

A 6-inch shell came in on the starboard quarter, passed through the starboard deck, the crew's galley, the upper deck on the port side, and burst against the splinter bulkheads.

This was to become the most important shell-hit in the action, as will be seen later. Apart from wrecking the galley, it destroyed an ammunition hoist and the electric supply to the 15-cm shell hoists forward.

An earlier 6-inch shell from either the *Ajax* or *Achilles* had come in on the starboard bow, passed through the armoured shield of the starboard 4-inch anti-aircraft gun, penetrated the bakery and burst in the searchlight workshop. The gun was wrecked, the starboard ammunition hoist for the 4-inch guns put out of action, and the searchlight workshop and a sick bay destroyed.

One of the *Exeter*'s 8-inch shells had hit the armour belt above the armoured deck and splinter bulkheads and exploded. The armoured deck was dented and cracked but the shell did not penetrate it. Water flooded in and the whole area was filled with fumes, but the leaks were quickly sealed by repair parties.

A 6-inch shell from the starboard quarter passed through the fo'c'sle and detonated on the port side, tearing a hole three feet by six feet above the waterline. The fifth hit was also a 6-inch shell which went through the wooden cutter on the port side, wrecked the 4-inch ammunition hoist and rained splinters over the engine-room ventilation hatches.

The sixth hit was something of a surprise to the Germans. Earlier, in the B turret of the *Achilles*, there had been a temporary delay in the shell supply, and the gunhouse crews took the ready-use shells from their racks and fed them into the guns. When they ran out of armour-piercing shells they came to two practice projectiles resting in their racks.

'Go on, stuff them in too,' said Sub-Lieutenant Somerville, who was the Officer of Quarters.

And off they went. One of them missed. The other was described in the *Graf Spee*'s Damage Control report thus:

A 15-cm drill shell [sic] came from the starboard quarter, passed through the starboard hawser reel behind the officers' mess, the starboard torpedo loading station, the warrant officers' mess, and *several warrant officers' lockers on the port side between decks. Damage Control telegraph, Damage Control telephone and service conduits (*Wirtschaftsleitung*) between decks in Section III were destroyed.*

The seventh hit was on the fo'c'sle and the explosion started a fire in the Damage Control storeroom and caused a leak on the port side. The next, also a 6-inch shell, hit the shielded port of Captain Langsdorff's cabin and exploded in the pantry.

The forward AA command post was put out of action by the ninth hit, which struck the foremast, the ready-use ammunition locker of a starboard 3·7-cm gun, and exploded in the command post. Everyone at the gun was killed and the ammunition was set on fire and exploded.

There were several occasions when the 6-inch shells hit the *Graf Spee*'s armour and ricocheted outboard to burst in the sea. Three hit the armoured front of B turret, but the steel was too tough, and each ricocheted overboard without causing any damage.

The thirteenth hit wounded Captain Langsdorff. This was another 6-inch shell which went through the starboard side of the foremast underneath the flying bridge, through the deck directly underneath and the port side of the mast without exploding. But a large number of splinters flew off and one of them struck Langsdorff. He had previously been slightly wounded by a splinter.

This time he ordered his second in command, Captain Kay, to come to the flying bridge; but Langsdorff continued in command.

The next shell also hit the foremast, destroying the radio-photo room, and the fifteenth hit, an 8-inch shell from the *Exeter*, went through the Admiral's bridge and the mast without exploding. Successive 6-inch hits destroyed a 5·9-inch gun and killed its crew, wrecked the Night Control Station, and smashed two boats.

Although the pocket battleship had been hit several times without suffering a great deal of damage, splinters from hits and near misses had by this stage put a good deal of equipment out of action.

In the forward conning tower the training mechanism was destroyed, the big rangefinder on the flying bridge was wrecked, the aircraft was badly damaged, most of the searchlights were put out of action, and there were six leaks below the waterline.

The reserve radio transmitter was wrecked by shock, along with the radar ranging apparatus for the guns.*

The men in the most terrible of all plights were the British Merchant Navy officers who were prisoners in the *Graf Spee*. Locked in their quarters, they stood a good chance of being either killed by British shells or drowned should the *Graf Spee* be sunk.

As soon as the alarms had sounded all over the pocket battleship –after the *Exeter*'s mast had been sighted – their doors had been locked.

Captain Pottinger, of the *Ashlea*, wrote later:† 'We were told afterwards by Captain Langsdorff that we were in the safest part of the ship, also that we were behind armour.

'We could see nothing. At about 6 AM the battle commenced. There were repeated concussions, like the firing of big guns. We could not tell whether these were the guns being fired by us or shells striking us. We zig-zagged continually at high speed and heeled over so much that at times I thought we were going to capsize.

'At about 8 AM the firing eased a bit but we continued to zig-zag and fired occasional salvoes from our after 11-inch guns.

'The only view we could get of what was going on was through a small hole in the door through which we could get a running commentary on what could be seen by our several observers.

'We could see some men working an ammunition hoist. They all looked very anxious. From what we could tell, things were not going too well with them. The dead were being piled up outside and the stench was awful. We could see men with rubber gloves on washing down the corpses with hoses. This may account for the report we used gas.

'We could also hear and see men being sick all over the place, some probably from fear and others from the gruesome sights around them.'

Captain Edwards, of the *Trevanion*, had an even better view. In his report he says that the *Graf Spee* was hit about two minutes after she first opened fire,‡ and later on he could feel more shells bursting on board.

The shell which wrecked the pantry came through a bulkhead and hit a

---

*It is not clear from German reports whether the radar was working at all during the action. It frequently broke down because of vibration from the ship's engines.
†In his report of the sinking of his ship.
‡This may well have been the hit referred to by the *Exeter*'s Director Gunner (see page 123): he reported a hit near the funnel with the fifth or sixth salvo.

beam above them, making a hole. Captain Edwards climbed up to look out, and he could see one of the aircraft had vanished.

At 0740 when Commodore Harwood decided to break off the action until nightfall, thirty-seven of the *Graf Spee*'s officers and men had been killed and fifty-seven wounded. And Langsdorff had had enough.

After receiving a report of the damage he went round the ship to make his own survey with his second in command, Captain Kay. He chatted with the wounded, praised certain men, and did what he could to cheer up his crew. But they were far from being the cheerful, confident youngsters who had gone into battle.

Returning to the bridge after seeing for himself what damage the three small cruisers had caused, he said to his Navigator, Korvettenkapitän Wattenberg: 'We must run into port, the ship is not now seaworthy for the North Atlantic.'*

> The Captain expressed this opinion with certainty, and ordered the Navigating Officer to check whether Montevideo or Buenos Aires was the best harbour for that purpose.
>
> The Navigating Officer advised Montevideo, considering the shallow water of the Indio Channel (possibility of fouling the engine cooling water with mud).
>
> The Captain agreed with this proposal. The strong dependence of Uruguay on England from a political standpoint was not known to him to the full extent.†

It now remained to report to Berlin, and Langsdorff drafted a signal to the Operations Division of the *Seekriegsleitung* in which he briefly described the battle and the *Graf Spee*'s action damage.

The log of the pocket battleship said:

> The Captain signalled his desire to enter Montevideo at the same time as he reported on the battle to the Operations Department. He understood that it would be impossible to sail out again, and thought the ship would be interned. Before he ran into Montevideo he received the answer from Operations. 'Agreed, Commander-in-Chief'.

Wattenberg laid off a course for the River Plate, and Langsdorff

*From the *Graf Spee*'s action report.
†Ibid.

ordered a speed of twenty-three knots. On the horizon to the north-east and south-west were the two British cruisers. Ahead, although no one realized it, lay the graves of the *Graf Spee* and her Captain.

XVII

Guarding Achilles' Heel

'WHEN THE action was broken off,' Captain Parry wrote later, 'my own feelings were that the enemy could do anything he wanted to. He showed no sign of being damaged; his main armament was still firing accurately; the *Exeter* was evidently out of it; and so he only had two small cruisers to prevent him attacking the very valuable River Plate trade . . .

'It was therefore rather astonishing, when we turned back a few minutes later, to find the enemy steaming off at a fairly high speed to the westward.'

Commodore Harwood ordered the *Ajax* to shadow from the *Graf Spee*'s port quarter and the *Achilles* from her starboard quarter. The time was 0830, the weather was perfect, apart from the increasing wind, which was kicking up a bit of sea; and the *Graf Spee*, despite her diesel engines, obligingly continued to make fairly continuous funnel smoke, so the task of shadowing at long range – then about fifteen miles – presented no difficulties.

Earlier the Commodore had naturally been very anxious about the *Exeter*, the heavyweight of his team, and before the *Ajax* lost her wireless aerials he signalled to Captain Bell: *Join me. What speed have you available?*

But the *Exeter* did not reply: Chief Petty Officer Telegraphist Harold Newman had not yet succeeded in rigging his jury aerials. *Ajax* called her up for more than twenty minutes, not knowing what had happened. Deciding finally that her wireless had been put out of action, Commodore Harwood ordered the Seafox to find her. To Lt Lewin went the signal: *Tell* Exeter *to close.*

Lewin returned after half an hour and signalled: Exeter *severely damaged and joining you as best she can.* Even from the aircraft the cruiser had looked a terrible mess. Kearney, the observer, reported: '*Exeter* was closed about eighteen miles south of the action. She was obviously hard hit and in no condition to fight another action. The position, course and speed of the squadron was passed to her, the aircraft flew over her in the direction of the Flag, and returned to *Ajax*.'

Lt Lewin wrote later: 'I have never seen such a shambles, anyway in a ship which survived. Her mainmast was moving perceptibly as she rolled.'

The Commodore had now to let the Admiralty, merchant ships in the area, Admiral Lyon, and the *Cumberland* know what was going on. His first signal, which was to give the Admiralty the news that he had found the *Graf Spee*, was, as mentioned earlier, at 0615:

> IMMEDIATE; *One pocket battleship 034° south 049° west course 275° degrees.*

This had been followed with a signal to the *Cumberland* to join him as soon as possible. Then at 0637 the *Ajax* transmitted a curt and dramatic signal:

> *Am engaging one PB;* Exeter, Achilles *in company.*

This was followed by a further 'pot-boiler' at 0717 to keep Admiral Lyon, the Admiralty and the *Cumberland* in the picture:

> *Am engaging one PB in lat 34° south, long 49° west.*

Later, when the *Ajax*'s wireless was out of action, Commodore Harwood signalled to the *Achilles*:

> Broadcast in plain language to GBMS:* One PB 34° south, 50° west, steering 275 degrees, report to Admiralty.

The *Achilles* then found that all her own aerials were down and it took some time to rig new ones. By then the Commodore had sent a further signal, this time to the *Cumberland*. Captain Parry later reported to him that the messages had been sent but 'I have only one leg of aerial left.'

Then, to the Admiralty and Admiral Lyon, Harwood made the following signal:

> IMMEDIATE; HMS Ajax, *HMS* Achilles, *HMS* Exeter *have been*

*GBMS – General Broadcast to Merchant Ships.

heavily engaged. Have withdrawn from daylight close action owing to shortage of ammunition. HMS Exeter *hauling away due damage, two turrets out of action in HMS* Ajax. *Pocket battleship has undoubtedly been hit. I am shadowing.*

On board the three cruisers there was now plenty to be done. In the *Exeter* there was the task of making the ship seaworthy, in the *Ajax* and *Achilles* repairing damage and shadowing.

All three also had the heartbreaking job of preparing for the burial service. In the *Exeter* it took place at 1545, and her log records: 'Buried at Sea Capt H.R.D. Woods, RM, Lt-Cdr J. Bowman-Manifold, Sub-Lt D.H. Tyler, Midshipman J. Rickcord and forty-seven ratings killed in action. Missing believed killed in action Sub-Lt C.A.L. Morse and one rating.'

Despite all that the ship's doctors could do, several more ratings died of wounds later in the day. (When the ship arrived at the Falkland Islands three days later fifty-nine ratings were taken ashore to hospital, and one man died six hours after she anchored.)

The *Ajax* hoisted the Seafox inboard after Lt Lewin made a fine landing – the observer later reported: 'Conditions were the worst of any in which the aircraft had previously been recovered.'

In the *Achilles*, as Captain Parry's wounded legs were stiffening up, he gave Lt Washbourn permission to leave the DCT to visit each gun turret, have a yarn with the men and tell them what was going on. He later reported to Captain Parry: 'I found everyone in magnificent heart . . .'

Then there was the question of the reward to be settled. Captain Parry had said, soon after the war started, he would give £1 to the first man to spot a German warship, and the time had now come to pay up. The rating who had reported the first sight of smoke to Washbourn was sent for, and Captain Parry handed over a pound note.

The rating, after pocketing it, said: 'Well, sir, it wasn't me that first saw it; it was ——.' Thus the *Graf Spee* cost Captain Parry another pound.

While the ship settled down into the shadowing routine, Captain Parry glanced over the side of the bridge and noticed a number of men wandering around, apparently aimlessly, on deck. He asked what they were doing and was told, 'They're collecting souvenirs, sir.'

By then it was time for the much-delayed breakfast – huge slices of bread with fried bacon in between were taken round to all the quarters.

The guns' crews, still fresh after firing an average of 156 rounds a gun, left their turrets and sat on deck in the sunshine to attack their meal, sum up their chances, and digest the news given them by Lt Washbourn.

It was then that Washbourn heard the comments made about him at the beginning of the action by a stoker, who had not then appreciated that the *Graf Spee* had arrived on the horizon.

The stoker had emerged from a hatchway grumbling about 'Flicking gunnery shoots so flicking early in the flicking morning and why couldn't the flicking Gunnery Jack (Officer) wait till after breakfast?'

At that point in his colourful monologue three large fountains, the manifestation of three 11-inch shells from the *Graf Spee*, rose close alongside. The stoker, commenting 'Cor, this ain't no flicking place for me!', hastily returned down his hatchway.

Outwardly all that the *Achilles* had to show of the action were splinter holes, damage on the upper deck – mostly caused by the after guns firing on a forward bearing – and the paint very badly blistered along the barrels of the guns.

So the two ships continued to shadow the *Graf Spee*, and an indication of how they felt is given in an extract from a letter written by one of the *Achilles*'s officers six weeks later:'. . . We talk loudly now about that phase of the operations as "The Chase", but it didn't seem like that at any time then. It was incredible to us that she should be running away from one and a half rather battered little cruisers, both very short of ammunition. And why, oh why, didn't she turn aside to polish off the *Exeter* and make it something of a material victory if a moral defeat?'

At 1010 she did turn aside to snap at the *Achilles*, which, over-estimating the pocket battleship's speed, came up too close on her tail. She turned suddenly and fired three salvoes of 11-inch shells. The first fell short, and Captain Parry immediately altered course to dodge the second salvo, which burst close alongside as the cruiser turned. The third burst in her wake and would have probably hit had Captain Parry not rapidly side-stepped.

On this occasion a Marine, before making for cover, paused a moment as the shells burst close astern to comment: 'Blimey, they're after our Heel.' It was with this in mind that Captain Parry put down a smoke screen and zig-zagged at a more respectful distance.

During the next hour both ships were able to make a proper check on armament and ammunition left, and it was found that the original hurried estimates, made while the guns were still firing, were wrong.* The *Achilles* had roughly estimated that she had 60 rounds for A turret, 90 for B, 90 for X and 100 for Y; now she reported to the Commodore that she had 173 for A, 239 for B, 140 for X and 100 for Y. The *Ajax*, too, found she had roughly double her original estimate.

This was cheering news, since no one was very certain what the *Graf Spee* was going to do next, and the prospect of being caught without ammunition and with fuel running low was not very encouraging for anyone.

The *Achilles*'s ammunition report had just been signalled to the *Ajax* when, at 1103, a merchant ship was sighted close to the *Graf Spee* and seemed to be blowing off steam. A few minutes later the *Graf Spee* called up the *Ajax* by wireless, using the cruiser's pre-war call sign, and said:

Please pick up lifeboats of English steamer.

This was the first indication that the enemy was the *Graf Spee* and not the *Admiral Scheer*, and the *Ajax* did not reply; but within fifteen minutes she was close enough to the steamer to see that her boats were still hoisted and there were men aboard. She was the *SS Shakespeare*, and the *Ajax* signalled:

Are you all right? If so hoist International 'C'.

Flag C of the International Code was hoisted on one of the *Shakespeare*'s signal halyards.

Have you received a message from Admiral Graf Spee?

Yes, replied the *Shakespeare*, whose crew were still agreeably surprised to find themselves alive after the passage of the pocket battleship.

Do you require assistance? If not, hoist 'No'.

Once again the flag hoist was run up in the *Shakespeare*: no, she did not need help.

---

*In the whole action the *Achilles* fired 340 rounds from A turret, 349 from B, 290 from X and 263 from Y turret. Altogether she fired between 210 and 220 broadsides.

Keep continuous watch on 500* kcs, ordered Commodore Harwood, and the *Ajax* steamed off after the *Graf Spee.*

For the *Shakespeare* it had been a very narrow escape. The *Graf Spee's* log records: 'While steering towards La Plata a large 5,000-ton English steamer was ordered to stop with a warning shot and to send the crew into the boats. The captain had the intention of torpedoing the steamer if the crew left the ship. He radioed a message to the *Ajax.*

'Since the crew of the steamer did not leave the ship, the Captain abandoned his intention of sinking the ship in view of the probable reception of his own crew in Montevideo.'

So the chase continued; and for a while it became almost routine. Both cruisers continually altered course and speed to keep the *Graf Spee* in sight, zig-zagging from time to time in case Langsdorff should be tempted to open fire again.

At noon the *Exeter,* her jury wireless aerials rigged, answered the Commodore's signal asking her maximum speed:

Eighteen knots. One gun in Y turret available in local control. All other main armament permanently out of action. One 4-inch gun available only. No air in ship.

This was followed twenty minutes later with: *All guns out of action.*

Half an hour later Captain Bell asked: *Do you know where* Admiral Scheer *is?*

He was having great trouble steering a reasonable course since he had only a boat compass, and he could not steam at more than eighteen knots because the damaged bulkheads would not stand it. Although the list to starboard had been taken off by pumping fuel oil over into the tanks on the port side, the *Exeter* was still three feet down by the bows.

The Commodore realized now that the gallant ship had no further fighting value, and he ordered Captain Bell to make for the Falkland Islands.

From Captain Parry's report: '1534–1542. The masts of a vessel were sighted to the north-westward and reported to you [Commodore Harwood] by V/S. When first seen the masts had the appearance of a

*The international Distress frequency.

151

*merchant vessel but six minutes later a streamlined funnel appeared
. . .'*

The lookout reported masts bearing Green 45 and Washbourn had
swung the *Achilles*'s DCT round on to it. He was unable to recognize
what little he could see of the ship; but the over-all impression was
ominous. She appeared to have a truncated funnel and the high fighting
superstructure of a man-o'-war.

She was like nothing in the recognition manuals – everyone in the DCT
agreed on that point. They had not been given any photographs of the
Admiral Hipper class of German cruisers, but a recent signal had given
them enough details to sketch a rough silhouette.

The idea quickly caught on, and Washbourn called down the voicepipe to Captain Parry: 'The ship bearing Green 45 looks very like a
Hipper to us.'

Whatever thoughts crossed Captain Parry's mind at being told that
one of Germany's latest heavy cruisers, mounting eight 8-inch and a
dozen 4-inch guns, was likely to join in the already unequal fight, he
merely said: 'I think I'll close a little further before reporting, Guns.'

Washbourn decided to get another opinion and climbed up through
the hatch to the Captain of Marines, saying: 'See what you make of it.'

He looked at the card and then took up his binoculars. After what
seemed an age he put them down and said glumly: 'That's her all right.'

Washbourn climbed back into the DCT and reported to Captain
Parry: 'I am afraid there's no doubt now, Sir . . .'

'All right,' Captain Parry replied, 'I'll make the enemy report.'

In a few moments a signalman was flashing to the *Ajax*: *Emergency.
Enemy in sight bearing 297 degrees.*

The strange ship was broad-on the *Achilles*'s starboard bow, while the
Ajax was nine miles away on the port beam. The Commodore signalled:
What is it?

Captain Parry replied: *Suspected 8-inch cruiser. Am confirming.*

For the Commodore this was grim news. The two cruisers were in no
state to take on another enemy in a fight which could have only one
result. But the sudden appearance of a German heavy cruiser would
explain the *Graf Spee*'s anxiety to get away to the westward – she had led
them into a trap.

Harwood ordered the *Achilles* not to engage the new enemy and sent off a signal to the *Exeter* warning her to keep away from the coast. Lewin was told to get ready to fly off again in the Seafox.

By then, however, the hull of the strange ship had risen over the horizon and could be seen from the *Achilles*. Everyone was vastly relieved when she was identified as a British merchantman – the ss *Delane*. Her streamlined funnel had given her the appearance of one of the *Hipper* class at long range. And very thankfully Captain Parry signalled to the *Ajax: False alarm.*

While the two cruisers broadcast warnings to Allied merchant ships who might be lying in her path, the *Graf Spee* continued on her westward course, and the Commodore was by now fairly certain she would enter the Plate.

That raised several problems for him. The estuary of the River Plate, dividing Uruguay on the east from Argentina on the west, is in fact a huge bay forming a half circle, with the river entering in the middle. Its size can be gauged by the fact that from Lobos Island on the Uruguayan side of the bay to Cape San Antonia on the Argentinian side is 120 miles of open sea.

Yet three widely separated deep-water channels can be used to enter the River Plate. The northernmost is between the English Bank lightship and Cumberland Shoal, the second between English Bank and Rouen Bank, and the southernmost, which is nearly thirty miles wide, between the Rouen Bank and the Argentine coast.

The city of Montevideo lies on the east bank of the river where it empties into the bay, while Buenos Aires lies 115 miles farther up-river on the Argentine side, being reached by the Indio Channel.

The *Graf Spee* was approaching the great bay obliquely; and if she was in fact making for the Plate she would enter on the eastern side. But she could round English Bank and double out again in the darkness, since night would have fallen before she reached the coast.

There were several things Langsdorff could do; and the Commodore, like a maritime Sherlock Holmes, tried to put himself in the German's position and deduce what his intentions were.

To do this successfully Harwood had to ask two questions – how badly damaged was the *Graf Spee*, and why had she broken off the action? Unfortunately, he could only guess at the answers.

Briefly, Harwood had to plan for the pocket battleship entering either

Montevideo or Buenos Aires, or doubling back in the darkness and making a dash for the broad Atlantic, trying to escape the pursuing cruisers in the night – not a difficult task, since these were the days before radar; and although Langsdorff did not know it, they would be out of fuel long before reinforcements arrived.

Shortly before 1400 the Commodore signalled to Captain H.W. McCall, the Naval Attaché at Montevideo, that the *Graf Spee* was heading direct for the Plate, and requested him to arrange for Lobos, English Bank, the Whistle Buoy off Montevideo entrance, Recalada light vessel and San Borombon Bay – on the west side – to be watched. He stressed the need for negative reports from areas in which the *Graf Spee* was not sighted.

Within nine hours Captain McCall reported that all arrangements had been made and the areas would be watched by tugs and aircraft.

To Captain Parry the Commodore signalled:

If enemy passes west of Lobos Achilles *is to follow him.* Ajax *will proceed south of English Bank in case he doubles out. Be careful you are not caught at dawn up sun as even if he anchors he may come to sea at any time. He is not to be relied on to respect territorial waters.*

Shadowing continued without incident until 1852, when lookouts in the *Ajax* saw the *Graf Spee* altering course to starboard and noticed her after turret training round in their direction. The three guns started elevating, and at once Captain Woodhouse put the *Ajax* on a zig-zag course in case the Germans started shooting.

The range was thirteen miles, and for a few minutes nothing happened. At 1913 the pocket battleship started making white smoke, then she fired a salvo which burst between 400 and 600 yards short. Immediately Captain Woodhouse altered course to port and a second salvo burst in the cruiser's wake as she turned.

The *Graf Spee*, her gesture of defiance apparently made, turned back on to her original course.

Sunset was due at 2048, and the after-glow would obviously silhouette the *Graf Spee* very nicely, whereas the two cruisers would be hidden against the darker eastern sky. But in order to keep in touch after dark the two cruisers would have to close the range before 2000, and they started creeping nearer.

By this time the coast of Uruguay was in sight, and Captain Parry took the *Achilles* as close inshore as possible. He had edged up to within eleven miles of the *Graf Spee* at 2055, and this no doubt irked the touchy Germans: they put down a smoke screen and fired three salvoes at the *Achilles*. The first two fell short and the third close astern.

This provoked Captain Parry into replying, so he too put down a smoke screen and fired five salvoes as he turned away. The *Ajax*, who was in a good position for flank firing, signalled that she had seen the *Graf Spee* straddled.

The Germans opened fire at the *Achilles* three times during the next hour; but Captain Parry did not take the bait. He was sure the Germans could not see his ship in the twilight and if he replied they would be able to plot his exact position from the flashes of his guns.

'None of these last efforts fell anywhere near us,' Captain Parry wrote later. 'But his cordite smoke being unexpectedly black, these salvoes created a smoke screen which made him very difficult to see; and it was not till two hours after sunset that he could again be distinguished unmistakably. His position then showed he was passing north of English Bank.'

The *Ajax* had earlier signalled *I am leaving her to you this side. Make frequent enemy reports,* and turned to port to guard the south-western exit from the Plate; at 2213, by altering course to the south slightly, Captain Parry had the pocket battleship neatly silhouetted against the lights of Montevideo, a city at peace where young couples danced in night-clubs, brightly-illuminated shop windows displayed their wares and war seemed a lifetime away; but at that moment it was less than seven miles.

From Commodore Harwood's dispatch: '. . . Graf Spee *proceeded north of English Bank and anchored in Montevideo roads at 0050.'*

'My chief preoccupation at that time,' he wrote, 'was how long did *Graf Spee* intend to stay there. The primary necessity was to keep to seaward of the *Graf Spee* if she came to sea again, and at the same time avoid being caught against the dawn light.

'At 2350 I ordered *Ajax* and *Achilles* to withdraw from the Plate. *Achilles* to patrol the area from the Uruguayan coast to a line 120 degrees from English Bank, and *Ajax* the southern area, both ships to move back into the Plate in their respective sectors after dawn.'

Everyone in both ships remained closed up at Action Stations all night while they kept guard on the stable doors. There was every chance that Captain McCall would be able to warn them if the *Graf Spee* got under way again; but once she was out of sight of the harbour she would rapidly disappear into the darkness unless one or other of the two waiting cruisers could get her silhouetted against the lights of the coastline and estimate her course.

For the captains of the two cruisers it was a worrying time; and both of them stayed on their bridges the whole night until after dawn.

XVIII

No Help at Hand

FOR THE time being, then, the two small cruisers, manned by weary but resolute men, stood alone between the enemy and the sea. If the *Graf Spee* could sink or elude either of them, then she would almost certainly escape into the vast area of the South Atlantic or even the Antarctic. Both the ships had been heavily engaged, and were short of fuel and ammunition (the nearest supply of the latter was Trinidad). They had no hope of destroying the *Graf Spee* unless they could engage her together; but this was likely to be impossible – at least at the beginning – since they had to watch different channels across the 120-mile stretch of the estuary.

The difficulties and dangers were many and great; and Commodore Harwood could look for little immediate assistance. The only trump cards now had to be played by the diplomats ashore; and the *Graf Spee* always had the last trick – she could weigh anchor and slip out whenever she wanted to, whatever the diplomatic rights and wrongs of the situation.

The Commodore wrote: 'I requested His Britannic Majesty's Minister, Montevideo [Mr E. Millington-Drake], to use every possible means of delaying *Graf Spee*'s sailing, in order to gain time for reinforcements to reach me. I suggested he should sail British ships and invoke the twenty-four-hour rule* to prevent her leaving.

'I learned that the *Ark Royal, Renown, Neptune, Dorsetshire, Shropshire* and three destroyers were all closing the Plate, but none of them could reach me for at least five days.

'*Cumberland* reported that she would arrive in the Plate at 2200/14th

*If a merchant ship of a belligerent nation sails from a neutral port, under International Law a warship of the opposing country is not allowed to sail for twenty-four hours.

December, having made the passage from the Falkland Islands in thirty-four hours . . .'

Meanwhile, in London the Admiralty was making its plans. Commodore Harwood's original enemy report had been received in Whitehall at breakfast time, and the signal was immediately taken to Admiral Pound, the First Sea Lord.

He realized the unequal odds facing Harwood, but there was not much he could do until he had more news. And he had to wait more than two hours before the Commodore's signal arrived saying that the *Exeter* had been badly damaged and that he was breaking off the daylight action.

Here, in order, are the majority of the relevant signals which arrived at Admiralty that day.

Commodore Harwood to Forces K and X (intercepted by Admiralty):

IMMEDIATE: One pocket battleship 034° south, 049° west course 275 degrees.

Harwood to the *Cumberland* and Admiralty:

IMMEDIATE: HMS Ajax, *HMS* Achilles, *HMS* Exeter *have been heavily engaged. Have withdrawn from daylight close action owing to shortage of ammunition. HMS* Exeter *hauling away due damage, two turrets out of action in HMS* Ajax. *Pocket battleship has undoubtedly been hit. I am shadowing.*

Staff Officer (Intelligence), Freetown, to Admiralty:

British ship GCVQ (Doric Star) due 9 December has not arrived.

Harwood to Admiralty and Admiral Lyon (at Freetown):

MOST IMMEDIATE. Position, course and speed of pocket battleship 034° 44' south, 051° 40' west, 260 degrees, 22 knots, using call sign DTGS. HMS Ajax *and HMS* Achilles *shadowing.*

HMS Exeter *very badly damaged. One gun in local control remains in action. Speed reduced maximum eighteen knots. Have directed her to proceed to Falkland Islands. Aircraft reports twenty-five to thirty hits obtained on pocket battleship but he still has high speed.*

Staff Officer (Intelligence), Freetown, to Admiralty:

British ship Tairoa *due here 11 December has not arrived.*

Admiral Lyon to the *Cumberland:*

> *Proceed to sea with all dispatch and endeavour to make contact with HMS* Exeter *and/or Commodore CSAD who reports contact with pocket battleship. . .*

Staff Officer (Intelligence), Montevideo, to Admiralty:

> *Pocket battleship sighted fifteen miles east from Punta del Este being engaged by two cruisers.*

Admiral Lyon to the *Neptune*:

> *If fuel permits, proceed to Rio de Janeiro, complete with fuel, and join CCSAD off River Plate. If necessary take fuel from* [oiler] Cherryleaf *to reach Rio de Janeiro.*

Staff Officer (Intelligence), Montevideo, to Admiralty:

> *MOST IMMEDIATE: German pocket battleship anchored in Montevideo Roads 2350 today Wednesday.*

Staff Officer (Intelligence), Montevideo, to Admiralty:

> *German armoured ship understood locally to be* Admiral Graf Spee *now anchored in Montevideo.*

While these cryptic signals were gradually building up the picture for the First Sea Lord, he made the first moves to send reinforcements to help Commodore Harwood. But apart from the *Cumberland*, already steaming north from the Falkland Islands at thirty knots to get to the Commodore 1,000 miles away, there were no British warships within 3,000 miles of the Plate.

Force I (the cruisers *Cornwall* and *Gloucester* and the carrier *Eagle*) were at Durban, more than 4,000 miles from the Plate, and as they were at the disposal of Admiral Lyon he ordered them to Cape Town 'with all dispatch', intending to give them further orders when they arrived, since by then the situation would be clearer.†

Cumberland had received only garbled signals from the Commodore but her captain, on his own initiative, had already put to sea.

†A few hours later, after they had left Durban, the Admiralty put these ships under the command of the C-in-C, East Indies, for work in connection with some important convoys, and they were recalled to Durban.

The cruisers *Sussex* and *Shropshire*, Force H, were on their way to Cape Town, and Admiral Lyon ordered them to proceed to the Cape 'with all possible speed', refuel and sail for Freetown. However, when he lost Force I he ordered both ships to stay at the Cape.

The *Dorsetshire*, which was at the Cape on the day of the battle, was ordered to sail for the Plate, 3,600 miles to the westward. The *Shropshire* followed her two days later, also bound for Montevideo. She was due to arrive on 23 December.

Three thousand miles to the north along the South American coast, 600 miles from Pernambuco, the carrier *Ark Royal* and the *Renown*, Force K, were on their way to meet the *Neptune*, which was coming south with her destroyers when the Commodore first sighted the *Graf Spee*.

The *Renown* was short of fuel, and as she had barely enough to reach the Plate and none for a long chase, Admiral Lyon ordered Vice-Admiral Wells, commanding Force K, to meet the *Neptune* and then go to Freetown to refuel. This would take them in the opposite direction to the Plate, but Freetown was the nearest British port to which Admiral Lyon could send them to fuel; and from his point of view diplomatic difficulties might prevent him from using a neutral port.

The First Sea Lord, directing operations in the Admiralty, quickly realized this and had the power to invoke the Foreign Office's help. He signalled to Admiral Lyon:

> *Force K is to proceed to River Plate, fuelling at a South American port or from an oiler.*

This would save them more than 2,000 miles, but the diplomats would have to put in some hard work. The First Sea Lord then signalled Admiral Lyon:

> *Report where Force K will fuel. Pressure is being applied by Ambassador so that they can fuel at Bahia or Rio de Janeiro should you select either of these places.*

These signals were repeated to Vice-Admiral Wells in the *Ark Royal* and the First Sea Lord followed them up with a message telling him to leave the destroyers (*Hardy, Hostile* and *Hero*) behind if they were likely to delay him. Admiral Lyon then ordered him to refuel at Rio de Janeiro, which was on the direct route and 1,000 miles north of the Plate. He at once increased speed to twenty-five knots.

Thus the *Ark Royal* and *Renown* could reach Rio by 17 December and would want twelve hours to refuel, and they would still be 1,000 miles – forty hours' steaming – from the Plate; the *Neptune* would reach Rio about twelve hours after Force K; the *Dorsetshire* would not get to Montevideo from South Africa before 21 December, and the *Shropshire*, which had later been ordered to sail, was not due until 23 December.

So at dawn on 14 December, when the Commodore's two cruisers began their daylight vigil in the Plate estuary, they knew that, apart from the *Cumberland* joining them that evening, there would be no further reinforcements until the *Ark Royal* and *Renown* and *Neptune* arrived in five days, and the *Dorsetshire* in seven days.

XIX

Langsdorff Decides to Scuttle

DAYBREAK on the 14th found every available man in the *Graf Spee* hard at work. The bodies of the thirty-seven men killed in the action were being prepared for burial, and the fifty-seven wounded were to be removed ashore for treatment. Repair parties were busy plugging innumerable splinter and shell holes – the pocket battleship was estimated to have been hit more than fifty times – clearing away wreckage, repairing electric leads and making a list of special equipment necessary to make good some of the more extensive damage.*

The load on Captain Langsdorff's shoulders was, to a certain extent, being eased. At sea he had no one with whom he could discuss decisions – command of a ship is a lonely, isolated task. Now he had an abundance of talent to help him and was in direct contact with Berlin.

The German Naval Attaché at Buenos Aires immediately flew over to Montevideo with German civilian constructors and boarded the *Graf Spee*. The German Ambassador at Montevideo, Dr Otto Langmann, was already on board by the time he arrived.

Captain Langsdorff, by now almost completely exhausted by lack of sleep and worry, outlined the position to the two men: the *Graf Spee* was unfit to go to sea because of action damage and he could not feed his men properly because the galley was wrecked. He had sixty-one British Merchant Navy officers on board and he proposed to free them almost immediately. And it was essential that he should discover what British reinforcements were due.

Dr Langmann, a stockily-built and testy little man who wore pince-nez, then told Langsdorff of the mistake he had made in entering a

*See Appendix D.

Uruguayan harbour, instead of going to Buenos Aires where the atmosphere would probably have been more cordial.

The British and French Governments, he said, would very soon be exerting the strongest pressure on the 'politically weak' Uruguay to make sure the *Graf Spee* was either allowed to stay no more than the seventy-two hours* allowed by International Law or that she was interned if she overstayed that period.

Then both Langmann and the Naval Attaché went ashore for a conference with the Uruguayan Foreign Minister, Dr Guani.

Meanwhile the *Graf Spee*'s Engineer, Korvettenkapitän Klepp, and the German civilian constructor from Buenos Aires were making a detailed inspection of the whole ship to estimate how long it would take – bearing in mind local facilities – to get her ready for sea. The major items on their list were for small leaks in Sections I–III and several more about six inches in diameter at and under the waterline at Section XIII on the starboard side, and two in Sections V and XIV, and one about five inches in diameter at the waterline at Section X on the port side. The underwater holes had been plugged, but the others, along with several eight-inch holes in the upper deck, would have to be welded. The galley would also need a good deal of work on it. There was some damage to fighting equipment which would have to be made good if the *Graf Spee* was to go into action effectively again. And there was also an unexploded British shell, embedded in the hull, to be removed.

Klepp and the constructor talked it over and decided that a minimum of fourteen days would be needed for the crew and civilian workmen with equipment to get the ship ready for sea. They reported their findings to Langsdorff. He immediately passed them on to Dr Langmann, who found himself in something of a quandary. He wanted to get as long a stay as possible for the *Graf Spee*; but on the other hand he did not want to reveal to the British the extent of the damage. In the end he sent a Note to the Uruguayan Foreign Minister requesting permission for a stay of fourteen days.

At the conference at the Foreign Ministry, Langmann and the Naval Attaché put their case to Dr Guani as strongly as they could; and it was finally agreed with him that a Uruguayan Technical Commission should inspect the ship later that afternoon to determine what repairs were needed.

*In fact Britain was pressing for only twenty-four hours on the ground that as the *Graf Spee* had steamed into harbour at high speed she was obviously seaworthy.

So at 1900 a Uruguayan Navy commander and an engineer officer arrived on board and were shown round by Klepp. They agreed some repairs were necessary to make the ship seaworthy, but no amount of questioning by the Germans would get them to say how long they considered would be required. They had first to report to their superior officers, they explained.

Thus, in a way hardly satisfactory to the Germans, the *Graf Spee*'s first day in Montevideo ended. In Berlin, Grand Admiral Raeder had received a brief radio report from Captain Langsdorff describing the damage and his immediate intentions; and with Ribbentrop, the German Foreign Minister, was anxiously awaiting a cable from Dr Langmann giving Uruguay's decision on the time to be allowed.

In Whitehall that day the Admiralty had been working closely with the Foreign Office. All available warships were, as described earlier, steaming to Commodore Harwood's assistance; now it was up to the diplomats to do their juggling.

Ideally, the Admiralty would have liked to see the *Graf Spee* interned; but failing that they wanted her to be allowed to stay for four or five days until the British reinforcements arrived off the Plate.

But it was vitally important that the Germans should not guess that. Otherwise, as soon as the *Graf Spee* realized that there was still only the *Ajax* and *Achilles* waiting for her outside, she might well make a dash for it and sink both the cruisers before escaping.

There were, therefore, three things to be done. The first one was to kick up a fuss in Montevideo and request that the *Graf Spee* should not be allowed to stay for more than twenty-four hours, thus making it appear that Britain was anxious for the *Graf Spee* to sail as soon as possible. The Germans would naturally assume the British had several warships just over the horizon, waiting to fall on the pocket battleship with vicious enthusiasm.

The second was to 'plant' stories that British Navy heavy warships were in fact already in position; and the third was to make sure the *Graf Spee*, despite Britain's apparently sincere and stern protests, did *not* sail. As Commodore Harwood had already suggested, this could be done for a few days by sailing British merchant ships and claiming twenty-four hours' grace.

Instructions were cabled to Mr E. Millington-Drake, the British

Minister in Montevideo, and the following signal was sent to Commodore Harwood, in the *Ajax*, and to Admiral Lyon in Freetown:

> *Foreign Office have instructed HM Minister, Montevideo to use every endeavour to get* Spee *interned. Arguments to be used are (A) if ship is seaworthy, Hague Convention does not permit repairs and she must leave after twenty-four hours or be interned, (B) if she is not seaworthy same is true, as there is wide support for the view that no shore facilities or extension of time may be granted for repairs and damage sustained in action.*
>
> *Foreign Office have added for Minister's own information that if Uruguayan authorities will not accept these arguments we should prefer that the ship remains four or five days.*

Meanwhile the *Ajax* and the *Achilles* continued on guard during the day and night of 14 December. The Commodore received various signals telling him when it was anticipated the reinforcements would arrive. The *Cumberland* joined him at 2200 after her dash from the Falkland Islands, and he ordered her to cover the sector between Rouen Bank and English Bank, with the *Achilles* to the north of her and the *Ajax* to the south.

'Should *Graf Spee* come out,' he wrote later, 'she was to be shadowed and all ships were to concentrate sufficiently far to seaward to enable a concerted attack to be carried out.'

That night after dark Captain Parry decided to take the *Achilles* right in close, and he found that it was possible to see anything moving in the entrance channel silhouetted against the lights of the town.

However, the Commodore said they must not commit any warlike act so close in. Although it was outside the three-mile limit, which was the only form of territorial waters which Britain recognized, Argentina and Uruguay between them claimed the whole Plate Estuary.

* * *

Next day, Friday, 15 December, Captain Langsdorff had the melancholy task of attending the funeral of the *Graf Spee*'s dead in a cemetery outside Montevideo. Hundreds of people lined the streets watching the cortège – a naval band forming a vanguard of brassy melancholy – move through the city, and a few German sympathizers gave Nazi salutes.

At the cemetery Langsdorff, in white uniform, with seven medals on his left breast and the Nazi eagle emblem sewn on the right, his left hand on the hilt of his sword, spoke a short funeral oration over the coffins, each of which was draped with a Nazi flag.

He then stepped to each of the coffins in turn and sprinkled earth over it. His face was drawn, and there were dark rings under his eyes. His uniform was creased and he looked very weary. Finally he stood back, flanked by German petty officers who were the pall-bearers, and with the German Ambassador and several civilians standing behind him. Every German man and woman present then stood to attention and raised their right arms stiffly, in the Nazi salute. All except Langsdorff. His left hand still clasping the hilt of his sword, he brought his right hand up to the peak of his cap in the old naval salute. He was oblivious to the sharp eyes of Dr Langmann, who realized that the photographs being taken by Press cameramen would very shortly be printed on the front pages of newspapers all over the world.

One of those newspapers, the *Washington Post*, wrote of 'the tribute offered by the English merchant seamen who were formerly prisoners of Captain Langsdorff. They, at the graveside, honoured the German sailors killed by British guns . . . Restored to freedom in Montevideo, they placed on the coffins of the German dead a wreath inscribed "To the memory of brave men of the sea from their comrades of the British Merchant Service".'

Later in the day Langsdorff, back on board the *Graf Spee*, received disturbing reports from the German Embassy in Buenos Aires about the strengthening of the British forces off the Plate. It was said that the *Ark Royal* and *Renown* had left Cape Town on 12 December* for an unknown destination; and furthermore chartered private planes flying over the Plate Estuary had sighted four British cruisers.

Then, to cap this, one of the *Graf Spee*'s gunnery officers personally reported sighting from the Director Control Tower a large warship which he considered to be the *Renown*; and on the horizon he saw what seemed to be the *Ark Royal* and two or three destroyers.

People ashore working for the Germans reported sighting several warships and the *Cumberland* was 'definitely identified'.

So the rumours and reports came in to Langsdorff. Some were inspired by the British Admiralty and some by people genuinely wishing to help

*When they were, in fact, off Pernambuco.

the Germans. But it was the gunnery officer's report which worried Langsdorff most of all.

At the same time the German Ambassador was being told of the Uruguayan Government's decision on the *Graf Spee*'s stay in port. She was to be allowed seventy-two hours, and any extension 'was not acceptable'. Their decision was based on the report of their Technical Commission, which said that seventy-two hours was adequate to make good the damage.

'The Uruguayan Government and populace were not unfriendly to the Germans,' the Germans later recorded, 'and the Foreign Minister had agreed that the time should commence from the time of the return to the shore of the Uruguayan Technical Commission. By this time *Spee* would have been nearly ninety-six hours in harbour from the time of her arrival.

'The German Ambassador, in his telegram to the Foreign Office, attributed the Uruguayan Government's decision to "the extraordinary economic pressure with which they were being treated by England and France".'

Early next day, 16 December, after spending the night considering the news from Dr Langmann, Captain Langsdorff dispatched a signal to the Naval High Command in Berlin, in which he outlined the situation and requested instructions. He said:

(1) Renown *and* Ark Royal *as well as cruisers and destroyers off Montevideo. Close blockade at night. No prospect of breaking out to the open sea and getting through to Germany.*

(2) *Intend to proceed to the limit of neutral waters. If I can fight my way through to Buenos Aires with ammunition still remaining I shall endeavour to do so.*

(3) *As a break-through might result in the destruction of* Spee *without the possibility of causing damage to the enemy, request instructions whether to scuttle the ship (in spite of the inadequate depth of water in the Plate Estuary) or to submit to internment.*

To his appreciation of the situation the German Ambassador added his own version in a telegram to the German Foreign Office:

No argument concerning legal rights can alter the necessity for an urgent decision regarding Spee. *Superior enemy naval forces which have been clearly observed from on board* Spee *make it appear to the Commanding Officer quite out of the question to shake off shadowers and thus achieve a successful break-through to Germany. From this point of view the fourteen days' stay would not alter the situation and could only assist the concentration of enemy naval forces.*

I am at one with the Naval Attaché regarding the internment of the vessel as the worst possible solution in the circumstances. It would be preferable in view of the shortage of ammunition to blow her up in the shallow waters of the Plate and to have the crew interned.

In Berlin, however, the Foreign Office still seemed unable to grasp the situation. Ribbentrop, whose temper when thwarted always overcame his limited reasoning powers, was unused to having small countries standing up to him. The rule of law was of little interest and had no bearing on the situation as far as he was concerned. Was not he the man Hitler – after the signing of the treaty with Russia – described as 'a second Bismarck'?

But apparently he failed to realize that Uruguay was not standing alone: eleven American Republics, including the United States, had a vital interest in the outcome, since the Havana Convention of 1928, to which the United States and several South American countries were signatories, was involved.

The British request for no more that twenty-four hours' stay was, of course, based on three Articles of the Hague Convention of 1907 – Article XI which forbids belligerent warships, unless individual nations have local laws to the contrary, to stay more than twenty-four hours in the territorial waters of a neutral power; Article XIII, which obliges a neutral country to notify a belligerent warship to leave its waters within twenty-four hours; and Article XIV, under which a belligerent warship may not prolong its stay beyond twenty-four hours except on account of damage or stress of weather.

Regarding this last Article, the ruling of the Havana Convention was that 'damage' did not cover damage caused by enemy action.

The British Minister had also drawn Uruguay's attention to Article XVIII of the Hague Convention which said that repairs to belligerent warships must be only those absolutely necessary to make her seaworthy and must not add to her fighting efficiency.

Thus the Uruguayans had been more than fair in granting seventy-two hours, starting after the twenty-four hours the *Graf Spee* had already spent in port.

Nevertheless, Ribbentrop replied to Dr Langmann by cable saying that the Uruguayan Government's decision was completely incomprehensible 'having regard to the conditon of the *Spee* and of the legal position'. Dr Langmann and Captain Langsdorff were ordered to seek to prolong the authorized stay and to 'counter with the greatest possible energy the influence of the British'.

At Dr Langmann's meeting later in the day with the Uruguayan Minister of Defence, this armchair directive proved impossible of fulfilment as the Minister appeared 'completely in the English camp and was the person chiefly responsible for the unfavourable decision* of the Uruguayan Cabinet'.

Further evidence of the German Foreign Office's wishful thinking and lack of realism came in another telegram an hour or so later:

According to English Press reports the Ark Royal *is in the Plate area. As you know we believe the* Ark Royal *has been sunk. By order of the Fuehrer you are to attempt to take photographs of the supposed* Ark Royal. *Signal results and forward photographs.*

The Germans were unable to charter an aircraft to make a reconnaissance . . .

Whatever Berlin's view of the situation, neither Dr Langmann nor Captain Langsdorff was very optimistic. Various articles considered to be of historic interest were taken ashore from the *Graf Spee* for dispatch to Berlin. They included the Battle Ensign worn during the action, a picture (which was damaged by shell splinters) of the late Admiral Graf von Spee, and the ship's bell.

In Berlin, having received Captain Langsdorff's signal, Admiral Raeder reported to Hitler at 1300 to put forward his suggestions concerning the pocket battleship and to get a decision on her fate. Also present at the meeting were Brigadier-General Jodl, who was Chief of the Operations Staff of the German High Command, and Commander von Puttkamer, a member of Admiral Raeder's staff.

The minutes of the meeting say that Admiral Raeder reported that at

*Nevertheless, the Uruguayan Chamber of Deputies, which ordinarily is far from being a unified body, subsequently voted unanimously unqualified approval of all that the Government had done with regard to the *Graf Spee*.

least two weeks were needed to make the *Graf Spee* seaworthy and that Uruguay had granted only seventy-two hours. The Foreign Office had been requested to continue their efforts to gain more time but 'this appears hopeless, however, as Britain and France are exerting great pressure, and Uruguay will conform to their wishes. Uruguay is unreliable as a neutral, and is not able to defend her neutrality. Internment in Montevideo is therefore out of the question.

'A break-through to the Argentine, which is stronger,' Raeder added, 'could be considered, since this would permit us to retain greater freedom of action. The captain of the *Graf Spee* has proposed a break-through to Buenos Aires, and he requests a decision as to whether, if the prospect is hopeless, he should choose internment in Montevideo or scuttle the ship in the fairly shallow waters of the Plate.'

Raeder then read out Langsdorff's signal, and gave his views. He could not recommend internment in Uruguay, and the right course, he said, would be an attempt to break through, or, if necessary, to scuttle the ship in the River Plate. He read the signal he proposed sending to Langsdorff.

Hitler, who had been listening carefully to what Raeder had to say, then declared he too was opposed to internment 'especially since there is a possibility that the *Graf Spee* might score a success against the British ships in the break-through'. He approved of the proposed instructions for Langsdorff.

These instructions, sent as Radiogram 1347/16 to the *Graf Spee* at 1700 said:

(1) *Attempt by all means to extend the time in neutral waters in order to guarantee freedom of action as long as possible.*

(2) *With reference to No. 2. Approved. [Langsdorff's proposal to put out to the neutral boundary and, if possible, fighting through to Buenos Aires.]*

(3) *With reference to No. 3 [if destruction was certain, should Langsdorff scuttle the ship or allow her to be interned]. NO internment in Uruguay. Attempt effective destruction if ship is scuttled.*

Signed: Raeder.

Later that evening Dr Langmann cabled from Montevideo that he had attempted to get the time limit extended but had failed, and Admiral Raeder sent a further signal to Captain Langsdorff:

As envoy reported impossibility of extending time limit, instructions according to Radiogram 1347/16 Nos. 2 and 3 remain in force.

During the afternoon and evening of 16 December, while Raeder and Hitler discussed these instructions, Captain Langsdorff had been preparing for a break-through. He had received reports from Rio de Janeiro and other sources which he and the Naval Attaché considered reliable, that the *Renown* and the *Achilles* had requested permission to enter the port, the latter to put wounded ashore. The *Ark Royal* was also reported off Rio de Janeiro, outside territorial waters.

Then the Harbourmaster of Montevideo informed Captain Langsdorff that a British steamer had sailed at 1815 that day and that in consequence the *Graf Spee* could not, under the Hague Convention, put to sea until twenty-four hours had elapsed – i.e. until 1815 next day.

This news appalled Langsdorff. His best chance of making a successful break-through depended mainly on being able to make a dash for it, hoping to take the waiting British warships by surprise. But now, unable to sail before 1815 on the 17th, with his seventy-two hour time limit expiring at 2000, he had only one and three quarter hours in which to select a sailing time.

The British had obviously sailed the steamer with this fact in mind, commented Langsdorff. He called a meeting which was attended by Kay, his Executive Officer, Wattenberg, his Senior Navigating Officer, two other officers, and the German Naval Attaché to consider the alternatives to breaking through to Germany.

Langsdorff began the meeting by saying that the seventy-two hours granted were not enough to patch the holes in the ship's hull and restore her seaworthiness. In other respects too, he considered the condition of the *Graf Spee*, as already described, precluded any idea of breaking through to Germany, even should she succeed in getting through the British forces off the Plate.

But, he told them, there was a possibility of putting to sea and, with the ammunition remaining, destroying one or more of the enemy; but the shallow water of the Plate was a handicap. If the *Graf Spee* should receive a hit and have her draught increased by flooding, she would ground and then be more or less defenceless, and the British would be able to shoot her to pieces. They might then be unable to prevent secret equipment falling into enemy hands.

On the other hand, said Langsdorff, it was out of the question to stay longer than the authorized time: if the *Graf Spee* stayed in harbour after 2000 next day, it was likely that the British ships would be summoned in and a naval battle would develop in the port.

'The severance of relationships between Uruguay and Germany would be the inescapable result of such an incident,' he added.

The break-through to Buenos Aires was then discussed, and it was agreed that it was impossible. The main reason was that, with the cooling-water intakes for the engines in the ship's bottom, there was the danger, in the shallow and muddy waters of the Plate, that they would get blocked up, causing the engines to run hot, and the ship, perhaps already in action with the enemy, would run into difficulties. In addition, they agreed, it was very questionable whether the Argentine would allow any longer period for repairs than Uruguay. The long approach channel to the Plate would also be disadvantageous for any subsequent attempts to put to sea.

Admiral Raeder's instructions forbade internment. Thus, said Langsdorff, the only alternative was to scuttle the ship outside territorial waters . . .

He gave instructions for his officers to prepare for this eventuality, but he warned them that scuttling was not to be ordered until he conferred again with the Ambassador.

The Ambassador, as mentioned in Raeder's second telegram to Langsdorff, had had a two-hour interview with the Uruguayan Foreign Minister that evening, and at times the conversation became very heated.

Dr Langmann, desperately seeking a few more days' grace, had demanded sufficient time to permit friendly negotiations; but the Foreign Minister was adamant. Seventy-two hours was all the time that could be permitted under international law.

Langmann was playing for high stakes and he put up every argument he could muster, but the Foreign Minister would not budge. Finally the angry Ambassador requested an audience with the President, but the Minister insisted that no interview could be granted unless the Ambassador acknowledged the seventy-two hour time limit. Langmann realized he was beaten. Hot and angry, he left the room to report to Berlin and to Langsdorff.

It was well after midnight that Langsdorff, with a heavy heart, then wrote a long official letter to the Ambassador in which, at the end, he made known his decision. It said:

Admiral Graf Spee   Montevideo
                                                                                            17:12:39

To: The German Ambassador Otto Langmann.

Your Excellency,

[The letter begins with the usual courtesies and he thanks the people of Uruguay for the reception he and his crew had been afforded.]

It was to my great regret amid these demonstrations of true human sentiments a jarring note was struck.

(1) By reason of what you have told me regarding your interview with the Foreign Minister of the Republic of Uruguay I am forced to regard as final and binding the time limited fixed as 2000 on 17:12:39 – before which time the *Admiral Graf Spee* must put to sea even if the repairs vitally necessary to make the vessel seaworthy cannot be completed by then.

I hereby register a formal protest against the decision of the Government of Uruguay.

(2) In accordance with Article 17 Chapter XIII of the Hague Convention, permission for warships of belligerent powers to remain in a neutral port may be granted for a period sufficient to carry out such repairs as are essential for the safe navigation of such vessels.

As far back as the year 1914 there was a precedent for this in South America. For several weeks the cruiser *Glasgow* lay in port carrying out repairs.

After an expert survey of the damage, I requested a period of fifteen days to carry out repairs in respect of the damage which compromised the seaworthiness of my ship.

The commission of experts sent by the Uruguayan Government was in a position while on board my ship to ascertain that the fighting capacity of my vessel (by which I mean the engines and armament) had suffered to such a small extent that there was no need for me to utilize the period of time I originally requested in order to increase her fighting capacity.

The said commission was able to ascertain that the hull of my ship gave evidence of damage, the repair of which was essential to the seaworthiness of the vessel.

In addition, it was patently obvious to this commission that the cooking installations and bakery on board were in a damaged condition – and that it was essential (considering the large crew borne) that these installations be in good working order before a long period on the high seas could be contemplated.

Article 17, Chapter XIII of the Hague Convention is concerned with damage such as this which I have described.

On the basis of a communication made to you by His Excellency the Foreign Minister, a committee of experts appointed by the Minister of Defence declared that a period of seventy-two hours would be sufficient to make good the damage. The decision of the Uruguayan Cabinet was based on this.

In spite of strenuous efforts it was not possible, in the time allotted, to repair the damage to my ship with the means at our disposal in Uruguay. This could have been ascertained beyond all doubt at the time, if a further investigation had been carried out on board.

(3) I hereby make formal declaration that the constructor entrusted with repairing the damage to my ship was obstructed by the port authorities on 16 December for a space of some hours after 1800, none of the men engaged for the work was permitted to come aboard. Permission for this was finally granted only after an official from the German Embassy had intervened.

I hereby declare that the decision of the Government of Uruguay compels me to leave the harbour of Montevideo with a ship which could not be sufficiently repaired to ensure the maximum safety of navigation.

To put to sea in such a vessel would bring danger upon my crew (over 1,000 men) by negligence. When I say 'danger' I do not mean such danger as would be involved in an action with the enemy. I am referring exclusively to the danger that would inevitably menace a ship at sea in such a condition.

(4) The decision taken by the Cabinet of the Republic of Uruguay is therefore a flagrant violation of the efforts to humanize warfare which led to the signing of the International Convention of the Hague.

It is abundantly clear that the difference between the attitude of the

Uruguayan people and the Uruguayan officials (except with the instance I have dealt with under Clause 3) on the one hand, and the position of the Uruguayan Government on the other hand, is attributed only to the influence of some interested parties.

Although I had the technical facilities to hand, I personally refrained from bringing to bear pressure of any kind.

Early on the morning of 13 December, I engaged the British cruiser *Exeter* on the high seas. The British cruisers *Ajax* and *Achilles* took part in this action. After the *Exeter* had been put out of action I decided to make for Montevideo to repair the damage to my vessel. I was aware that the British Government recognizes only the three-mile zone (even in the waters of the River Plate). As soon as my ship had reached the zone over which the countries contiguous to the Plate claim national condominium (and in spite of the British interpretation of this claim as it was known to me) out of respect of the two peace-loving nations I abstained from further part in the action. I should stress particularly the point that in spite of a favourable tactical position and in spite of good visibility I did not open fire on a British cruiser standing off the Isla de Lobos until the enemy had fired on my ship and shot had fallen close.

(5) I do not recognize the grounds for the decision of the Government of Uruguay – nevertheless I shall respect the time limit imposed. Inasmuch as the Government of Uruguay refuses to grant me time to make my ship seaworthy as laid down in the Hague Convention, I am not minded to place my ship (which has suffered no diminution of its fighting powers during the action) under the control of the Government.

Under the circumstances I have no alternative but to sink my ship. I shall blow her up close inshore and disembark my crew if this may be possible.

Signed: Langsdorff (Captain).

This letter to the Ambassador was almost certainly written for its possible propaganda value at a later date; and it throws little real light on the subject.

In the first place, having arrived in Montevideo and landed his wounded, both Langsdorff and the Skl in Berlin might have guessed that few if any effective reinforcements could reach Commodore

Harwood for many hours. It was obvious than the *Ajax* and *Achilles*, waiting outside, must be even shorter of ammunition than the *Graf Spee* professed herself to be. And Langsdorff was certainly not desperately short of fuel – the *Tacoma* was in any case in Montevideo, civilian supplies were available, and the *Altmark* was still at sea.

His own public assessment of the action damage affecting the *Graf Spee*'s seaworthiness does not tally with the damage reports from the ship which were subsequently captured by the Allies after the war.* Her engines and fighting efficiency, he admits, were not affected. He was at present unable to cook hot meals for his crew and there were holes in the hull – but all were temporarily patched and shored up.

It is possible the ship might be said not to have been in first-class condition to face a winter's gale in the North Atlantic; but with the *Altmark* waiting for him to the south, still undetected, there was no reason why he should not wait in a more equable climate until the spring before attempting to get back to Germany.

The knowledge that the *Ajax* and *Achilles* were still waiting outside could not, on the 14th, have been a very great deterrent to a determined ship should Langsdorff have sailed from Montevideo in the darkness. Captain Bell had managed to get the shattered *Exeter* back to the Falklands; and the damage to the *Graf Spee* was negligible by comparison. Once clear of the lights ashore, the chances of evading the cruisers were good. Commodore Harwood, at least, was under no illusions about the difficulties he faced. Referring to 16 December, after the *Cumberland* had joined him a few hours before the time limit expired next day, he wrote with typical understatement: 'The difficulty of intercepting *Graf Spee* who had so many courses of action open to her will, I feel sure, be realized.' He told his captains afterwards that he put their chances at about thirty per cent, and to his wife, while the *Ajax* steamed up and down on guard, he wrote: 'Things are tricky at the moment as we don't know if he is coming out again. I have a most difficult problem to catch him again. If he escapes me all the good we have done will be upset – not all, but a lot of it. The mouth of the Plate is so wide and there are so many ways out that it is very difficult. Probably another battle – and who knows? I hope for the best. If yes or no, you will know before you get this . . .'

A British officer in one of the cruisers wrote later to a friend

*See Appendix D.

describing the action, and added: 'Our wait outside, the "Death Watch" as the Yankee [radio] running commentaries called it, with our little "pop guns" was perhaps a little more trying. As you probably know by this time the fleet which assembled outside were entirely the products of the distorted imagination of the BBC announcer ably aided by TL [Their Lordships – the Admiralty], I presume. After thirty-six hours one lumbering great mastodon, *Cumberland*, blundered up, but we had little faith in her, except as the obvious target for the Teutons' first attentions.'

XX

Graf Spee *Scuttles Herself*

EARLY ON 17 December, shortly after writing his letter to the Ambassador, Captain Langsdorff received a signal from Berlin approving his decision to try to break through to Buenos Aires, but for the reasons mentioned he had already decided instead to scuttle his ship.

Shortly before 0300 he returned on board to supervise the preparations. From the chart of the Plate Estuary, it was obvious that the *Graf Spee* would not be totally submerged when scuttled because the water was so shallow, and the Germans had to ensure that as much equipment as possible should be destroyed so that prying British eyes would not be able to discover too much afterwards.

Arrangements were also made during the morning for the disembarkation of officers and men from the *Graf Spee*, and also for tugs to take off the personnel who would actually form the scuttling party. Langsdorff decided his crew should be taken to Buenos Aires, since he hoped for better treatment from the Argentine Government. Dr Langmann also agreed to take several of the pocket battleship's officers on the staff of the Embassy at Montevideo, in the hope that some of them would be able to get back to Germany and report personally on the cruise and the last days of the *Graf Spee*.

During the morning it was rumoured that the previously reported intention of the *Renown* to enter Rio de Janeiro had been abandoned, and by now she could be off the River Plate. But there was no further news for Langsdorff about the *Ark Royal* and *Achilles*.

Then at 1300 the German Ambassador in Rio de Janeiro sent an urgent message: the *Ark Royal* and *Renown* had just arrived there. Langsdorff received the news philosophically. Perhaps he wondered if the Embassy staff at Rio were taking photographs of the allegedly sunken carrier in order to convince Berlin that she was still afloat. He considered the arrival of the two warships did not disprove the fact that they had been seen off the Plate from the *Graf Spee* on the 15th, since they could have covered the 1,000 miles to Rio in two days.

He then estimated that the British force waiting outside Montevideo included cruisers (among them the *Cumberland*), which in the event of the *Graf Spee*'s departure would shadow in order to bring the *Ark Royal* and *Renown* and eventually further powerful forces into contact, and he therefore saw no cause to alter his decision to scuttle.

The BBC, the Press and the agents of both sides had done a good job in creating a powerful British force lurking over the horizon just off Montevideo – indeed, they had been helped by the *Graf Spee*'s officers as well; but in fact on 17 December it was still the mixture as before – the *Ajax*, with Commodore Harwood on board, the *Achilles* and the *Cumberland*.

As the hours went by, the tension in the three ships was increasing. The *Graf Spee* had to sail by 2000, and it was generally felt she would leave a skeleton crew on board to fight it out. The prospect was not altogether a pleasing one.

The *Ajax* and *Achilles* had been guarding the entrance to the Plate for four days now. On the 15th, after the *Cumberland* had joined him, the Commodore decided to start refuelling his force. The *Olynthus* was ordered to go to the Rouen Bank and the *Ajax* met her there. The Commodore told the *Cumberland* to wait in sight to the northward, so that she could give a warning should the *Graf Spee* slip out without her sailing being reported from Montevideo itself.

The weather, however, was bad and a strong wind kicked up a nasty sea in the shallow waters of the Estuary. Only 200 tons of oil had been pumped over to the *Ajax* before wires – including the spans of two hurricane hawsers – started parting.

During the morning the Commodore had completed his plans for guarding Montevideo and he sent the following policy signal to the other two cruisers:

My object destruction. Necessitates concentrating our forces. In-creased risk of enemy escape accepted. Achilles *is now to watch north of English Bank and* Cumberland *to west of English Bank, latter showing herself off Montevideo in daylight. If enemy leaves before 2100, ships in touch shadow at maximum range — all units concentrate on shadower. If enemy has not left by 2100, leave patrol positions and concentrate in position 090 degrees San Antonio 15 miles by 0030;* Ajax *will probably join* Cumberland *on her way south.*

If enemy leaves Montevideo after sunset, Cumberland *is at once to fly off one aircraft to locate and shadow enemy, if necessary landing in a lee, risking internment, and trying to find a British ship in the morning. If plan miscarries, adopt plan 'B', all units concentrate in position 36° south 52° west at 0600.*

The only criticism of the plan was made by a few officers who, referring to the first words of the signal, asked rather wryly: 'Who's going to be destroyed?'

The Commodore then sent the *Cumberland* the same signal that he had dispatched to the *Exeter* and *Achilles* the day before the battle,* describing how on the signal ZMM they would divide into two divisions. The *Cumberland*'s name was substituted for that of *Exeter* which appeared on the original. Thus in the event of going into action against the *Graf Spee* the *Ajax* and *Achilles* would again form the First Division and the *Cumberland*, with her eight 8-inch guns, would form the Second.

The Commodore was, as mentioned earlier, receiving valuable information every two hours from the Staff Officer (Intelligence) in Montevideo. He reported that the *Graf Spee* had landed a funeral party that morning and, later, had been granted an extension of her stay up to seventy-two hours.

'It appeared that she had been damaged far more extensively than I had thought likely,' the Commodore wrote afterwards, 'and had been hit 60 to 70 times in all.

'The British ship *Ashworth* was sailed at 1900 and the *Graf Spee* accepted the edict that she would not be allowed to sail for 24 hours after this. At the same time I could feel no security that she would not break out at any moment . . .'

In London, the Admiralty of course were busy with the task of concentrating more warships in the Plate area and, by discreet

*See page 94.

propaganda, spreading alarm and despondency among the Germans in both Montevideo and Berlin.

As it seemed quite possible that the SKL might well have ordered U-boats to head for the Plate area to help the *Graf Spee* escape, and since cruisers make good targets yet are ill-fitted for tackling submarine attacks, Force K was warned by Admiral Lyon that the destroyers should join as soon as possible, although *Ark Royal* and *Renown* were not to wait for them.

This was followed up by a signal from the First Sea Lord telling Vice-Admiral Wells that the *Ark Royal* was to arrive in the Plate area as soon as possible and not wait for the *Renown*.

By this time the First Sea Lord had received reports from Montevideo about the interrogation of the British Merchant Navy officers freed from the *Graf Spee* – reports which told an extraordinary story of a tanker named the *Altmark* which had been acting as a supply ship to the pocket battleship, and which now held more than 300 British prisoners of war. The only details available were her tonnage, probable speed, rough silhouette, the fact that she carried concealed guns, and that she had last refuelled the *Graf Spee* on 6 December in an unknown position.

As the commanding officer appeared to be a complete Nazi, it seemed probable that the only way to rescue the Britons on board would be by capturing the vessel.* The submarine *Severn*, on her way to the Plate, was therefore ordered to reconnoitre Trinidada Island to see if the *Altmark* was hiding in the vicinity. The First Sea Lord's signal ordered 'As 300 British merchant seamen on board [she] should be shadowed but do not torpedo.'

*   *   *

On Saturday, 16 December, the *Ajax* and *Cumberland* met as planned at 0030 and together they steamed towards Montevideo. The *Ajax*'s Seafox

*The *Altmark* in fact evaded all British warships until 15 February 1940, when she was reported off Trondheim, Norway. The destroyer *Cossack* was one of a force of ships ordered to sweep along the Norwegian coast. The *Altmark* was sighted and she ran into Jossing Fjord, inside the territorial waters. The Norwegians were obstructive and the First Sea Lord ordered Captain Vian, commanding the *Cossack*, to offer the Norwegians joint escort of the *Altmark* to Bergen or, failing that, to board her. The Norwegians would not co-operate and the *Cossack* went in, slid herself alongside and boarded the *Altmark* with the now famous cry 'The Navy's Here!'

was catapulted off to make a reconnaissance of the harbour, but Lt Lewin had strict instructions not to fly over territorial waters. However, he and Kearney did not have any luck – thick mist prevented them seeing anything, but they reported being fired on in the vicinity of the Whistle Buoy.

This seemed to indicate that the *Graf Spee* was trying to break out, taking advantage of the mist, and all three ships went to action stations. However, a report by radio from the Staff Officer (Intelligence) in Montevideo shortly afterwards indicated that she was still in harbour. No one was very disappointed: the prospect of blundering into a pocket battleship in the mist, possible at a range of a few yards, was not a welcome one, even for keen and hardy gunnery officers.

'I informed His Britannic Minister, Montevideo, of the firing on our aircraft,' the Commodore wrote, 'and suggested that an investigation into this might be a way of delaying *Graf Spee* sailing. He replied, however, that it was definitely not *Graf Spee* who fired, and that it had possibly been the Argentine guard gunboat at Recalada, or in some other position.'

Lewin, by this time, was very tired and had developed a habit which was worrying Kearney. He was keeping watch on and watch off in the *Ajax*, as well as making extensive reconnaissance flights over the Estuary, and sometimes he almost dropped off to sleep. Kearney would not notice this until the aircraft started doing strange things, and he used to shout at the top of his voice to warn Lewin before matters got out of hand.

While the cruisers had been closing Montevideo, the First Sea Lord sent the Commodore a signal which indicated Britain's attitude towards the claim for a twelve-mile limit on territorial waters. It said:

> IMMEDIATE: *You are free to engage* Graf Spee *anywhere outside the three-mile limit.*

The Commodore wrote: 'I decided to move my patrol into the area north and east of English Bank, as I considered that a battle in the very restricted water just outside the three-mile limit of Montevideo was impracticable, owing to the lack of sea room and possibility of "overs" landing in Uruguay and causing international complications.'

The latest news from Montevideo was to the effect that the *Graf Spee* was still repairing damage, having obtained assistance from the shore, and had provisioned. 'It was reported as unlikely that she would sail that night; on the other hand, once again I did not feel able to rely on such an optimistic report,' Harwood commented.

During the evening a more welcome signal arrived for the Commodore, and the first thing he noticed when it was handed to him was that instead of being addressed to 'Commodore Commanding South America Division' it was prefixed 'Rear-Admiral Commanding South America Division'.

It said:

From Naval Secretary.* IMMEDIATE. In recognition of the gallant and successful action fought by HM ships Ajax, Achilles *and* Exeter *against the German battleship* Graf von Spee [sic], *the First Lord desires me to inform you that His Majesty has been pleased to appoint Commodore Henry Harwood Harwood to be Knight Commander of the Most Honourable Order of the Bath; and that Captain W.E. Parry, HMS* Achilles, *C.H.L. Woodhouse, HMS* Ajax, *and F.S. Bell, HMS* Exeter, *to be Companions of the same Order.*

Commodore Harwood has also been promoted to be Rear-Admiral in His Majesty's Fleet to date from 13 December, the date of the action.

This was followed by a signal from the First Sea Lord, which said:

Their Lordships desire to express to you, the captain, officers and ship's company of HM ships Ajax, Achilles, *and* Exeter, *their high appreciation of the spirit and determined manner in which the action against the* Admiral Graf Spee *was conducted.*

It was a fitting and stimulating end to the day. Tomorrow the *Graf Spee*'s time limit expired and a battle seemed likely. Harwood ordered that instead of the three ships remaining all night in the first degree of readiness (i.e. everyone at their night stations), they could assume the third degree (a proportion only to be closed up).

The spirit of the men, who had had very little sleep for four days and nights, was shown by the fact that when the order was passed round a unanimous request was received from all quarters that they would prefer to remain closed up all night.

*i.e. Sir R.H. Archibald Carter, Secretary to the Board of Admiralty.

The squadron spent the night patrolling on a north and south line five miles to the east of the English Bank Light Buoy, and the *Olynthus* went to sea with orders to be at Rouen Bank by 1000 if the *Graf Spee* had not broken out.

The events of the next day, Sunday, 17 December, are best told in the words of Rear-Admiral Harwood:

'I ordered *Achilles*, who was getting low in fuel, to oil from *Olynthus* off the Rouen Bank during the forenoon. *Ajax* and *Cumberland* acted as lookouts at visibility distance during the operation. The squadron then cruised in company off the south-east of the English Bank, remaining concentrated throughout the afternoon and ready again to take up the same night patrol as on the previous night.

'The SO (I), Montevideo, reported that *Graf Spee* had landed all her borrowed welding apparatus during this forenoon. We all expected that she would break out at any moment. I would like to place on record the fact that at this stage the most cheerful optimism pervaded all ships in spite of the fact that this was the fifth night of waiting for the enemy.

'At 1540 I received a signal that the *Graf Spee* was transferring between 300 and 400 men to the German ship *Tacoma* lying close to her in the ante-port. At 1720 a further report stated that over 700 men with their baggage and some provisions had now been transferred, and that there were indications that *Graf Spee* intended to scuttle herself.

'Shortly after this *Graf Spee* was reported as weighing.

'I immediately altered course to close the Whistle Buoy, and increased to 25 knots. *Ajax*'s aircraft was flown off and ordered to proceed towards Montevideo and report the position of *Graf Spee* and also *Tacoma*.

'*Graf Spee* left harbour at 1815 and proceeded slowly to the westward. *Tacoma* also weighed, and followed her out of harbour.

'I ordered my squadron to assume the First Degree of Readiness, in case *Graf Spee* intended re-transferring her crew from *Tacoma* outside the harbour, or intended to break out with or without her surplus crew . . .'

*   *   *

In Montevideo itself Captain Langsdorff, weary and disheartened, had almost completed the plans which would destroy the ship that had been his greatest command and would provide the Allies with powerful propaganda. From his own personal point of view he could not get away from the fact that, whatever mitigating factors there were, he would be a naval officer who had scuttled his ship. And having spent his early, formative years in the Kaiser's High Seas Fleet, he was considerably more sensitive about his personal honour than the type of men normally absorbed into the Nazi régime.

But to his own officers and men he remained outwardly as cheerful as ever, and he gave no indication of the struggle which was going on in his own mind. He was a Nazi and believed wholeheartedly in Germany; but like many other naval officers he had been shocked by Hitler's alliance with Russia. He believed that Bolshevism was the greatest enemy, and it may well be that the seeds of his apparent disillusionment with Hitler were sown with the signing of the Treaty.

Langsdorff considered it quite likely that the British cruisers, warned as soon as he weighed anchor, would steam in towards Montevideo and attack the *Graf Spee* as she was being scuttled; and if this happened there might be a heavy loss of life among his men.

To safeguard against this as much as possible he decided that the actual scuttling party should consist of only forty-three men – himself, Ascher, the Senior Gunnery Officer, Wattenberg, the Navigator, Klepp, his engineer, a sub-lieutenant and thirty-eight petty officers and ratings.

The bulk of the *Graf Spee*'s crew would be transferred to the *Tacoma*, anchored nearby in the harbour, before he sailed. But he dared not risk having the *Tacoma* make for Buenos Aires in case she was intercepted by the British cruisers. Instead he arranged for two Argentinian tugs and a barge to meet the *Graf Spee* and the *Tacoma* out to sea and take off all the German officers and crew, and the *Tacoma* could then return to Montevideo. Langsdorff guessed that the British, even if they realized what was going on, would not dare intercept three neutral vessels inside their own territorial waters.

There was much to do before the *Graf Spee* sailed on her last voyage, and the minutes sped by. All the secret papers on board which were not wanted by the Embassy were destroyed, and Langsdorff was furious when he found that one over-zealous officer had burned the Action Report which he had written. It was the only copy, and with it were the gunnery, damage control, torpedo and action control centre reports.

Between 1400 and 1600, boatloads of the *Graf Spee*'s crew were transferred to the *Tacoma*, and among the crowds of people watching from the shore were Britons whose task it was to relay the latest information to the waiting British cruisers. They counted the Germans in the boat as best they could, and estimated that in those two hours 900 men had been taken off the pocket battleship.

Langsdorff had already sent word to the Harbourmaster that the *Graf Spee* would sail at or shortly after 1815, and this news soon became common knowledge among the crowd. Langsdorff was told that a launch would lead him out of the harbour.

By now the great warship had become the centre of world attention: dozens of newspaper reporters and radio commentators of many nationalities had been gathering in Montevideo during the past three days, and several radio stations were broadcasting direct commentaries, which were, not unnaturally, being listened to with some interest aboard the British cruisers.

For the people of Montevideo it promised to be a dramatic Sunday afternoon, and crowds gathered along the Prado and other vantage points, eagerly watching the pocket battleship and commenting vociferously on every movement made by the Germans.

Then, a few moments after 1700 local time, a large Nazi ensign was broken out from the *Graf Spee*'s foremast, followed by a second from the mainmast, and slowly one anchor was weighed. A few minutes later the second cable rumbled up from the sea bed, and almost imperceptibly the pocket battleship began to move.

To the crowd the *Graf Spee* seemed a majestic sight as, without the help of tugs, Langsdorff manoeuvred her round until she was heading seaward. Then he increased speed; and with the Nazi ensigns streaming in the wind, the *Graf Spee* passed out through the breakwater on her last voyage. Fifteen minutes later the *Tacoma* sailed out, following the same course.

The crowd, by now numbering three-quarters of a million and standing on quays, breakwaters, piers and along the shore, were silent as the pocket battleship moved out through the seaward channel to the south-eastward. She still looked a powerful fighting machine, and many believed she would go into action, and that the talk of scuttling her was merely a ruse to mislead the British.

They could see an aeroplane – presumably British, flown off by one of the cruisers – approaching the warship, and farther out to sea were two tugs and a barge. What were they doing there? The crowd, the newspaper reporters and the radio commentators speculated freely and, as it happened, inaccurately.

Suddenly they saw the *Graf Spee* start altering course. She came round to starboard until she was heading westwards, towards the setting sun. She was going to Buenos Aires! She wasn't going to fight the British or scuttle herself after all!

The *Graf Spee* was now steering for the Recalada pontoon, marking the entrance to the channel to Buenos Aires, but she had not gone far on her new course when she slowed down and then stopped. The two Argentinian tugs and the barge came alongside, and the rest of the pocket battleship's crew, with the exception of the scuttling party, scrambled over the side to the safety afforded by neutral flags. They had signed their own private peace, and few of them regretted it.

All this, however, was only the overture to the Wagnerian masterpiece, the preliminary bars which built up the tension while the latecomers of the audience shuffled into their seats and made themselves comfortable.

As the barge and the tugs drew away, the screws of the great warship started to turn almost reluctantly, and at Langsdorff's order a touch of the helm turned her towards the westward, where the sun, by now a deep crimson ball, was almost touching the rim of the land round the estuary.

But, unlike the Ulysses of Tennyson's inspiration, it was too late to seek a newer world; Langsdorff's purpose held, but it was not to sail beyond the sunset, and the paths of all the western stars, until he died; it was, more prosaically, to sail a few cables until the pocket battleship's bows nosed on to a mudbank. That was to be the *Graf Spee*'s Happy Isles; and it was ironic that Tennyson's next line reads 'And see the great Achilles whom we knew . . .'

Held on the mudbank, the overture ended with the rattling of the cable as an anchor was let go, and it mattered little whether there was good holding ground. At a signal launches came across from the *Tacoma*, now waiting 3,000 yards away, and went alongside.

Langsdorff waited alone with his hopes and fears while his men set the fuses of the scuttling charges, walking through an empty ship in which, for the first time in many months, there was no sound other than the metallic echo of their footsteps.

The time was 2040, and the scuttling party, their task completed,

187

climbed into the launches and were taken off to the tugs. All the vessels then moved off to a respectful distance.

The time selected for the fuses to go off had been chosen with the Teutonic flair for heavy drama, because at 2054, as the sun dipped below the coastline, a sudden flash of flame leapt from the ship, followed by a vast double explosion. The centre of the *Graf Spee* seemed to dissolve into swirling black smoke which twisted upwards in tortured spirals towards the darkening sky.

The pocket battleship's crew, scattered in the tugs, the barge and the *Tacoma*, stood to attention, giving the Nazi salute; and this indeed was the twilight of a god, a welded-steel god worshipped by nearly fifty score Nazi adolescents, and which was now disintegrating before their awe-struck eyes and upraised arms. Was it for this end that they had fought? They themselves did not ask the question; the Fuehrer had apparently said so, and therefore it was so. Blind faith supplies its own balm to bruised spirits.

But the first rumbling reverberation had not lost itself in receptive space before another curtain of flame leapt up aft, high above the masthead, to be followed by another explosion which seemed to erupt under the *Graf Spee*, lift her, and drop her back crumpled into the waiting sea. Wreckage showered out in neat parabolas, the mainmast collapsed like a stalk of corn before a scythe, and the great after turret, which had successfully withstood the shells of the British cruisers, was flung upwards as the magazine beneath exploded.

Now the violent dying spasms were over the self-induced cremation was to follow. Eager, seeking flames swept along the whole length of the ship; and ashore, while excited radio commentators regained their breath, the German Naval Attaché sent a cable to Berlin. Had his lords and master wished to use it as a dramatic libretto to this Wagnerian sham they would have been disappointed. It said:

> *Pocket battleship* Graf Spee *left Montevideo 1820* [German time]; *blown up by her crew 1954. Crew at present embarked in* Tacoma.

Just as the *Graf Spee* blew up, a British officer, Lt Cassells, was sent from Montevideo to report on the activities of the tugs and the barge.

'On arriving at the dockside,' he wrote, 'we heard the explosion in the *Graf Spee* and immediately boarded our tug. We had barely cast off when we were hailed by one of the port officials and instructed by him to take him on board.

'As we proceeded at full speed towards the wreck, it was evident that the port official knew absolutely nothing of what had taken place, and in fact he thought that some of the German crew were still aboard when the explosion occurred.

'We arrived alongside the *Tacoma* within twenty minutes of the explosion and found that the crew of the *Graf Spee* had already boarded one barge and two tugs . . . The port official hailed the ships and asked them under what instructions they were acting. He was informed that they were bound for Argentina in accordance with instructions from their company.

'The senior port official, Senor Riquero, then appeared in another tug and orders were received from him that the tugs were not to move away. However, one of these tugs proceeded away to the westward at full speed and was pursued.

'In addition to the tugs there were four of the *Graf Spee*'s boats under their own power, in one of which was Captain Langsdorff. As difficulty was being experienced in giving instructions to the German crew, Captain Langsdorff came aboard our tug to act as interpreter. The port official informed Captain Langsdorff that as he had no knowledge that the tugs and barge had orders to leave Uruguayan waters, it was imperative for them to return to Montevideo.

'The Captain at first thought that he had been stopped because of being accused of blowing up his ship in Uruguayan waters, and hastened to explain that he had been led to a pre-arranged spot, three miles off the coast, by a Uruguayan official tug and then gone one mile farther on his own initiative in order to avoid future arguments.

'In this connection the Captain remarked: "The English do not recognize a neutral territorial zone of more than three miles: that is why I sank my ship one mile farther out than the limit, so that I was free to act as I chose with the Argentine tugs and barge and the crew in them."

'The port official then pointed out it was not a question of the sinking of the *Graf Spee* but the behaviour of the Argentine tugs and barge with which he was concerned.

'He insisted on an explanation of their apparently unauthorized transport of men and baggage and of their movements generally. Captain

Langsdorff reported that he had received full permission from the Uruguayan authorities to proceed to Argentina.

'As the port official had no knowledge of this, he was not prepared to accept the Captain's statement and it was therefore decided to hail a Uruguayan naval gunboat which had just arrived on the scene.

'The commander of the gunboat had also received no instructions and he therefore sent a wireless message for orders. The reply was that the Germans were to be allowed to proceed without hindrance.'

Rear-Admiral Harwood and his three cruisers heard the news when Lewin and Kearney, who had watched the whole act, signalled:

Graf Spee *has blown herself up.*

Captain Parry wrote later: '. . . One realized that the drama was over. Both *Ajax* and ourselves simultaneously had ordered all hands on deck; and CSA then ordered us to take station ahead of him.

'We were both steaming as fast as we could in the shallow water some thirty miles east of Montevideo, which made the ships almost unmanageable. But as we passed *Ajax* everybody went mad and cheered and yelled themselves hoarse.

'We then eased down while *Ajax* hoisted in her aircraft. Her pilot complained that no one seemed to be taking any interest in him. However, in he came. By this time it was dark. I suddenly heard another roar coming out of the darkness, and there was *Ajax* passing us only about 100 yards away, while both ships' companies again yelled at the tops of their voices.

'Ahead of us there was visible a red glow in the sky, flickering up and down like a bonfire; and as we approached it turned into a sort of witch's cauldron blazing away in the sea a few miles west of the Montevideo channel . . .

'Soon after midnight, having gazed our fill on this unique sight, we turned south; and all those who could do so turned in to enjoy their first real night's rest for some days.'

XXI

Langsdorff Shoots Himself

CAPTAIN LANGSDORFF and his crew were housed in the Naval Arsenal in Buenos Aires, and while the *Graf Spee* still burned like a livid torch, a grim warning to those who cared to accept it, Berlin tried to turn her ignominious end into a propaganda victory. But even by Nazi standards they had little enough to go on.

An hour after the scuttling the German Ambassador in Montevideo protested to the Uruguayan Foreign Minister that the neutrality laws had not been properly observed; and at the same time he published Captain Langsdorff's letter which set out the alleged contraventions.

The first offical announcement made in Berlin about the scuttling was to have said briefly, 'The time necessary to make the *Graf Spee* seaworthy was refused by the Government of Uruguay. In the circumstances Captain Langsdorff decided to destroy his ship by blowing it up.' According to Admiral Raeder, however, the second sentence was altered to include the phrase 'on the personal orders of the Fuehrer' (underlined) and later altered again to read '. . . Under the circumstances the Fuehrer ordered Captain Langsdorff to destroy the ship by blowing her up. This order was put into effect outside the territorial waters of Uruguay.'

At the same time an urgent telegram was sent from Berlin to the German Ambassador in Montevideo:

> *Please give no further releases or reports of any sort to the Press concerning the sinking of the* Graf Spee. *This applies also to Langsdorff's letter. Anything further that is to be revealed will be released from here.*
> *Signed, Ribbentrop.*

The Nazi Foreign Minister was still smarting from the rap over the knuckles applied by Uruguay with her strict interpretation of international law, and he did not want to risk any indiscretions by his envoys or, for that matter, by Langsdorff.

The *Tacoma*, meanwhile, had been ordered back to Montevideo by a Uruguayan warship, and her captain was put under arrest, charged with violating port regulations. Four members of the *Graf Spee*'s crew were found on board and they too were arrested and charged with blowing up their ship. (They were subsequently released.)

On Monday morning Captain Langsdorff awoke in Buenos Aires to find himself attacked in the local newspapers as a coward and a traitor to the tradition of the sea because he had not gone down with his ship. This came as a deep shock to him, since he had expected a great welcome from the Argentinians.

Now, with thirty-seven of his men buried on Uruguayan soil, twenty-eight in hospital at Montevideo, four more in jail there and the rest detained in Argentina, he considered his duty was almost done.

One task remained: to prevent, if possible, the internment of his crew. During the day representations were made to the Argentine Government, claiming that as the *Graf Spee*'s crew were now ship-wrecked seamen they were not subject to internment.

However, the Cabinet decided next day that they should be interned and the cost would be charged to the German Government. This news was taken to Captain Langsdorff by the German Ambassador, Baron von Thermann, and it was unofficially stated that it meant, in effect, that officers would be interned in Buenos Aires city under parole, and the crew would be sent to the interior, under the control of local authorities.

During the later afternoon Langsdorff decided that he would like to speak to all his crew in private, and they were assembled in a large room while guards kept all unauthorized people away from the building. Subsequent reports of what he said to his men vary considerably. Some say that he told them of a telephone conversation with Hitler in which he declared that the *Graf Spee* ought to sail out and fight, but that Hitler ordered him to scuttle her. However, in the light of the documents subsequently captured at the end of the war, excerpts from which have already been given in this narrative, this has been shown to be completely untrue. Langsdorff had never pressed to be allowed to fight, and he certainly never had a telephone conversation with Hitler, whose instructions were given in the first instance to Admiral Raeder.

All the reports agree on one thing, that his closing words to the men assembled before him were:

'A few days ago it was your sad duty to pay the last honours to your dead comrades. Perhaps you will be called on to undertake a similar task in the future.'

Only a few of the officers fully understood the significance of his words; and they were confirmed later when Langsdorff gave his personal effects, including his camera, as keepsakes to certain officers, saying, 'Take these; I will not need them any more.'

After saying good-night to his crew and saluting them – using the old Navy salute, not the Nazi one – he left with some of his senior officers. When approached by newspaper correspondents, he said, with his usual courtesy, 'There's no story tonight, but there will probably be a big one for you in the morning.'

Then, after talking with him for three hours, his officers left the room. It was now nearly midnight, and Langsdorff sat down at a desk and wrote three letters. One was to his wife, another to his parents, and a third to Baron von Thermann. It said:

Buenos Aires
19:12:39.

To: The Ambassador, Buenos Aires.
Your Excellency,

After a long struggle I reached the grave decision to scuttle the pocket battleship *Graf Spee* in order to prevent her from falling into enemy hands. I am convinced that under the circumstances no other course was open to me, once I had taken my ship into the trap of Montevideo. For, with the ammunition remaining,* any attempt to fight my way back to open and deep water was bound to fail. And yet only in deep water could I have scuttled the ship after having used the remaining ammunition, and thus been able to prevent her falling to the enemy.

Rather than expose my ship to the danger of falling partly or completely into enemy hands after her brave fight, I have decided not to fight but to destroy the equipment and scuttle the ship. It was clear to me that the decision might be consciously or unwittingly mis-

*In fact he had nearly half the 11-inch outfit left: see Appendix D.

193

construed by persons ignorant of my motives as being attributable partly or entirely to personal considerations. Therefore I decided from the beginning to bear the consequences involved in this decision.

For a captain with a sense of honour, it goes without saying that his personal fate cannot be separated from that of his ship.

I postponed my intention as long as I still bore responsibility for decisions concerning the welfare of the crew under my command. After today's decision of the Argentine Government, I can do no more for my ship's company. Neither will I be able to take an active part in the present struggle of my country. I can now only prove by my death that the fighting services of the Third Reich are ready to die for the honour of the flag.

I alone bear the responsibility for scuttling the pocket battleship *Admiral Graf Spee*. I am happy to pay with my life for any possible reflection on the honour of the flag. I shall face my fate with firm faith in the cause and the future of the nation and of my Fuehrer.

I am writing this letter to Your Excellency in the quiet of the evening, after calm deliberation, in order that you may be able to inform my superior officers, and to counter public rumours if this should become necessary.

(signed) LANGSDORFF,
Captain.
Commanding Officer of the sunk
pocket battleship *Admiral Graf Spee*

This letter completed and sealed, Langsdorff unwrapped an ensign of the old Imperial German Navy, and took out his revolver.

At 0830 next morning one of his officers came to the room and found Langsdorff dead, his body lying on the ensign. The fact he had not used the Nazi ensign is perhaps the best indication of Langsdorff's final attitude to that régime.

During the afternoon the German Embassy issued a communiqué which said: 'According to a letter he wrote to the German Ambassador he said that he had decided from the first moment to share the fate of his superb vessel.

'Only by excercising powerful self-control, and by considering the responsibility which devolved upon him for the safe disembarkation of the crew, composed of more than a thousand young men, was he able to postpone his decision until he had fulfilled his duty, and made a complete report to his superiors.

'This mission was completed last night, and the destiny of a brave sailor, who has written another glorious page in Germany's naval history, was fulfilled.'

The funeral of Captain Langsdorff took place the next afternoon at the German cemetery in Buenos Aires, and was attended by the *Graf Spee*'s officers and crew, members of the Argentine armed forces, the German Ambassador, and Captain Pottinger, master of the *Ashlea*, who represented the captains of British merchantmen who had been prisoners in the pocket battleship.

Epilogue

AFTER AN uneventful fortnight following the scuttling, Rear-Admiral Harwood arranged to visit Montevideo in the *Ajax* and sent the *Achilles* to Buenos Aires. Both ships were given great receptions, and on 5 January they met off English Bank for the last time. The *Ajax* was to sail for England, and Rear-Admiral Harwood transferred his flag to the *Achilles*, which for the next twenty-four days remained the flagship of the South America Division.

When the *Achilles* was due to leave for New Zealand to have a refit, the cruiser *Hawkins* arrived to take over as flagship and early on 29 January the Admiral transferred to her. The *Achilles* steamed off to collect mail off the Whistle Buoy at the entrance to Montevideo and rejoined the *Hawkins* in the evening.

Then the *Achilles* received a signal telling Captain Parry to proceed in execution of previous orders. The time had come for the last of the three cruisers which fought the Battle of the River Plate to say goodbye to Rear-Admiral Harwood, leaving him flying his flag in a ship manned almost entirely by reservists and which had no association with the events of the past few weeks.

The *Achilles* steamed close to the *Hawkins*, with the band playing 'For He's a Jolly Good Fellow', and the crew singing at the tops of their voices. They ended with an entirely spontaneous three cheers and the 'Maori Farewell'.

The Admiral signalled 'My best wishes to you all. I have so enjoyed flying my flag in your happy ship. Goodbye and good luck'.

While aboard the *Achilles* the Admiral had taught the wardroom a new South American method of cutting for drinks with dice, called 'Bidai Bidou'. Now several officers asked Captain Parry's permission to signal

'Bidai Bidou'. This was given, but the two words had to be repeated several times before *Hawkins*'s signalman understood it. The Admiral answered '653' – the one throw that defeats 'Bidai' and 'Bidou'.

Just before he transferred to the *Hawkins,* the Rear-Admiral received a letter from the First Sea Lord, and it said:

11th January, 1940

My dear Bobby
You can have no doubt in your mind about what we feel here and your determined and courageous handling of the *Graf Spee.*

I do not mind telling you that when we got the news of the first sighting I thought the Huns had all the luck as the first contact of one of his pocket battleships was being made in that area in which we had the weakest hunting unit, and what is more, not only were the two ships of the unit separate, but they were running up against the weakest ship of the pair.

I think the manner in which all your ships went for her baldheaded must have had a great moral effect and largely influenced the *Spee*'s subsequent unintelligible actions. She must have realized that *Exeter* had only one gun in action when she dropped out of the fight, and why the *Spee* did not turn on her and finish her off, I cannot imagine.

Even if all our ships had been sunk you would have done the right thing. As things turned out I am delighted that you did not have *Cumberland* with you – so even had you sunk the *Spee* it would not have been so glorious an affair.

Your action had a great effect in two ways. Firstly it has set a standard for this war, a matter of great importance.

Secondly it has reversed the finding of the Troubridge court martial and shows how wrong that was.

Little did we think when we were shipmates so many years ago in the Mediterranean what Fate had in store for us, but Fate has been kinder to you even than to me, because you have been allowed to command a British force in a successful action at sea. That can never be my lot.

You seem to have had a wonderful reception at Montevideo, but not more than you deserve.

Yrs ever
Dudley Pound

Appendix A

Extracts from an analysis, dated February 1940, of the role of the *Admiral Graf Spee* in the Battle of the River Plate, produced by the German Inspectorate of Naval Ordnance, the Naval Gunnery Experimental Command, and the Naval Gunnery School:

'ASSUMPTIONS REGARDING THE ACTION:
Before considering the method of using the guns, it must be mentioned that, according to the available reports, the fight would not have taken place if *Spee* had not desired it.

Her decision was based on the erroneous assumption that she had only one cruiser and two destroyers against her. For *Spee* sighted the mastheads of the enemy as early as 0552, range 31,000 metres, while she, owing to her smoke, was not identified until 0610.

GUNNERY TACTICS:
The *Spee*, with a broadside of six 11-inch guns and four 5.9-inch guns was opposed by *Exeter* with six 8-inch guns and *Ajax* and *Achilles* with a total of sixteen 6-inch guns.

Fire was opened at 0617.

In principle no enemy ships should be left uncovered by our guns; a division of armament to engage three targets (that is one turret on *Exeter*; one on *Ajax* and the secondary armament on *Achilles*) is precluded because of the slow rate of fire of the main armament and the consequent technical difficulties.

The principle must be: "Use the main armament against the main enemy". Therefore under the conditions of the action the following distribution of fire would have been correct:

Main armament against *Exeter*; secondary armament against *Ajax* and *Achilles*.

Despite the contradictory British statements it may be assumed the *Spee* distributed her fire in this way. The short shift of target to the light cruisers when they threatened the *Spee* with their torpedoes was ineffective; therefore the main armament, which had been holding the *Exeter* well, was taken off its target, thus giving the *Exeter* temporary relief after several hits which she had suffered after opening of fire.

Unfortunately the reports do not show *which* ship turned *first*. Was it *Spee* to avoid danger from torpedoes, or was it *Exeter* in order to avoid *Spee*'s fire, or was it a manoeuvre made "in accordance with a predetermined plan"?

According to the track chart *Exeter* turned about 0623, while *Spee* followed round at 0625. It is not clear why *Spee* did not immediately turn about, but left off firing at *Exeter* and turned her fire on to the light cruisers for a short period. If the *Spee* considered the light cruisers (which had in the meantime approached to within 16,000 metres) as the more dangerous enemy, then only the fire of the main armament over a longer period would have had any prospect of damaging the light cruisers or of forcing them away.

The northerly course chosen by *Spee* made it temporarily more difficult for the cruisers to fetch over to the other side; this move by *Spee* increased the *Exeter*'s range. In spite of this, between 0631 and 0634 *Spee* inflicted such severe hits on *Exeter* that she had to turn away to the south making black smoke.

If at 0634 *Spee* had followed this move by turning to the south-west then, whilst maintaining or reducing the range, she could have engaged the already damaged opponent with her main armament from a favourable position in regard to the wind. If, because of smoke, *Exeter* was out of sight, then on a still more southerly course *Spee* could have engaged the light cruisers for a longer period not only with her secondary armament but also with her main armament. From the course steered by *Spee* this was possible intermittently with the after turrets.

It may be assumed that, if *Spee* had decided at that time to continue to use her main armament on the *Exeter*, the latter would have been put completely out of action much earlier; and *Spee* would not have encountered the difficulties in engaging the light cruisers which occurred between 0710 and 0715 when *Exeter* was actually disabled.

According to our analysis the British light cruisers, independently of the courses of *Spee* and with more progessive closing range, obtained a position far more unfavourable to the pocket battleship.

The actual course of the engagement resulted in the light cruisers in time becoming the main opponent, so that the *Spee* should have used her main armament against these. She could do this the more easily since two turrets were already out of action in *Exeter* at the latest by 0710, and since *Exeter* had scored no decisive hits on *Spee*.

This statement is made without prejudice to the earlier possibility of sinking the *Exeter* (after 0634).

However, as soon as she was being effectively hit by the British light cruisers she had to shift target to them. It would therefore have been desirable by 0710 at the latest for *Spee* to have used the whole of her main armament against the British cruisers. Every minute after this increased the danger of torpedoes.'

The German experts go on to enlarge on this theme and then say:

'From 0712 onwards, however, *Spee* engaged in a purely retreating action which was dictated by the worries about torpedo hits – apart from the possible considerations as to the operational use of the ships.

Although torpedo hits were avoided, this was at the cost of numerous shell hits which were sustained by the ship. The effective use of *Spee*'s gunnery was reduced by the constant changes in course, the unfavourable bearings and the hindrance through smoke and blast, and finally the frequent changes of target.

The *longer* the ship's guns can fire on one target with a steady ship's course the *greater* are the chances of success. As can be seen from this action, the principle has not been changed despite new mechanical devices.

EFFECTIVE GUNNERY:
Apparently the main armament of *Spee* inflicted most severe damage on the *Exeter* which reduced her speed and finally made her useless as a fighting unit. According to reports the effect of the secondary armament was unsatisfactory and – at least against the *Exeter* – not of decisive importance.

According to available data the least danger for pocket battleships is at a range of between 16,000–18,000 metres, where an 8-inch shell does not yet penetrate the horizontal armour with a favourable angle of impact . . .*

CONCLUSIONS:

It must be stressed that these criticisms are the result of "armchair" deliberations and are in no way meant as a criticism of the decisions of the Commanding Officer of *Spee* during the action.'

---

* By this, the Germans presumably meant that at a range of *less* than 16,000 metres an 8-inch shell might penetrate the vertical armour, while at a range *greater* than 18,000 metres it would be falling so steeply that it might get through the horizontal armour. Between 16,000–18,000 metres, apparently, neither would happen.

Appendix B

Extract from the War Diary of the Operations Division of the German Naval Staff, 16 January 1940:

'The task of commerce raiding was very well carried out by the *Spee* . . . *Conclusion from the action:* Timing unfavourable. Battle was deliberately accepted. The question as to whether disengagement was subsequently possible cannot be answered, but if the decision was once made to fight it out then it was necessary for the action to be pressed home with all resources until the principal opponent had been sunk.

The course of the action demonstrates the great difficulty and abnormal risk for a pocket battleship in engaging two or three cruisers, since even a few relatively minor but unlucky hits can rob her of the utilization of her main asset – the wide Atlantic.

The strategic effect of the *Spee*'s operation was very considerable.'

Appendix C

British, Allied and neutral merchant shipping losses 1939–45

Cause	Tons	Ships	Percentage
U-boat	14,687,231	2,828	68·1
Aircraft	2,889,883	820	13·4
Mines	1,406,037	534	6·5
Surface raiders*	1,328,091	237	6·2
E-boats	229,676	99	1·1
Unknown	1,029,802	632	4·7
	21,570,720	5,150	

* The total consists of:

Warships	498,447	104	2·3
Merchant raiders	829,644	133	3·9

It will be seen that although only 6·2 per cent was sunk by surface raiders, the actual tonnage is considerable.

Appendix D

Battle damage to the *Admiral Graf Spee*, 13 December 1939: reports of departments. (These documents were captured at the end of the war.)

GUNNERY

MAIN BATTERY:
1. Foretop rangefinder destroyed by fragments, otherwise nothing out of action, no derangement of fire-control and turrets.
2. Ammunition supply: 324 rounds (ammunition expenditure during the battle 378 rounds).

SECONDARY BATTERY:
1. Starboard target indicator in the conning tower.
2. Current supply for the hoist for the forward magazine group.
3. Ammunition hoist, No 1, port, destroyed.
4. Port, No. 3, 15-cm gun mount: gun shield badly battered, elevating mechanism jammed.
5. Ammunition supply: 423 rounds.

ANTI-AIRCRAFT:
1. Forward AA command post out of action from a hit in the foundation.
2. AA No. 1 from a hit in left half.
3. Right gun barrel of AA No 11, dented from a large shell fragment, barrel unusable.
4. Starboard forward 3·7-cm elevating gears and left sighting mechanism damaged from shell fragments.

5. Starboard chain hoist for 10·5-cm ammunition hoist destroyed.

6. Chain hoist bushing of the port 10.5-cm ammunition hoist shot away (temporarily out of action).

7. Ammunition supply: 2,470 rounds of 10·5-cm; full supply of 3·7-cm and 2-cm.

SEARCHLIGHTS:

1. Cables for searchlights No 2 and No 6 shot away.

2. Mirror for searchlight No 5 destroyed by fragments (replaced).

TORPEDO:

Caused by hits –

1. Port torpedo train angle indicator (*TRW – Torpedo-richtungsweiser*), through direct hit in the foundation, all cables shot away.

2. Starboard foremast director (shock effect of a shell passing through the platform railing and from fragments).

3. Torpedo distance converter (*l/e Wandler*), through detonation of a 20·3-cm shell in the transverse corridor, between decks, Section XI.

4. Head telephone, torpedo reporting station, through fragments.

5. Starboard loading station, through a direct hit.

6. Starboard spread firing apparatus (lamps destroyed by vibration, apparatus in use later without illumination).

Through other causes –

1. Current supply for the spread firing apparatus and training mechanism, groups 1 and 2 of the port set of tubes. (Cause unknown. Current was at a later time available. A disturbance, which appeared often during practice of battle exercises, and at that time was found to be caused by a poor circuit connection at the switch panel.)

2. From gas pressure [blast] from B turret: effect on the tube banks.

3. Wall telephone of torpedo work room.

COMMUNICATIONS:

1. Dispatch tubes sending and receiving room shot away.

2. Transmitter of the reserve radio room fouled.

3. Both DF rangefinders (*Goniometerkreuzrahmen*).

4. A long-wave and three short-wave aerials, four receiving aerials and four on the funnel.
5. Radio photo post from direct hit.
6. Radio direction finder from shock. Radar gear from shock.

SHIP'S HULL:
Large hole in ship's side, Section XV port, in the upper-deck (sealed off by damage control).

PERSONNEL LOSSES:

37 dead.
57 wounded.

After running into Montevideo, the following damage outboard was determined:
1. An approximately 15 cm-long crack in the between decks, section IV, port.
2. Several leaks about 15 cm diameter in the upper deck, section VIII, port.
3. A dent in the upper deck, section VIII starboard, about 15 cm long.
4. A leak about 10 cm in diameter at the waterline of section X port. A trim tank full of water.
5. Several leaks about 15 cm in diameter at and under the waterline, section XIII, starboard. (Trim tanks XII 4.6 and XII 4.8 full of water.)

Battle damage which could not be repaired with the equipment and materials aboard the Admiral Graf Spee:
Forward AA command post.
Starboard AA gun mounting.
Right barrel, port AA gun mounting.
Starboard chain hoist.
15-cm hoist 1, port.
Rangefinder, foretop.
Starboard foremast apparatus.

Port torpedo training mechanism.
Torpedo ranging device.
Torpedo tube 11.
Spread (torpedo) apparatus, starboard.
Starboard torpedo filling room.
Turning gear for [aircraft] catapult.
Bow protection gear.
Radiators for after part of ship.
Service conduits, after part of ship.
Fire-fighting piping, section X, upper deck. [Firemains.]
Deck duty petty officers' bath.
Hole in the freeboard, Section XV, port.

Appendix E

Hit No	Place	Damage	Time required
1	Detonation of a 15-cm shell in upper deck by amm hoist, No 1 port, secondary battery.	Port, No 1 hoist out of action. Current supply of forward group re-established with emergency power supply.	5 hours.
2	Shell through left side No 1 AA mounts.	Destroyed part cut away, English sight from 7·5-cm gun sight built in. AA shooting impossible. Only to side.	On 16 Dec. ready for use.
2	Detonation by starboard 10·5-cm amm supply installation, upper deck.	Stbd chain hoist of 10·5-cm amm hoist destroyed.	Not repairable.

3	20·3-cm shell between decks, Section IX.	Cable and remote controls to foretop damaged.	Repaired by noon, 14 December.
5	Shell through chain hoist port 10·5-cm amm hoist.	Brass bushing shot away. Bushing exchanged.	
9	Splinter in starboard 3·7-cm gun mount forward.	Elevating mechanism overhauled, shafts put in order.	6 hours.
9	Detonation in the foundation of forward AA command post.	Gyroscope section out of action, cables and telephone connection repaired.	7 hours
17	15-cm shell hit left side protective shield of port No 3 gun mounting.	Bent portion of shield cut away, cable repaired, helix shaft overhauled, elevating gear still works with difficulty.	Conditionally operative on 15 Dec.
18	Shell through night-control station.	Cables for searchlights 2 and 6 shot away; cable for searchlight 6 repaired.	4 hours.
near miss	Splinter in forward post.	Gearing dismantled, helix and 'segment' overhauled.	6 hours.

near miss	Splinter in flying bridge rangefinder.	Apparatus for range-finding out of action.	Not repairable.
near miss	Large fragment in right barrel of AA 2.	Right barrel dented and unusable.	Not repairable.
near miss	Splinter in searchlight 5.	Mirror destroyed: exchanged with a spare reflector.	3 hours.

Appendix F

Additional awards to officers and men of the cruisers *Ajax*, *Achilles* and *Exeter*.

APPOINTED TO THE DISTINGUISHED SERVICE ORDER:
Captain D. H. Everett, MBE (*Ajax*); Cdr D. M. L. Neame (*Achilles*); Cdr R. R. Graham (*Exeter*); Lt I. D. de'Ath, RM (*Ajax*), Lt R. R. Washbourn (*Achilles*); Cdr (E) C. E. Simms (*Exeter*).

CONSPICUOUS GALLANTRY MEDAL:
Able Seaman W.G. Gwilliam (*Exeter*); Sgt S.J. Trimble, RM (*Achilles*); Marine W.A. Russell (*Exeter*); Stoker P.O'Brien (*Exeter*).

HMS AJAX

DSC
Lt-Cdr D. P. Dreyer; Lt N. K. Todd; Lt E. D. G. Lewin; Warrant Shipwright F. H. T. Panter; Warrant Engineer A. P. Monk; Gunner R. C. Biggs.

DSM
Petty Officer A. E. Fuller; Chief Mechanician W. G. Dorling; Stoker B. Wood; Stoker F. E. Monk; Shipwright D. Graham; Electrical Artificer J. W. Jenkins; Sgt R. G. Cook, RM; Marine T. S. R. N. Buckley; Petty Officer C. H. C. Gorton; Petty Officer J. W. Hill; Leading Seaman L. C. Curd; Able Seaman R. D. Macey; Able Seaman R. McClarnan; Stoker R. Perry.

HMS ACHILLES

DSC
Lt G. G. Cowburn; Surgeon-Lt C. G. Hunter; Gunner E. J. Watts; Gunner H. T. Burchell.

DSM
Able Seaman E. V. Shirley; Ordinary Seaman I. T. L. Rogers; Boy A. M. Dorsett; Chief Petty Officer W. G. Bonniface; Petty Officer W. R. Headon; Petty Officer A. Maycock; Able Seaman H. H. Gould; Acting Chief Mechanician L. Hood; Chief Stoker W. J. Wain; Chief Yeoman L. C. Martinson; Chief Petty Officer Telegraphist W. L. Brewer; Chief Ordnance Artificer G. H. Sampson; Cook A. G. Young; Sgt F. T. Saunders, RM.

HMS EXETER

DSC
Cdr C. J. Smith; Cdr. R. B. Jennings; Lt A. E. Toase, RM; Surgeon-Lt R. W. G. Lancashire; Midshipman R. W. D. Don; Warrant Shipwright C. E. Rendle.

DSM
Engine Room Artificer J. McGarry; Engine Room Artificer F. L. Bond; Sgt A. B. Wilde, RM; Acting Petty Officer H. V. Chalkley; Sick Berth Chief Petty Officer C. D. Pope; Petty Officer C. F. Hallas; Stoker J. L. Minhinett; Acting Leading Airman E. A. Shoesmith; Plumber G. E. Smith; Joiner F. Knight; Petty Officer W. E. Green; Chief Mechanician J. A. Rooskey; Able Seaman A. J. Ball; Petty Officer S. J. Smith; Engine Room Artificer T. G. Phillips; Master-at-Arms S. A. Carter; Sick Berth Attendant E. T. Dakin.

Index

213